MISSIONAL CHURCH

THE GOSPEL AND OUR CULTURE SERIES

*A series to foster the missional encounter of the gospel
with North American culture*

Craig Van Gelder

General Editor

• •

Volumes now available

Darrell L. Guder, et al., *Missional Church: A Vision for the
Sending of the Church in North America*

George R. Hunsberger and Craig Van Gelder, editors, *The Church
between Gospel and Culture: The Emerging Mission in North America*

Forthcoming

George R. Hunsberger, *Bearing the Witness of the Spirit:
Lesslie Newbigin's Theology of Cultural Plurality*

Craig Van Gelder, editor, *Confident Witness — Changing World*

Darrell L. Guder, *The Continuing Conversation of the Church*

MISSIONAL CHURCH

*A Vision for the Sending of the Church
in North America*

Darrell L. Guder

Project Coordinator and Editor

Lois Barrett
Inagrace T. Dietterich
George R. Hunsberger
Alan J. Roxburgh
Craig Van Gelder

William B. Eerdmans Publishing Company
Grand Rapids, Michigan / Cambridge, U.K.

266
Gud

Printed in the United States of America

02 01 00 99   7 6 5 4 3

Library of Congress Cataloging-in-Publication Data

Missional church : a vision for the sending of the church
in North America / Darrell L. Guder, project coordinator
and editor ; Lois Barrett . . . [et al.].
        p.   cm.
Includes bibliographical references.
ISBN 0-8028-4350-6 (pbk. : alk. paper)
1. Missions — Theory.   2. Missions — North America.
3. Christian leadership.   4. Twenty-first century.
I. Guder, Darrell L., 1939-   . II. Barrett, Lois.
        BV2070.M573   1998
266′0097 — dc21   97-32962
                                            CIP

Contents

Project Team Members

The writers of this volume recognize that we are located — ethnically, ecclesially, geographically, and intellectually. We identify important aspects of that location here and invite people of other locations into conversation about what we are proposing.

LOIS BARRETT is an ordained Mennonite minister who serves as the Executive Secretary of the Commission on Home Ministries of the General Conference Mennonite Church in Newton, Kansas. She is a graduate of the Associated Mennonite Biblical Seminaries, Elkhart, Indiana, and earned her Doctor of Philosophy degree in the field of historical theology from the Union Institute, Cincinnati, working on the figure of Ursula Jost, a sixteenth-century Anabaptist noted for her ecstatic spirituality. She has served as a pastor of a network of house churches in Wichita, Kansas. Dr. Barrett drafted chapter five, "Missional Witness: The Church as Apostle to the World."

INAGRACE T. DIETTERICH is an ordained United Methodist minister who serves as the Director of Theological Research at the Center for Parish Development in Chicago, Illinois. She is a graduate of Wartburg Theological Seminary and completed her Doctor of Philosophy degree at the University of Chicago, working under David Tracy on the theology of the Holy Spirit in a trinitarian context. Dr. Dietterich drafted chapter six, "Missional Community: Cultivating Communities of the Holy Spirit."

DARRELL L. GUDER is an ordained minister in the Presbyterian Church (U.S.A.) who serves as the Peachtree Professor of Evangelism and Church Growth at Columbia Theological Seminary, Decatur, Georgia; at the beginning of the project, he was Benfield Professor of Evangelism and Mission at Louisville Presbyterian Theological Seminary. He completed his Doctor of Philosophy degree at the University of Hamburg and has served in educational and pastoral positions in the German and North American churches. Dr. Guder drafted chapter one, "Missional Church: From Sending to Being Sent"; chapter eight, "Missional Structures: The Particular Community"; and chapter nine, "Missional Connectedness: The Community of Communities in Mission."

GEORGE R. HUNSBERGER is an ordained minister in the Presbyterian Church (U.S.A.) who serves as the Professor of Missiology at Western Theological Seminary in Holland, Michigan. He studied theology at Reformed Theological Seminary in Jackson, Mississippi, and completed his Doctor of Philosophy degree at Princeton Theological Seminary on Lesslie Newbigin's theology of cultural plurality. He has been a campus minister, a pastor, and a mission worker in East Africa. He is the Coordinator of the Gospel and Our Culture Network. Dr. Hunsberger drafted chapter four, "Missional Vocation: Called and Sent to Represent the Reign of God."

ALAN J. ROXBURGH in an ordained Baptist minister in Canada who studied theology at Fuller Theological Seminary, completed a Master of Theology at the University of Toronto in philosophical theology, and the Doctor of Ministry degree at Northern Baptist Seminary in Chicago, Illinois. When the project began, he was Professor of Evangelism and Mission at the McMaster Divinity School of the University of Toronto. At present he is the pastor of West Vancouver Baptist Church. Dr. Roxburgh drafted chapter seven, "Missional Leadership: Equipping God's People for Mission."

CRAIG VAN GELDER is an ordained minister of the Christian Reformed Church who serves as Professor of Domestic Missiology at Calvin Theological Seminary, Grand Rapids, Michigan. He studied theology at Reformed Theological Seminary, and earned the Doctor of Philosophy degree in Missions at Southwestern Baptist Theological Seminary, followed by the Doctor of Philosophy degree in Administration in Urban Affairs at the University of Texas in Arlington. He also serves as a church consultant on urban and missional issues. Dr. Van Gelder drafted chapter two, "Mission Context: Understanding North American Culture," and chapter three, "Missional Challenge: Understanding the Church in North America."

Missional Church:
From Sending to Being Sent

As we move toward the end of the century, more and more commentators are proposing their versions of the "great new fact of our time." Among the many great new facts suggested, Christians in North America would likely point to two. On the one hand, during the twentieth century Christianity has become a truly worldwide movement, with churches established on every continent and among every major cultural group. The great modern missionary movement has been, despite all the controversy and debate, a truly successful enterprise. On the other hand, while modern missions have led to an expansion of world Christianity, Christianity in North America has moved (or been moved) away from its position of dominance as it has experienced the loss not only of numbers but of power and influence within society.

The United States is still, by all accounts, a very religious society. The pollsters affirm that Americans and Canadians believe in God, pray regularly, and consider themselves religious. But they find less and less reason to express their faith by joining a Christian church. North American religiosity is changing profoundly by becoming more pluralistic, more individualistic, and more private. Religion fits into North American secularism in a remarkable synthesis that the student of religious behavior finds fascinating. But for the Christian who takes the gospel of Jesus Christ seriously, this religiosity is a weighty challenge.

It is not the purpose of this book to duplicate the many studies of the changing religiosity of North American society. For our purposes, the result of the process is important. The Christian church finds itself in a very different place in relation to its context. Rather than occupying a central and influential place, North American Christian churches are increasingly marginalized, so much so that in our urban areas they represent a minority movement. It is by now a truism to speak of North America as a mission field. Our concern is the way that the Christian churches are responding to this challenge.

The reactions to this shifting ecclesial scene[1] in North America have been diverse. Extensive research on this topic has spawned a boom in the field of religious sociology, accompanied by an explosion in the number and variety of publications. At the same time, consulting agencies and programs whose sole aim is to help changing churches cope with their changing situation have proliferated. One can find a workshop or seminar on virtually every aspect of churchly life. The typical religious bookstore in North America overflows with books on successful churches with "add-water-and-stir" instructions on how to follow their example, how-to manuals for every conceivable problem a struggling congregation might face, and analyses of the myriad crises with which the church is grappling.

The crises are certainly many and complex: diminishing numbers, clergy burnout, the loss of youth, the end of denominational loyalty, biblical illiteracy, divisions in the ranks, the electronic church and its various corruptions, the irrelevance of traditional forms of worship, the loss of genuine spirituality, and widespread confusion about both the purpose and the message of the church of Jesus Christ. The typical North American response to our situation is to analyze the problem and find a solution. These solutions tend to be methodological. Arrange all the components of the church landscape differently, and many assume that the problem can be solved. Or use the best demographic or psychological or sociological insights, and one can redesign the church for success in our changing context. All it takes, it would seem, is money, talent, time, and commitment.

One should not be surprised that, in this time of crisis, the megachurch appears to many as a successful and eminently North American way to move from problem to problem solving. No doubt we can learn much from the emergence and proliferation of nontraditional churches that now dot the margins of our urban centers. The contrast between

---

1. "Ecclesial" refers to the church not only as an institution but also as a 'called out people' whose purpose is linked to God's mission. See p. 153, note 19.

2

their success and the persistent malaise of traditional denominational churches sets in high relief the crises of the latter. Moreover, the vast array of programmatic and methodological solutions on the market today only underlines the scope of the crisis.

The basic thesis of this book is that the answer to the crisis of the North American church will not be found at the level of method and problem solving. We share the conviction of a growing consensus of Christians in North America that the problem is much more deeply rooted. It has to do with who we are and what we are for. The real issues in the current crisis of the Christian church are spiritual and theological. That is what this study is about.

The Genesis of Our Study

This book arises out of a study and research process inaugurated by the Gospel and Our Culture Network. The Network emerged in North America in the late 1980s as the continuation, on this side of the Atlantic, of the Gospel and Culture discussion initiated in Great Britain during 1983 by the publication of Bishop Lesslie Newbigin's short monograph, *The Other Side of 1984: Questions for the Churches.*[2] The concerns raised by the bishop were certainly not new. But as a missionary statesman and leader who had returned after decades in India to minister in Britain, Newbigin analyzed with penetrating clarity the challenge presented by the changing context of Western society. In a word, what had once been a Christendom society was now clearly post-Christian, and in many ways, anti-Christian. Newbigin brought into public discussion a theological consensus that had long been forming among missiologists and theologians. He then focused that consensus on the concrete reality of Western society, as it has taken shape in this century. His conclusions have mobilized Christian thinkers and leaders on both sides of the Atlantic.

The missiological consensus that Newbigin focused on our situation may be summarized with the term *missio Dei,* "mission of God."

2. Lesslie Newbegin, *The Other Side of 1984: Questions for the Churches,* was published originally by the British Council of Churches for a year-long discussion program in Britain. It was reissued by the World Council of Churches in Geneva in 1984, and was disseminated in the United States by the National Council of the Churches of Christ in New York.

This consensus emerged out of the theological reflection on the amazing missionary expansion of the last three hundred years. Without discounting the remarkable response of men and women in previously unevangelized cultures, and the emergence of strong and vibrant Christian churches across the world, many began to be concerned about the shape of that mission. It became increasingly clear that Western mission had been very much a European-church-centered enterprise. The gospel to which we testified around the world had been passed along in the cultural shape of the Western church. This church was the result of centuries of Western cultural tradition that we define in this book as "Christendom." The subtle assumption of much Western mission was that the church's missionary mandate lay not only in forming the church of Jesus Christ, but in shaping the Christian communities that it birthed in the image of the church of western European culture.

This ecclesiocentric understanding of mission has been replaced during this century by a profoundly theocentric reconceptualization of Christian mission. We have come to see that mission is not merely an activity of the church. Rather, mission is the result of God's initiative, rooted in God's purposes to restore and heal creation. "Mission" means "sending," and it is the central biblical theme describing the purpose of God's action in human history. God's mission began with the call of Israel to receive God's blessings in order to be a blessing to the nations. God's mission unfolded in the history of God's people across the centuries recorded in Scripture, and it reached its revelatory climax in the incarnation of God's work of salvation in Jesus ministering, crucified, and resurrected. God's mission continued then in the sending of the Spirit to call forth and empower the church as the witness to God's good news in Jesus Christ. It continues today in the worldwide witness of churches in every culture to the gospel of Jesus Christ, and it moves toward the promised consummation of God's salvation in the *eschaton* ("last" or "final day").

We have learned to speak of God as a "missionary God." Thus we have learned to understand the church as a "sent people." "As the Father has sent me, so I send you" (John 20:21).

This missional reorientation of our theology is the result of a broad biblical and theological awakening that has begun to hear the gospel in fresh ways. God's character and purpose as a sending or missionary God redefines our understanding of the Trinity.

4

Mission [is] understood as being derived from the very nature of God. It [is] thus put in the context of the doctrine of the Trinity, not of ecclesiology or soteriology. The classical doctrine of the *missio Dei* as God the Father sending the Son, and God the Father and the Son sending the Spirit [is] expanded to include yet another "movement": Father, Son, and Holy Spirit sending the church into the world.[3]

This trinitarian point of entry into our theology of the church necessarily shifts all the accents in our ecclesiology. As it leads us to see the church as the instrument of God's mission, it also forces us to recognize the ways in which the Western church has tended to shape and fit the gospel into its cultural context and made the church's institutional extension and survival its priority. As we have used the tools of biblical scholarship carefully, we have begun to learn that the biblical message is more radical, more inclusive, more transforming than we have allowed it to be. In particular, we have begun to see that the church of Jesus Christ is not the purpose or goal of the gospel, but rather its instrument and witness. God's mission embraces all of creation. "God so loved the *world*" is the emphasis of the beloved gospel summary in John 3:16. This does not mean that the church is not essential to God's work of salvation — it is. But it is essential as God's chosen people "who are blessed to be a blessing to the nations" (Gen. 12).

Bishop Newbigin and others have helped us to see that God's mission is calling and sending us, the church of Jesus Christ, to be a missionary church in our own societies, in the cultures in which we find ourselves. These cultures are no longer Christian; some would argue that they never were. Now, however, their character as a mission field is so obvious as to need no demonstration. The issue for the Christian church is its faithful response to this challenge. But that is also its problem.

Neither the structures nor the theology of our established Western traditional churches is missional. They are shaped by the legacy of Christendom. That is, they have been formed by centuries in which

---

3. David Bosch, *Transforming Mission: Paradigm Shifts in Theology of Mission* (Maryknoll, N.Y.: Orbis, 1991), 390. This formulation reflects the Western tradition, of course; our Orthodox colleagues uphold the missionary nature of God while emphasizing that the Father sends both the Son and the Spirit.

Western civilization considered itself formally and officially Christian. This legacy may be described as the Constantinian system, because this presumption was seeded in the fourth century, when the Roman Emperor Constantine granted the Christian church special favors and privileges. In subsequent centuries, the Christian church shaped the religious and cultural life of all Europe. The cultures that resulted in Europe and later in North America are called Constantinian, or Christendom, or technically the *corpus Christianum*. In this book, when we speak of Christendom we are referring to the system of church-state partnership and cultural hegemony in which the Christian religion was the protected and privileged religion of society and the church its legally established institutional form. Even when the legal structures of Christendom have been removed (as in North America), the legacy continues as a pattern of powerful traditions, attitudes, and social structures that we describe as "functional Christendom."

In the ecclesiocentric approach of Christendom, mission became only one of the many programs of the church. Mission boards emerged in Western churches to do the work of foreign mission. Yet even here the Western churches understood themselves as sending churches, and they assumed the destination of their sending to be the pagan reaches of the world that needed both the gospel and "the benefits of Western civilization." In like manner, Western churches also developed home mission or inner mission, as the emerging secularism of Western societies presented us with new challenges. But it has taken us decades to realize that mission is not just a program of the church. It defines the church as God's sent people. Either we are defined by mission, or we reduce the scope of the gospel and the mandate of the church. Thus our challenge today is to move from church with mission to missional church.

One needs only to visit North American congregations to find that the church-centered approach to mission is alive and well. Congregations still tend to view missions as one of several programs of the church. Evangelism, when present, is usually defined as member recruitment at the local level and as church planting at the regional level. The sending-receiving mentality is still strong as churches collect funds and send them off to genuine mission enterprises elsewhere. Indeed, the main business of many mission committees is to determine how to spend the mission budget rather than view the entire congregational budget as an exercise in mission.

As denominational and centralized structures diminish in importance and power, local congregations are beginning to see their own context as their mission. But even with that shift, few have taken the necessary steps to redefine themselves as missionary by their very nature.

This gap between theological reorientation and actual practice is still reflected in much North American theological education. The doctrine of the church, ecclesiology, can and is still taught with little or no reference to the church's missionary vocation. Mission, or missiology, is a somewhat marginalized discipline, taught usually as one of the subjects in practical theology. There is little curricular evidence that "mission is the mother of theology."[4]

The obvious fact that what we once regarded as Christendom is now a post-Constantinian, post-Christendom, and even post-Christian mission field stands in bold contrast today with the apparent lethargy of established church traditions in addressing their new situation both creatively and faithfully. Yet this helpfully highlights the need for and providential appearance of a theological revolution in missional thinking that centers the body of Christ on God's mission rather than post-Christendom's concern for the church's institutional maintenance.

Like the Gospel and Culture discussions that spawned it, this book focuses on the need for such a theological revolution and seeks to propel that movement by reshaping the way we do our theology of the church. For this reason, we ask ourselves here, What would an understanding of the church (an ecclesiology) look like if it were truly missional in design and definition?

Our Research Approach

The Gospel and Our Culture Network brings together "Christian leaders from a wide array of churches and organizations who are working together on the frontier of the missionary encounter of the gospel with North American assumptions and perspectives, preferences and practices." In its discussion to date, the Network's participants have worked on three major thematic areas. We have addressed North American culture by trying to "discern the shifting worlds so radically reshaping our lives and the places where God is at work in them." We have probed

4. Martin Kähler, *Schriften zu Christologie und Mission* (1908; repr. Munich: Chr. Kaiser, 1971), 190, as quoted in Bosch, *Transforming Mission,* 16.

the gospel by searching for "fresh ways in which the gospel gives us resources for a confident witness to Jesus Christ." We have sought to aid North American churches in developing "new forms of mission-shaped churches as the Spirit calls us to be faithful people of witness."[5] Out of this discussion emerged the present research project to explore the possible shape and themes of a missiological ecclesiology for North America.[6]

The project method we have adopted is a simple one. A team of six researchers worked together intensively for three years to review the recent literature that, in our judgment, speaks relevantly to the missional challenge of North American culture, the crisis of the churches within that context, and the possible shape of a missional ecclesiology. To probe further, we invited four theologians whose work appeared to us especially helpful to meet and discuss these issues with the entire team. Those theologians were Justo Gonzales, Douglas John Hall, Stanley Hauerwas, and John Howard Yoder. We exchanged essays and chapters by writers across the theological and ecclesiastical spectrum. We wrote interpretive surveys and criticized them in long team meetings. Over this period of time, a set of themes began to crystallize that seemed to us to be essential for a missional ecclesiology in North America. We assigned each other the responsibility to draft expositions of these themes, using the literature already available and our own discussions as our resources. As we drafted, we critiqued and even rewrote each other's work. We struggled with our shared assumptions and our differences, sought to define our terms, and arrived at a consensus that, we trust, will serve to stimulate more discussion of the crucial issues of a missional theology of the church.

The reorientation of our theology under the "mission of God" has been the central focus of our deliberations. We have accepted the definition of the church as God's instrument for God's mission, convinced that this is scripturally warranted. The definition of the term *church* itself continues to present challenges to us. Our team consists of theologians from Reformed, Methodist, Baptist, and Anabaptist traditions, although

---

5. The citations in this paragraph are taken from recent brochures of the Gospel and Our Culture Network. Much of the early reflection on these themes is captured in George R. Hunsberger and Craig Van Gelder, eds., *The Church Between Gospel and Culture: The Emerging Mission in North America* (Grand Rapids: Eerdmans, 1996).

6. This project has been made possible as part of a grant from the Pew Charitable Trusts to the Gospel and Our Culture Network.

we are ecumenically influenced enough to resist being identified too narrowly with any of our traditions. We continue to grapple with emphases and nuances when we consider the church as an alternative or contrast community, but we know that we cannot evade that distinctive edge to the church's calling. We have arrived at a shared consensus that our definitions of the church should focus on and arise out of the formation of particular communities of God's people, called and sent where they are as witnesses to the gospel.

We recognize that the term *culture* is exceptionally difficult to define. Neither Canada nor the United States is one single culture; rather they are themselves a complex of diverse and interwoven cultural traditions that are constantly forming new and challenging expressions. Several approaches to defining the term will become apparent to the reader. One can begin with a simple lexical approach: "The sum total of ways of living built up by a human community and transmitted from one generation to another."[7] But in our various discussions, we accent particular dimensions of culture that are important for our theological exposition and thus evolve a more complex understanding of culture as we proceed.

Our explorations have focused on North America, by which we mean Canada and the United States. Throughout our analysis of the North American context, we have concentrated on those contextual patterns that can in some sense be shown to be overarching, controlling, or perhaps dominating ones. Within North America numerous groups and subgroups embrace and embody cultural traditions whose roots live elsewhere than in the dominant patterns. These include Native American populations (the "first nations"), African-American populations, Asian-American populations, a diversity of European populations, Latin American and Hispanic populations, as well as many others. We cannot cover this broad variety here, but particular knowledge of the ethnicity and tradition of local people must always have the attention of any particular church. Every church must know its own unique ethnicity as well as the ethnicity of people around it.

Nevertheless, western European and North American societies have general, dominant cultural dynamics that shape how we view and live life as well as affect all the varied traditions that inhabit those societies. In real ways these dynamics are controlling because they frame

7. Newbigin, *Other Side of 1984*, 5.

9

and accommodate even the ethnic multiplicity. These powers we all encounter and must negotiate. They give the framework for social interaction and form the social institutions within which we all conduct our lives. It should be obvious that many cultural groupings in North America experience these dominant cultural dynamics as oppressive, exclusionary, and often racist. The thrust of the gospel exposition in this book is to define a missionary people whose witness will prophetically challenge precisely those dominant patterns as the church accepts its vocation to be an alternative community. The structures of leadership and community life must then carry through that prophetic vocation.

As one illustration of the plurality of cultures that we must keep in view, but also because the two large multicultural societies of North America, the United States and Canada, have shaped the general Western dynamics differently, this survey will show some of the distinctive patterns that differentiate these two societies.

We have recognized that these cultures are profoundly European in their formation, and so we have sought to take the historical ecclesiologies of the European traditions seriously in our work. We have not surveyed those complex traditions in detail, but we have recognized that we are heirs of a continuing struggle within the church to be faithful to its calling. We seek to be grateful yet critical in our reception of the generations of theological reflection that precede and instruct us. We have found in the four Nicene marks of the church a constructive place in which to explore and develop our traditional ecclesiologies for our missional context today. Of course, some of the European traditions will see themselves as underrepresented in our discussion, and we invite them to continue the conversation and broaden our understandings of a missional ecclesiology.

The centrality of the gospel as God's good news for all the world pervades our discussion from beginning to end. Our sense of the wonder of the gospel and the ways our traditions domesticate and reduce it has grown during our conversations and research. It has become particularly important to us to focus our discussion on Jesus' message and practice of the reign of God. A vast contemporary biblical discussion of this theme guides us in our thinking. We are persuaded that any responsible missional ecclesiology must be centered on the hope, the message, and the demonstration of the inbreaking reign of God in Jesus Christ.

As theologians of Protestant traditions, we have been guided by a shared conviction that the Scriptures are the normative and authoritative witness to God's mission and its unfolding in human history. This shared conviction has not prevented us from discovering a stimulating breadth of interpretive approaches within our little group, which reflects the breadth and diversity of perspectives in the Scriptures themselves. Yet we now agree that one must read Scripture from a missional hermeneutic, and we hope that our efforts will encourage biblical colleagues to help us better understand what that means and how to do it.[8]

Our path has led us to make the following fundamental affirmations as the basis for the vision we wish to portray. These should be the characteristics of a faithfully missional ecclesiology. With the term *missional* we emphasize the essential nature and vocation of the church as God's called and sent people:

1. A missional ecclesiology is biblical. Whatever one believes about the church needs to be found in and based on what the Bible teaches. Moreover, these biblical perspectives need to be made explicit. The biblical witness is appropriately received as the testimony to God's mission and the formation of God's missionary people to be the instruments and witnesses of that mission.

2. A missional ecclesiology is historical. When we shape our ecclesiology for a particular culture, we must take into consideration the historical development of other ecclesiologies. Today this means reading our Western history and the worldwide emergence of the church carefully. As part of our catholicity, we are guided by the Christian church in all its cultural expressions, those that precede us and those that are contemporary with us.

3. A missional ecclesiology is contextual. Every ecclesiology is developed within a particular cultural context. There is but one way to be the church, and that is incarnationally, within a specific concrete setting. The gospel is always translated into a culture, and God's people are formed in that culture in response to the translated and Spirit-empowered Word. All ecclesiologies function relative to their context. Their truth and faithfulness are related both to the gospel they proclaim and to the witness they foster in every culture.

4. A missional ecclesiology is eschatological. Our doctrine of the

---

8. See James Brownson, "Speaking the Truth in Love: Elements of a Missional Hermeneutic," in Hunsberger and Van Gelder, eds., *Church Between Gospel and Culture*, 228-59.

church must be developmental and dynamic in nature, if we believe that the church is the work of the creating and inspiring Spirit of God and is moving toward God's promised consummation of all things. Neither the church nor its interpretive doctrine may be static. New biblical insights will convert the church and its theology; new historical challenges will raise questions never before considered; and new cultural contexts will require a witnessing response that redefines how we function and how we hope as Christians.

5. A missional ecclesiology can be practiced, that is, it can be translated into practice. The basic function of all theology is to equip the church for its calling. If that calling is fundamentally missional, then what we understand and teach about the church will shape God's people for their faithful witness in particular places. A missional ecclesiology serves the church's witness as it "makes disciples of all nations, . . . teaching them to obey everything that I [Jesus] have commanded you" (Matt. 28:19-20).

The Divine-Human Tension in Our Enterprise

Sociological and organizational interests inform much of the contemporary discussion of the North American church. The results of those studies are informative and have helped us. But our task is solidly theological and practical in its focus. We do not approach the theme of the church with any objectivity. We are persuaded that it is God's creation for God's mission. Our purpose is the church's missional renewal. We are deeply conscious, as we work, of the necessary ambivalence that surrounds such an undertaking.

The church of Jesus Christ is, and has always been, clearly visible to the observing eye. This is as it was intended when God called it into being as a community that is distinctly God's people in the midst of a world of people whom God has made and upon whose lives God makes a claim. The Christian community is a real one. It is made of real people, and thus it is discernible.

We do not believe, however, that once the sociologist or historian describes a particular church as a fully human, thoroughly sociological organism, there is nothing more to say of it. While the church is always a real, human, social organism, it is also the body of Christ, a community

12

grafted into the life of God in its baptism and by the action of the Holy Spirit. Elements of it are true that are not made visible by the categories and presuppositions of the sociologist, elements that rest deep in its faith and hope in the divine promises on which it was birthed.

The traditional language of the "visible" and "invisible" church has become muddled in common usage. Much of the church uses it to represent a strong dichotomy between a supposedly invisible church—an idealized church composed of all true believers as known to the mind of God—and the visible church—the actual tangible human institutions called churches made up of people who ostensibly profess faith in Jesus Christ. The first is to be believed but is ultimately impossible to experience. The latter is what we live with but is hardly believable nor worthy of the biblical imagery used to describe the church. Under the impact of such thinking, followers of Jesus are kept from experiencing what is considered the true, invisible church because it is out of reach. Consequently they are left with little reason to live and work in the hope that the tangible, visible churches are important enough to God to warrant their prayers and tears.

The biblical imagery itself is instructive at just this point. The most glorious affirmations about the church, which include such images as the body of Christ, the household of God, and the temple of the Spirit, are used precisely to describe real human communities of the first century. The opening nine verses of Paul's first letter to the Corinthians say grand things about a church even though it was deeply troubled and troubling because it was full of real, human sinfulness. In the New Testament there is no dichotomy between a supposed invisible church and the visible one.

The point of the "visible-invisible" language is not that there are ultimately two churches, one ideal and one tangible. Instead, the one church is to be affirmed as real, tangible human communities marked and made to be much more than appears on the surface. The church is not just another human institution. It is the creation of the Spirit. To borrow the language of Hans Küng: the church is at once both visible and invisible, and this is always true of it.[9]

In this respect the church bears a marked resemblance to the incarnation of Jesus, who, being God, was equally real human flesh and life. It is no accident that the church is called the "body of Christ." It

9. Hans Küng, *The Church* (Garden City, N.Y.: Image, 1967), 59-65.

continues as an incarnate expression of the life of God. But no less than for Jesus, this expression means that the church always takes particular form, shaped according to the cultural and historical context in which it lives.

This shaping always moves in two directions. On the one hand, the church understands that under the power of God, the gospel shapes the culture of a society — its assumptions, its perspectives, its choices. The church knows this because the gospel is always doing that to the very culture that is its own. This gives an indication of God's vision for the church's transforming impact on its context. On the other hand, because the church is incarnational, it also knows that it will always be called to express the gospel within the terms, styles, and perspectives of its social context. It will be shaped by that context, just as it will constantly challenge and shape that context. The church lives in the confidence that this ought to be so, and that it is the nature of its calling for this to be so.

The church knows to expect a life full of ambiguities because it is shaped by its context as the gospel reshapes the context. Such a calling never leaves the church in a finished, settled, or permanent incarnation. Its vocation to live faithfully to the gospel in a fully contextual manner means that it can sometimes find itself either unfaithful or uncontextual. In addition, the human context that shapes it continues to change. Therefore the questions of its faithfulness are always fresh ones. The gospel of God is never fully and finally discerned so that no further transformation can be expected. The interaction between the gospel and all human cultures is a dynamic one, and it always lies at the heart of what it means to be the church.

The Components of a Missional Ecclesiology for North America

The church must constantly hear the gospel afresh in order to discern its faithful response. It must constantly examine how it has been shaped by its context and ask God to convert and transform it. But at certain times and places it is particularly urgent that the church both understand the shaping it has inherited from its context and hear the gospel's word that calls the church to alter its life. We are persuaded that the present is such a time and North America is such a place. Questions like these have been left too long unattended. A radical shift is taking place in the way our society sees the church's presence and the way that society assigns it a place in the scheme of things. Deep crisis points are now visible in the social order itself, and old rules are up for grabs.

The churches of North America live at this time and place. For the church to ask the question of its own identity and mission in this place and time, it must be clear about the nature of the cultural context that it shares and by which it is shaped. Only on that ground can we properly engage the issue of faithfulness to the gospel in incarnational terms.

We must therefore begin our investigation by attempting to define this context clearly. In chapters two and three, drafted by Craig Van Gelder, we provide, in broad strokes, a portrait of the North American cultural context and the formation of the church within that context. We do not say everything that could be said, and we need to keep pressing beyond these brief sketches. But in chapter two we offer a set of factors in North American cultures that especially impinge on the nature and faithfulness of the church. These are the shaping forces of the cultural context.

Chapter three adds a second layer to this portrait: the particular experiences of the church in the North American context and the way its identity and life have been shaped by that context. This chapter illustrates the effects of the context's shaping forces on the church's shaped forms as we have inherited them.

Building on this contextual and historical analysis, we turn to the theological heart of a missional ecclesiology. In chapter four, drafted by George Hunsberger, we explore the basic definition of the church as the people of God who are called and sent to re-present the reign of God. This vocation is rooted in the good news, the gospel: in Jesus Christ the reign of God is at hand and is now breaking in.

In chapter five, drafted by Lois Barrett, we build on this basic theology of the gospel and the church's vocation by expanding our understanding of the church as the apostle to the world. As such, the church sees the world through the biblical perspective of the principalities and powers, and functions in that world as an alternative community. Biblical thought informs our understanding as we consider what it means to be a "city on a hill," to take up Christ's cross, and to continue his ministry.

Chapter six, drafted by Inagrace Dietterich, explores the intimate relationship between the church's apostolate to the world and its distinctive ecclesial practices. These practices form the common bond for the missional church in all of its cultural expressions. Yet all these practices achieve their true essence only when they serve the community in its missional vocation.

In chapters four through six, then, we address the evangelical and missional understandings of the church that must find expression in the context described in chapters two and three. Shaping the church's response then becomes the agenda of the last three chapters of the book.

In chapter seven, drafted by Alan Roxburgh, we examine the nature and practice of missional leadership. We move from the historical process to the present crisis and propose an apostolic reorientation of our concept and practice of ecclesial leadership. Since missional leadership cannot be separated from the formation of missional communities, this chapter suggests a way of understanding the structure of the particular community that draws together both the contextual analysis and the theological content of the preceding chapters.

In chapters eight and nine, drafted by Darrell Guder, we propose the structural implications of a missional ecclesiology both for the particular community, "the church in a place," and for the larger structures of connectedness of the church. Our attempt here is to establish some trajectories for responsible decision making as the organized church must take decisive action in a very unsettled context.

Finally, the reader will note that the authors' names are not attached to individual chapters. Our goal has not been to produce a book of discrete essays but instead to create a cohesive exposition of the missional calling and practice of the church. Although we have all served as primary authors of specific chapters, we have so incorporated each other's thinking, corrections, rewriting, and challenges that we can now offer this book as a jointly written contribution to the theological conversation in North America.

To enhance that cohesiveness, we have submitted our chapters to Dr. Milton J Coalter, who has edited them with a well-sharpened pencil, a commitment to clear expression, and an eye for the overarching themes that move throughout our study. The project coordinator, Darrell Guder, has done the final editing and also drafted this first chapter, using the thoughts and ideas of the entire team.

With a profound sense of gratitude to the Pew Charitable Trusts, the many discussion partners within the Gospel and Our Culture Network, and especially to each other within the team, we invite our readers to engage with us in this exploration of a missional ecclesiology for the churches in North America. Like so many others, we sense that this is a dramatic and decisive time in Christ's church. We trust and pray that our work will be seen as constructive and be used by God's Spirit for the missional renewal of the church.

In an incisive essay on the missional challenge of late postmodern Western culture, Diogenes Allen suggested that Christopher Fry had captured our situation well in his play *A Sleep of Prisoners*. Allen introduced the following quotation with these comments: "We remain captives within a mental framework that has actually been broken. We are like prisoners who could walk out of a prison because all that would enclose us has been burst open, but we remain inside because we are asleep. Christopher Fry, however, tells us that this is the time to wake up."

> The human heart can go to the lengths of God.
> Dark and cold we may be, but this
> Is no winter now. The frozen misery
> Of centuries breaks, cracks, begins to move;
> The thunder is the thunder of the floes,
> The thaw, the flood, the upstart Spring.
> Thank God our time is now when wrong
> Comes up to face us everywhere,
> Never to leave us till we take
> The longest stride of soul men ever took.
> Affairs are now soul size.
> The enterprise
> Is exploration into God.[10]

---

10. Diogenes Allen, "The Fields Are White for the Harvest," in Arnold Lovell, ed., *Evangelism in the Reformed Tradition* (Decatur, Ga.: CTS Press, 1990), 17-18.

• 2 •

Missional Context:
Understanding North American Culture

The gospel is always conveyed through the medium of culture. It becomes good news to lost and broken humanity as it is incarnated in the world through God's sent people, the church. To be faithful to its calling, the church must be contextual, that is, it must be culturally relevant within a specific setting. The church relates constantly and dynamically both to the gospel and to its contextual reality.

It is important, then, for the church to study its context carefully and to understand it. The technical term for this continuing discipline is *contextualization*. Since everyone lives in culture, the church's careful study of its context will help the church to translate the truth of the gospel as good news for the society to which it is sent. Moreover, because culture is not neutral, this discipline will assist the church to discern how it might be compromising gospel truth as it lives out its obedience to Christ the Lord.

In order to contextualize responsibly, the church must assess its culture critically, discerning and unmasking its philosophical foundations and values. This book is about developing a missional ecclesiology for North America. We begin with an examination of the historical foundations and values that have shaped our culture. Although many of these cultural patterns are common to all of North America, we will need to distinguish aspects that are unique to the United States and Canada. To arrive at the understanding of North American culture we need for our task, we will consider, first, modernity's pervasive influence in shaping the ideas and values that characterize our societies. Then we will consider the shifts now taking place with the emergence of the postmodern condition, and their implications.

Constructing the Modern Way of Life

Anywhere, North America, Mid-1990s: Modernity—What Have You Done to Us?

It was an all too typical Monday morning for Hank. He was on the car phone talking with his office while stalled in the morning traffic on the 409 Bypass. The weekend had been difficult. It was his weekend with his two kids. The divorce had become final not long ago. Between trips to the soccer game and the dance recital on Saturday, there had been that two-hour wait at the hospital's prime care unit while the doctor set his son's broken collarbone. Nothing serious, but it all seemed to take so much time. Trying to handle the details of life seemed complex and overwhelming sometimes.

Complex and overwhelming! That also described what was going on with the phone call. Hank's company was the target of a takeover by a larger corporation, and the rumor on the street was that there would be significant downsizing in middle management, which very likely would affect Hank's position. As an African-American he had always felt that the deck was stacked against him. After everything it took to land this job, it seemed as if it could evaporate in an instant.

The technological developments in his area of engineering were driving a host of changes. Sometimes it seemed that no one was in charge. Everyone just seemed to be reacting to change. Hank needed to have his report filed by 8:30, and with traffic running this slow he wasn't going to be there in time. The phone call would at least enable him to have his secretary transfer the report electronically from his workstation.

His secretary Mary was single, charming, and quite efficient. The recent reprimand by his boss, suggesting that Hank's behavior toward her was close to sexual harassment, had arisen out of her misunderstanding of his intentions. He had simply been doing what seemed like innocent flirting. Why had she gotten so upset? Sometimes he wondered if he really understood white people, even though his life had come to be surrounded by so many of them.

His divorce hadn't helped. It wasn't a messy affair, just a drifting apart after ten years and two kids — two people on different wavelengths living separate lives in the same suburban house. What seemed strange was how alone he now felt living for the first time in an apartment. It was an upscale place, but it seemed so isolating. And what a hassle to sort out the divorce. It seemed as if the last few months had been a constant process of dividing up wedding gifts and former friends.

Was this the success Hank had dreamed about for years, his way out of the ghetto? Was this the promised land? Was this what life was all about?

Complex, modern society is a reality for everyone in North America. No one has escaped being shaped by its pervasive influence. It has become the very air that we breathe. Hank's life circumstances reflect the reality of this "air," which includes such dimensions as:

- urbanized life with its complex patterns of social relationships
- multiple tasks and responsibilities that fragment time and space
- an economy shaped and driven by technology and its advances
- job, career, and identity defined by professionalized roles and skills
- submerged racial and ethnic identities in a stew-pot society
- the pervasive influence of change and rapid obsolescence
- bureaucratic organizations run by rules and policies
- individualized moral values concerning such matters as divorce and sexuality
- radical forms of individuality producing isolation and aloneness
- hunger for some overarching story to give meaning and structure to life.

The world of North America is a modern one. The modern way of life that makes up our reality is the product of numerous social, political, economic, and religious developments. For the most part, however, these various forces stem from a common foundation. They were given their impetus by the ideas and values associated with the historical intellectual movement known as the Enlightenment. This movement consisted of a series of intellectual developments whose origins lie in seventeenth- and eighteenth-century Europe.

The intellectuals of the Enlightenment were engaged in a noble effort to assert and foster a greater measure of personal freedom. To do so, Enlightenment thinkers searched for alternatives to the authoritarian constraints of established monarchies and religious hierarchies as well as an alternative to the claims of truth grounded in historical tradition and biblical teaching. Renaissance humanism from the fourteenth through the sixteenth centuries had prepared the way for this development by placing renewed emphasis on the individual. In the sixteenth century the Protestant Reformation also reinforced this focus by stressing the importance of individual responsibility in relationship to one's personal salvation. Sixteenth-century Europe welcomed these movements toward more personal freedom. But European societies in the seventeenth and eighteenth centuries were still structured under the controlling authority of ruling kings and state churches.[1]

It was the theorists of the Enlightenment who postulated a new three-pronged alternative for achieving personal freedom. First, rather than tying one's personal identity and destiny to monarchs or the church, they proposed a counterprinciple. One's personal identity and destiny should be the self-construction of a rational, autonomous individual. This is what sociologists have come to call the "modern self." Second, to establish this premise, it was necessary to formulate a different approach for determining what is true, one specifically based on human reason or rationality. Third, with this as the basis for constructing the modern self, a new notion of what constitutes the social order emerged. The whole spectrum of Enlightenment thought is quite complex and far more nuanced than this brief summary. But for our purposes, it will be helpful to explore the origins of these three motifs that lay at the core of emergent modernity and have been major factors in reshaping the church in this era.

Rationality and Reason

The struggle of early Enlightenment thinkers to establish an alternative method for discovering truth is clearly illustrated in the experience of Galileo (1564-1642). After Galileo's empirical observations confirmed Copernicus's (1473-1543) theory that the earth rotated around the sun, church and state authorities forced Galileo to recant his view because they believed that the Bible taught a different cosmology. Their challenge to Galileo raised the question whether the Enlightenment thinkers' approach to the use of rationality and reason, rooted primarily in the tradition of Greek philosophers, would be allowed to stand on its own merits. Would they have the freedom to pursue their studies without

---

1. See especially the discussion by Bard Thompson, *Humanists and Reformers: A History of the Renaissance and Reformation* (Grand Rapids: Eerdmans, 1996).

intervention from controlling authorities who used political and religious tradition to define the limits of what was considered true?

A number of other things contributed to this shift in the foundations for discovering truth. Francis Bacon (1561-1626) proposed the rational use of logic and the scientific method as the source for knowing.[2] Some thinkers like René Descartes (1596-1650) believed that truths were innate within the human mind. They focused primarily on trying to employ the principles of rational logic to discover these self-evident truths.[3] This focus spawned an approach and method known as rationalism. Other thinkers believed that truth existed only as it could be observed and described. They sought to develop truth by using empirical research in the study of human experience. This research was then used by such as figures as John Locke (1632-1704) to construct hypotheses and laws out of the facts that were discovered. This method became known as empiricism.[4] In time, the empirical method became the normative way to determine what is true.

These two alternatives for determining truth, though fundamentally different in approach, shared a commitment to employ a rational method as the key to guaranteeing the discovery of what is true. Enlightenment thinking propelled a move away from the notion of truth as embedded within a tradition or revelation to a notion of truth as discovered through the use of rational method. This represented a foundational watershed in human thought.[5] This shift of perspective within emergent modernity focused attention on the matter of epistemology — the study of the nature of truth and the methods used to discern it. Although most early Enlightenment thinkers assumed the validity of the Christian faith, before long the newly developing scientific method, with an epistemology that increasingly focused on empiricism, would be used to cancel out the God-hypothesis (see David Hume, 1711-1776).[6]

Enlightenment thinkers believed that they were introducing a liberating conception of truth. But in fact their methods for perceiving truth reduced the truth that they sought to illumine in at least three ways.

2. Howard Becker and Harry E. Barnes, *Social Thought from Lore to Science,* 2 vols. (New York: Dover, 1961), 1:386-87.

3. Ibid., 2:462-63.

4. Ibid., 1:390-96.

5. Peter T. Manicas, *A History and Philosophy of the Social Sciences* (New York: Blackwell, 1987), 11-13.

6. Ibid., 14-15.

First, their truth tended to become instrumental since they privileged only that which could be experienced. Second, they claimed objectivity by privileging scientific discovery as the only sure truth. Third, they validated only what was measurable by privileging facts over values. Recent examination of these limitations is leading many to reassess the usefulness of the Enlightenment's confidence in empirical reason as the basis for knowledge.

The Autonomous Self

The power and influence of various institutions, including the church, monarchies of various sorts, the feudal system, and the guild, shaped the identity of the individual in medieval Europe. In this context, personal interests and freedoms were submerged within larger corporate interests.[7] A primary goal of the Enlightenment was to formulate a new basis for individual identity as the key to increasing personal freedom. While theorists pursued this effort along the divergent paths of rationalism and empiricism, they shared in common a basic understanding of the individual as a rational and autonomous self. Those taking the approach of rationalism lodged final authority inside the human mind instead of relying on authority from outside sources such as tradition or revelation as determinative. By using the mind and employing logic and reason, they viewed the individual as capable of discerning self-evident truths (see Descartes). Those taking the approach of empiricism regarded the human mind as a blank slate on which human experience was written. The key for the empiricist was for the rational, autonomous individual to use reason to organize that experience into discernible truths (see Locke).[8]

While different in method, each approach fostered the creation of the modern self, the self-contained individual capable of discerning truth and constructing knowledge. This capacity to develop such truth and knowledge provided the basis for achieving personal freedom. The individual would then presumably reach full potential with such freedom. Great optimism surrounded this dream of constructing a society on the foundation of this combination of objective, scientific truth and the rational, autonomous individual.

7. Thompson, *Humanists and Reformers,* 63.
8. Manicas, *History and Philosophy,* 11-12.

Social Contract

During the sixteenth century, a number of political thinkers formulated conceptions of society that were based on the application of scientific knowledge to the social realities of life. But most of these efforts, like that of Thomas More's (1478-1535) *Utopia,* still limited individual freedom by tying the social order tightly to the rule of a strong monarch.[9] In time, an alternative to the rule of such sovereigns was proposed in the form of the social contract theory. This democratic doctrine provided a way to affirm the social reality of life while preserving the integrity of personal freedom. It recognized that persons made choices out of personal self-interest. The difficulty, however, was how to construct a social order from this starting point. This difficulty was overcome by positing that the collective effect of individuals choosing out of rational self-interest would lead to the promotion of the common good in the whole of society (see Thomas Hobbes, 1588-1679).[10]

Although Hobbes continued to defend the need for the monarch, it was not long before others like John Locke and Jean-Jacques Rousseau (1712-1778) moved beyond Hobbes by shifting the focus of the social contract toward a more democratic basis.[11] They held that rational, autonomous persons had natural rights, and by entering into a social contract people could affirm and protect these rights. It soon became evident that such a social contract could also serve as the basis for constructing political challenges to the status quo. Both the American and French revolutions need to be understood as natural extensions of the logic of social contract theory.

Social contract theorists were not naïve, however, regarding the potential for abuse within human nature. Such figures as Charles de Montesquieu (1689-1755) recognized that a social contract required the construction of institutions that together would achieve a separation and balance of power.[12] Such a society, they assumed, would make significant progress through the proper use of science in social management. This combination of the scientific method with the expectation of historical progress became known as logical positivism (see

9. Becker and Barnes, *Social Thought,* 1:314-19.
10. Ibid., 388-89.
11. Ibid., 390-92.
12. Manicas, *History and Philosophy,* 32-36.

Auguste Comte, 1798-1857).[13] Once this view took hold, it functioned as the dominant philosophy in the social sciences until the 1960s.

Underlying this constellation of theories was the basic motivation to free persons in modern society from arbitrary restrictions. When persons enjoyed true freedom, these theorists believed that the full potential of human life could be realized. They considered this notion of freedom the more natural state of the human condition. Freely choosing, autonomous individuals, deciding out of rational self-interest to enter into a social contract in order to construct a progressive society, became the central ideology of modernity. Here lies the foundation for the call to freedom and human rights of the past two hundred years, people waging battle with civil and religious authority structures all along the way. Modernity is the story of this struggle to create society on the bases of objective scientific truth and the construct of the autonomous self. The United States and Canada are two of the nations that bear this imprint most directly.

Facets of the Modern Self

Modernity developed out of both the intellectual currents of the Enlightenment and the emerging patterns in the political, social, and economic realms of life. The ideas important to modernity found ways of embedding themselves into the concrete social structures of life. Modernity has increasingly put its stamp on virtually every nation of the West and, to one degree or another, all the other nations of the world. It has become what Lesslie Newbigin has called the most pervasive culture of the world and one of the most resistant to the Christian gospel.[14]

As already noted, at the heart of modernity's emergence lies a confidence in the autonomous, rational self. To understand the contemporary cultures of North America and the circumstances that the church inhabits, it is important to look more closely at the particular forms that the modern self has taken. This is true because the identity for persons and their institutions, including Christians and churches, is rooted in the conception and structure of the modern self. Five features of the modern self are offered here as a cluster of facets that form its character.

13. Ibid., 56-64.
14. Lesslie Newbigin, *Foolishness to the Greeks* (Grand Rapids: Eerdmans, 1986).

The Modern Self as Citizen with Rights and Freedoms

A profound political truth is acted out every time a grade-school child in the United States stands at attention, with right hand placed over heart, and states the pledge of allegiance to the flag. This political act symbolizes a key institutional development within modernity that took effect in the formation of the modern nation-state. The nation-state as a political construction was the logical extension of rational principles and social contract theory. It is implicit within social contract theory that persons possess a collective identity that supersedes the family, ethnicity, or cultural tradition. The nation-state became an ideological framework for implementing this identity (see Johann Herder, 1744-1803).[15] It guaranteed citizens personal rights and freedom in exchange for their primary allegiance to the state.

The concept of the modern nation-state emerged within the debates surrounding the American and French revolutions. During the nineteenth century, a whole series of values attached themselves to this construct. These included historical progress, social Darwinism, racial theory, and the superiority of Western civilization. The consolidation of the German federation under Bismarck (1815-1898) clearly institutionalized the structure of the modern nation-state. What was not fully clear then, but became painfully evident on the battlefields of World Wars I and II, was the capacity of such nation-states to use the rights and freedoms of citizens as a down payment in support of nationalistic agendas achieved through military power. In other words, an unresolved tension exists between modernity's protection of a citizen's rights and freedoms and its demands on a citizen's allegiance and civic responsibilities. An illustration of this tension occurred in the 1960s when American college students burned their draft cards as an act of civil disobedience, both to thwart the government's requirement that they serve in the military action in Vietnam and to protest the government's involvement there. The modern self is shaped, along the lines of this tension, to be a loyal citizen in the interest of personal freedom.

15. Ibid., 76-84.

The Modern Self as Consumer

A trip to a contemporary shopping mall to purchase a pair of pants symbolizes another profoundly shaping institutional development within Western modernity. The selections confronting the shopper are extensive, including not only the endless choices among styles, colors, and fabrics, but also choices about whether to shop in one of the four major anchor stores or in one of fifteen specialty shops. This multiplicity of choices is one of the many end products of the way the economy took form in modernity. Capitalism arose as one of the shaping institutions of modernity and has steadily become the organizing principle of the economics of the modern world.

According to Adam Smith (1723-1790), an economy greatly increases its capacity to produce and expand wealth through the growth, concentration, and investment of capital.[16] As Western societies increasingly organized their economies along those lines, profound societal changes followed. Persons migrated from the basically self-sufficient economic unit of the family toward an expanding array of wage-earning jobs in the factories and commerce of growing towns. With this shift, economic viability and vulnerability became a function of the technological changes that constantly reshaped the means of production. As products were standardized, mass-produced, and more readily available, new processes for marketing, advertising, and conspicuous consumption became the order of the day. This economic system stimulated the growth of modern cities and an urban style of life as people moved into cities to fill the new jobs created by mass production techniques.

All these developments and the spiral of change they entailed continue today on a global scale. The fuller effects of the capitalist economy are now becoming evident in what some describe as the third stage of capitalism: consumer capitalism.[17] This third type of capitalist economy pressures the consumer to increase consumption, whether such consumption is really needed or not, in order to sustain growth and profitability.[18] The modern self as consumer is both pawn and player in

---

16. Ibid., 45-47.

17. The earlier stages were laissez-faire capitalism and welfare-state capitalism.

18. Fredric Jameson, "Postmodernism, or, the Cultural Logic of Late Capitalism," *New Left Review* 46 (1984): 53-92.

this economic game: pawn because each person is the object of the push to consume, and player because each person depends on the jobs of the marketplace that drive the culture of consumption.

The Modern Self as Constructed Roles and Identities

When asked to identify themselves today, people commonly refer to their career, job title, employer, or educational achievements. This response illustrates how the culture of modernity roots a person's identity in one's achievements and place in the social order, especially the economic social order. What identifies people is their function — what they do rather than their character or their personal qualities.

The issue of personal identity for the modern self is closely related to the formation of the modern bureaucracy.[19] The capitalist economy required the formation and management of large-scale organizations. While large organizations have existed throughout history, what was unique in the late nineteenth century was the effort to bring a rational, scientific design to them.[20] Positions became job descriptions with detailed responsibilities and defined limits of power; policy manuals standardized procedures; authority, delegation, and decision making were structured vertically, from top to bottom, using a host of middle managers. Moreover, industrial innovators like Frederick Taylor (1856-1915) added to the conception of the modern bureaucracy by defining principles of scientific management for shaping the life of such organizations.[21]

This scientific approach to managing organizations gave birth to a wide spectrum of sophisticated skills and techniques for governing human behavior in service to organizational goals. Individuals live out modern urban life within the milieu of multiple large-scale organizations that shape the roles they play and the identities they carry. For the

19. Charles Perrow, *Complex Organizations: A Critical Essay,* 2nd ed. (Glenville, Ill.: Scott, Foresman, 1973), 3-5.

20. In his monumental work to analyze and interpret the new dynamics, Max Weber (1864-1920) has provided scholars a conceptual framework for understanding the rational-legal character of the modern bureaucracy that was emerging by the turn of the century.

21. Perrow, *Complex Organizations,* 63-65.

modern self defined in these terms, the constructed identity inherent within modern bureaucratic life often generates a tension between personal individuality and one's organizational role. The modern self as a constructed set of roles and identities leaves unresolved issues within the fuller development of modernity.

The Modern Self as Product of Technique

Entering the auditorium of a community church that conducts a contemporary worship service can be a moving experience. The combination of seating arrangement, staging, variations in lighting and sound amplification, as well as orchestration of the presentation are all part of the arsenal of technological tools and techniques that enhance the desired ambiance of the service. Such an experience illustrates a fourth development in modernity shaping the modern self: the rapid growth of science-based technology with its concomitant application of technique for the manipulation of the social and natural world. The expansion of technology and technique serves as the primary driving force behind the pattern of constant change so often associated with modernity. For all the pain and trauma it introduces, constant change has become the expected norm for most people.

The acceptance of technological and technique-driven change has spawned a number of important myths that are deeply embedded within modernity. One is that the new is somehow better and must necessarily replace the old once it is introduced. Another is that what is efficient is more desirable and must necessarily replace what is only workable. A third is that there is a technique solution to every problem, and science can address any and every problem we encounter if we just work at it with enough intelligence, or long enough: "We *can* do it, if we *will*."

While numerous other myths are associated with technology, this list is sufficient to illustrate the seductive character of this force within modernity.[22] The challenge to preserve individual choice and responsibility in the midst of the expanding applications of new technologies

22. For discussion of the influence of technology and technique in modern society, see Jacques Ellul, *The Technological Society*, tr. John Wilkinson (New York: Random House, 1964); and *The Meaning of the City*, tr. Dennis Pardee (Grand Rapids: Eerdmans, 1970).

and techniques creates a real tension for most people. The modern self is a product of life amid the constant search for the new and the efficient through the employment of technology and technique. Sometimes on the receiving end of another's technique for social solutions, sometimes wielding the technique oneself, the modern person becomes defined on the one hand as a manipulable piece of the social machine, and on the other hand as the supremely capable master of the social and natural worlds.

The Modern Self of Feeling, Intuition, and Desire

As much as modernity's development has been driven by its vision of the rational, it has exhibited another side. That other side constitutes a powerful and parallel countermovement, largely in reaction against modernity's tendencies toward a planned, rationalized, bureaucratized, technicized, and commodity-driven world. This alter ego of rational modernity is what became known in the nineteenth century as romanticism, and in the twentieth century as modernism. Modernism is the birth-twin of modernity, but the two are not identical twins. The twentieth-century movement of modernism attempted to capture in the arts and literature the side of the human spirit that is emotive, affective, intuitive, and experiential. The world of modernity increasingly produced what Max Weber (1864-1920) called the iron cage effect, where life is lived amid institutional structures produced by human values, but these structures no longer provide a place for these values. As this effect occurred, modernism pushed past all the boundaries of convention, principle, and essential forms. In essence, it embodied a reaction against the limits of instrumental reason.[23] Most clearly evidenced in the arts, this dynamic movement played itself out in a series of artistic expressions, including impressionism, expressionism, abstract art, and chance. The human spirit, the movement believed, could not be contained within the construction of the modern self as an autonomous individual making rational choices. The result was a search to find meaning by exploring feeling, experience, and desire.

A contemporary rock concert offers a vivid illustration of the impulses expressed in modernism. The twelve-foot video screens projecting

23. Becker and Barnes, *Social Thought*, 2:531-32.

images of the action on stage accentuate the visual experience. The amplification of music through massive loudspeakers heightens the emotional impact. The rhythms, lyrics, costumes, and choreography intensify human desires, often expressed in sexual and sensual ways. The massive concentration of bodies moving together in rhythm quickens human feelings. In such a setting, experience becomes the main text; verbal content and cognitive meaning function only as subtexts.

This counterpulse within the larger development of modernity is as shaping of the modern self as is its rational side. But they produce an inherent tension for the modern person. On the one hand, we are defined by experience and feeling; on the other hand, we are driven to live by rational processes. Here is evidence of yet another unresolved issue within the fuller development of modernity.

The modern self is the dominant construct for how people think of themselves within contemporary Western societies, including those of North America. This construct is based on ways for discovering truth and developing knowledge that took form in the Enlightenment, with its confidence in instrumental reason and scientific knowledge. The modern self exists within a social order structured around citizenship and nation-state authority. Its shaping dynamics include the possession of personal rights, perpetual consumption, development of a constructed identity, the use of efficient technique, and a search for intense experience. Each of these dynamics creates an unresolved tension. As with all human cultures, modernity creates such a complex web of understandings and impulses that lines of tension are to be expected. But such tension lines are the points at which change and further development take place. We shall see how these unresolved issues are now fueling a revisioning of truth, self, and society toward what many call postmodernity, or the postmodern condition. These same fault lines also constitute some of the greatest challenges facing the churches of North America as they seek to witness faithfully to Jesus Christ by announcing and demonstrating the reign of God in their appointed place.

United States and Canadian Variations on the Theme

Before coming to those matters, however, it will be helpful to provide a more particular description of how modernity has taken shape within the North American context. Reflections till now have given a general view of modernity as it has formed the Western world. Each part of that world, and each ethnic or regional community, has experienced the impact and form of modernity in a unique way from its specific vantage point in different parts of the world. Here we will show the particular forms modernity has taken in the North American context by further indicating the nuances of its differences within the experiences of the United States and Canada.

This should not be taken as a denial that there are numerous variations and particularities of modernity as it has been experienced within each country. Indeed, the multiethnic and multifaceted character of life within each nation is itself a significant part of the form modernity takes. This book is based on the conviction that a full analysis of the context of any North American church's life and calling must take all those facets of local character and experience into account. It is obviously beyond the scope of this book to attempt a full portrait of the myriad diversities involved. What is offered here in the comparison between the United States and Canada is an initial illustration of the way particularity must be distinguished. We offer it both as an important element of difference in itself, and as a model for the closer look at diversity that must be added.

The United States' Version of the Modern Project

The application of modernity to the building of modern societies is often referred to as the "Enlightenment project" or the "modern project."[24] Several aspects of this project were uniquely woven into the story of what became the United States. One involves the timing of the nation's formation. The political framework for the fledgling United States was conceived as Enlightenment thought matured in the mid- to late eighteenth century. A focused application of Enlightenment principles organized U.S. constitutional thinking. The building of the new nation also coincided with the development of other primary institutional forms of the modern project. During this period, the frontier was settled, industry developed, and cities were built. Its special circumstances allowed the United States to build new institutional systems as it passed through its

24. David Harvey, *The Condition of Postmodernity* (New York: Blackwell, 1989), 12.

stages of growth and change in a somewhat orderly pattern over an extended period of time. In contrast, the application of the ideas and institutions of modernity in Europe had to replace historically rooted systems, and whole societies had to be reconstructed within a brief span of time. The unique situation of the United States fostered the myth in this country that social progress and managed institutional development were relatively easy to accomplish and could be offered as a realistic solution to any other nation.

Another aspect peculiar to the United States' version of the modern project involves the availability of extensive and seemingly endless resources. Massive immigration from Europe, large tracts of land on the frontier, and multiple natural resources fed the growth of the nation. These extensive resources in personnel, land, and raw materials allowed for distinct regional difference to emerge in the U.S. story, even as these variations continued to be blended into a common national identity. These resources also helped produce, over time, an extensive working class that became increasingly middle class in this century. The possibility of everyone attaining the middle-class ideal through hard work and education by taking full advantage of relatively equal opportunity became a significant component of the American dream.

The United States' version of the modern project was also significantly formed by a belief that the early English Puritan settlers transplanted to this country: that God had directly intervened to create a particular people in this place at this time. This sense of destiny has been a powerful force in the construction of the United States' national identity. Although religious in roots, this sense of destiny quickly took on a broader secular interpretation that has continued to commingle with its religious counterpart throughout the decades. It has had many manifestations, including the United States as moral example, safe haven, big brother, world policeman, and exemplar of the democratic ideal of freedom and rights.[25]

National myths like these are woven deeply into the consciousness of the U.S. people, although not all have shared them in quite the same way. Native American populations were forcibly removed from ancient homelands. Slaves were emancipated only at the cost of a civil war and then only to a partial freedom. Women won the right to vote only after

25. H. W. Brands, *The Reckless Decade: America in the 1890s* (New York: St. Martin's, 1995), 287-335.

a long, hard effort. Today an intense struggle to find ways to share a common story continues among diverse peoples.

Still, myths forming a common, national story powerfully moved the emerging mainstream psyche of the nation and provided a foundation for the assimilation of masses of diverse immigrants into the United States' context during the latter part of the nineteenth century. Sharing a common story was assumed to be rooted in the constitutional commitment that all could experience life, liberty, and the pursuit of happiness. These inalienable rights functioned as part of the great experiment of providing every person an equal standing before the law and an equal opportunity within the social, political, and economic order.

Canada's Version of the Modern Project

Unique factors influenced Canada's experience as well. One of the most significant and defining differences between the United States and Canada was Canada's constitutional formation. In the 1860s the province of Ontario led a confederation movement designed to move beyond England's direct rule. The English throne and Parliament concurred in this effort, and confederation was born as a political solution to buffer Canada from the expansionist interests of the United States while providing the government for a diverse set of provinces. This solution lacked any notion of destiny, any military battles, any brave heroes, or any national symbols. Consequently, most Canadians wear national identity lightly as they simply live out the freedoms and rights of their citizenship.[26] Canada lacks the type of national myths that provide for patriotic loyalty and personal sacrifice for a higher cause. The Canadian contribution to the victory at the World War I battle of Vimy and the celebration of Remembrance Day probably come closest to expressing such myths, but their role in shaping a corporate ethos is minimal.

Complicating the formation of a national identity was the bicultural makeup of the original confederation. Both English and French traditions were woven into the common fabric of confederation, and the Quebec question has been on the table ever since. This bicultural character made Canadians more tolerant of diversity and more committed, at least in

26. See the discussion by Richard Gwyn, *Nationalism Without Walls: The Unbearable Lightness of Being Canadian* (Toronto: McClelland and Stewart, 1995).

principle, to pluralism. It also produced a dilemma concerning how to adjudicate personal rights and freedoms equally and fairly. Canada as a nation embraced one of the most liberal applications of the Enlightenment notion of rights and freedoms. This openness within Canadian society is reflected in its citizenship, which since 1945 has not distinguished between native born and naturalized. It is also exhibited in an immigration policy that has readily accepted unlimited numbers of persons from throughout the world. The cultural pluralism that this openness creates today produces new kinds of pressures that overlay those associated with the original bicultural character of Canada.

Canada's initial confederation experience was more of a top-down process than a movement born from among the people. Federal-led solutions have been the norm for addressing Canadian developmental issues. Hence Canada functions more as a state-nation than a nation-state.[27] Throughout this century, Canada has had one of the most well-developed welfare policies for all its citizens. The state has likewise played a major role in the formation of national corporations and industries. Also of note is the role of the Royal Canadian Mounted Police in serving as a national police force beyond provincial supervision. This version of the democratizing traditions within the development of Canada has fostered the expectation that the government will provide solutions to problems. As long as tax revenues were strong, this system worked quite well. But in recent years, the expectation has fallen on hard times because of a declining economy.

Another feature in some respects unique to Canadian society is the incorporation of patterns of English civility into the shaping of a national culture. This tradition of civility functioned early as a dominant culture for the country as a whole, at least outside Quebec. But changes within Quebec and the increased presence of multiple ethnic populations in the other provinces have forced a shift in the importance and dominance of this tradition of civility. The social order increasingly searches for a new set of shared norms to guide public behavior. This shift has had consequences for the church. Its historical support of the earlier tradition of English civility has implicated the church in efforts to resist change.

The notion of rights and freedoms is deeply woven into the culture of modernity. This notion has taken a particular Canadian form in recent years. For decades Canada lived within its confederation without a writ-

27. Ibid., 19-27.

ten constitution. But the increased restlessness in Quebec, following the Quiet Revolution of the 1960s, stimulated a move toward independence. The constitutional solution, rendered largely through the political mastery of Pierre Trudeau, who served as Prime Minister of Canada, was embodied in the Charter of Rights and Freedoms passed in 1982. While intended to be a solution to the issue of Quebec, it actually opened wider the question of how to guarantee individual rights (section 15-1) while also insuring that historical deprivations of specific groups would be addressed (section 15-2).[28] The resulting picture is one of modernity sown in the wind and a "mosaic madness" returning in the whirlwind.[29]

The Emerging Postmodern Condition

Anywhere City/Suburb in North America: Reality Isn't What It Used to Be!

Bruce flicked through the various cable channels for the fifth time. He was bored and he was alone. The psychic network intrigued him for awhile. The personal testimonies seemed genuine enough, and he did have some interest in astrology. The after-hours channel was always a ready tease with the sweet-sounding invitations of good-looking women who wanted to "share your most intimate fantasies." The old Bond movie was interesting, but he had already seen it three times. What was there to experience that was new and different?

Life seemed kind of strange to him at the moment. He had recently broken off a long-term relationship with Kim after she had wanted to get more serious. He wasn't ready for any permanent commitment. He missed her and the sex that they had regularly shared, but he accepted the fact that life was moving on. What bothered him most at the moment was that he was so alone.

His job was okay in terms of the money he was earning, but he knew it wasn't taking him anywhere. But then, he wasn't sure that he wanted to go anywhere. The whole career thing in which his parents had been so caught up didn't hold much glamour. Big bucks, big houses, big cars, big bills, busy life — it all seemed kind of senseless.

28. Ibid., 165-81.

29. See the discussion in Reginald W. Bibby, *Mosaic Madness* (Toronto: Stoddart, 1990).

Sometimes he thought about God, not like his parents had with the church thing, but in more personal ways. He thought of himself as spiritual. Sometimes he talked with God, but it didn't make him feel less alone. One of his friends at work had recently gotten involved in some type of church that she had called "charismatic," and she had invited him to come with her. She kept telling him about the great music and the good feeling she got from the services. It had sounded interesting, up to a point, but he wasn't ready to have anyone put a God-trip on him.

One of the things he did think a lot about was how crazy the world was becoming. There had been that senseless killing last week in his city. Two kids had pulled a gun and shot a homeless person for no apparent reason. Then there was the tension in his neighborhood because Hispanics were moving in. The next thing you know he'd have to learn Spanish. No way! Let them learn how to speak English like the rest of us. Why didn't the government pass a law on that?

He realized that he was angry. He was not sure why, but he just felt angry. What kind of world was this anyway? He went back to surfing channels. After a while he picked up on the story lines of three different movies and settled in for another evening at home, constructing a collage of reality with his remote control.

The seemingly rational, objective, and managed world of modernity has undergone deep, significant shifts in recent decades. It is not merely that changes in our world demand new responses from us. The very foundations of society have changed. This shift in knowing and understanding "what is real" shapes the world Bruce inhabits. Often referred to as the "postmodern condition," this new world includes patterns such as:

- endless choices made available by technology
- loss of shared experiences
- meanings conveyed as surfaces and images
- transient relationships
- plurality of approaches to sexual expression and experience
- increasingly two-tiered economy with many dead-end jobs
- personal spirituality without the necessity of organized religion
- random violence and clashes between cultures
- feelings of anger or resentment because somebody's left us with a mess.

This emerging world, described as "postmodernity" or the "postmodern condition," means a shift in mood, style, and perspective from what had come to be known as "modernity." The use of the prefix *post-* betrays the fact that the extent and implications of this change are not yet fully clear. No fully descriptive word has emerged for what the culture is becoming. We only have a word that indicates what it appears to be moving away from. What is clear, however, is that significant changes are afoot that are transforming the way we understand truth, self, and society.

Scholars who trace the emergence of the postmodern condition have reached no clear consensus regarding either the scope of the change or the reasons for it. Some, like Anthony Giddens, argue that we are encountering just another phase of modernity, a radicalized version of it.[30] Others, with Jürgen Habermas, contend that the modern project of the Enlightenment is basically unfinished, having run aground on the problem of reason limited to its instrumental use and thereby failing to affirm its communicative value.[31] In contrast, Jean-François Lyotard proposed that the whole framework of Enlightenment thought that gave birth to modernity is faulty, and we cannot depend on it to move us forward.[32] In the midst of this range of interpretations and perspectives about the current change in culture, a number of illustrative theories point to some of its more pronounced features. These provide sketches of the leading edges of the cultural landscape of North America in which the contemporary church finds itself. They also show the lines of pressure and tension experienced in and by the contemporary culture.

Economics. Theorists like Frederic Jameson maintain that changes taking place in the economy explain the shifts that are occurring. They theorize that the rise of the third stage of capitalism, what most label as "globalized" or "consumer capitalism," explains much that is associated with the postmodern condition. In the postmodern condition, all of life is turned into commodities that can be marketed; managed, national economies are shifting toward a global economy with worldwide financial structures beyond the control of any one country; and a pervasive consumerism is required to keep the whole capitalist economy growing.[33]

Difference. Another group of observers agrees with Lyotard in stressing our growing awareness of difference as the key to understanding the

30. See Anthony Giddens, *The Consequences of Modernity* (Stanford: Stanford University Press, 1990).

31. Steven Best and Douglas Kellner, *Postmodern Theory: Critical Interrogations* (New York: Guilford, 1991), 233-46.

32. Ibid., 146-80.

33. See Jameson, "Postmodernism."

emergence of the postmodern condition. Modernity's assumptions of uniformity, the essential, and objectivity are all relativized in the face of this awareness. The reality of difference means that an external source for making choices no longer exists. In this condition, no metanarratives are available to guide individual choice or construct a social order in any authoritative manner.[34]

Desire. Analysts like Gilles Deleuze and Felix Guattari identify the dethroning of reason and the rise of feeling and desire as the basis for the shift to the postmodern condition. In this shift, intuition functions as the source of personal knowing, an intuition shaped by personal feelings and desires. This approach results in the privileging of every person and setting as both viable and valid for living life.[35] There are no shared norms to govern the larger society.

Power. Some thinkers, represented by Michel Foucault, conceptualize our understanding of the nature of power as the key to explaining the postmodern condition. In particular, the critical connection between power and knowledge is made. Conceptual frameworks, theories, or worldviews structure our understanding of reality. These mental pictures are not value-neutral; they are selective of certain preferences and tend to privilege certain elements of reality. Thus our understanding of all knowledge is laden with power relations. These authors suggest that how knowledge is structured and used is inherently a political process. This perspective challenges the claims of objectivity and factuality explicit in the Enlightenment method of scientific knowing. Understanding the true nature of power in relation to our rational knowing/knowledge redefines all relationships and all meaning.[36]

Simulation. Still others, working from the perspective of Jean Baudrillard, explain the postmodern condition in terms of the emergence of an image culture. Such a culture uses signs to represent real things. A condition of simulation increasingly becomes the new reality as the sign begins to replace rather than simply to substitute for the real thing that it is to represent. It is proposed that these signs and the simulation process are increasingly divorced from real things, producing a condition of virtual reality. In this condition, persons see the simulated as real.[37]

34. Best and Kellner, *Postmodern Theory,* 233-46.
35. Ibid., 76-110.
36. Ibid., 34-75.
37. Ibid., 111-45.

These various theories of the postmodern indicate some of the complexity of our task as we attempt to describe our present North American culture. While the theoretical perspectives regarding the post-modern condition may still be in the process of clarification, some expressions of this condition are readily visible in the North American context. In particular, there are significant changes in the three elements of modernity surveyed earlier: Enlightenment notions of truth, self, and society.

Relative Truth

It has become increasingly evident that no one stands outside a particular point of view when it comes to discovering truth. Claims of objectivity and appeals to factuality are now qualified by context, whether in regard to the chemist working in a laboratory or the biblical scholar working in a library of ancient texts. We now acknowledge that everyone works with basic assumptions about reality. This has shifted the focus from epistemology, the question of how we discover truth, to hermeneutics, the question of what assumptions one brings to the pursuit of truth. This move recognizes that all persons live within particular contexts. Therefore they possess specific cultural perspectives that are historically conditioned and shape the way they understand, see, and experience life. This tends to relativize every point of view.

The relative character of our knowing does not necessarily mean that we cannot know God or truth. It does mean, however, that we need to accept that our understanding of truth is always an interpretation relative to our context and cultural understanding. Therefore we need always to be open to other perspectives of interpretation and recognize that our understandings of truth are developmental in character. This recognition of a relativity of perspective is not the same thing as a thoroughgoing relativism that denies that any truth can be known.[38]

Another dynamic of the postmodern condition that touches on the way we discover or interpret truth originates in the critique of the limits of instrumental reason. The emerging postmodern approach to under-

38. See the discussion in ibid., 256-303, and also in Herbert W. Simons and Michael Billig, eds., *After Postmodernism: Reconstructing Ideology Critique* (Thousand Oaks, Calif.: Sage, 1994).

standing truth is more holistic by pointing to a variety of ways of knowing through rational intelligence, emotional intelligence, and intuitive intelligence. This variety dethrones modernity's privileging of instrumental reason as the source of objective facts. In its place, we find the more balanced perspective of using reason tempered by emotive and intuitive sources of understanding.

The Bible leads the church to experience in a similar way a more holistic understanding of truth than is emphasized in postmodernity's approach to knowing. For the church to live out an intimate engagement with the narrative of God's action in Jesus Christ that shapes its life and thought, it must use personal and communal ways of knowing that reach beyond the merely rational.[39] Falling into an ultimate relativism and subjectivity are always dangers within the emerging postmodern condition, but the postmodern worldview can nevertheless be conducive to establishing critical points of contact with a more holistic approach to knowing.

Decentered Self

The Enlightenment of the eighteenth century sought to promote individual personal freedom by constructing the modern self. During the nineteenth century, European philosophers addressed establishing the limits of personal freedom on the premise that the individual is rational and autonomous. The bankruptcy of this effort became evident, however, when they failed to secure any normative content common to all persons. When "god" died in the equation of modernity, it was only a matter of time before the modern self would also expire.[40] There are no reasons to sustain personal freedom beyond what Friedrich Nietzsche (1844-1900) referred to as the "will to power." All that remains is brute force and domination. The darker implications of this will to power became all too evident in the rise of Nazi Germany and the use of instrumental reason to construct the death camps of the Holocaust.

The collapse of confidence in the modern self coincided with new

39. Lesslie Newbigin, *The Gospel in a Pluralist Society* (Grand Rapids: Eerdmans, 1989), 222-23.
40. Robert Hollinger, *Postmodernism and the Social Sciences: A Thematic Approach* (Thousand Oaks, Calif.: Sage, 1994), 103-6.

developments in the social sciences. These developments shifted the focus away from an individual making rational choices to a quite different foundation for explaining human behavior. For instance, the emerging discipline of sociology moved the locus of attention to society's influence and social norms' shaping human behavior (Max Weber).[41] The new psychological theories of Sigmund Freud (1856-1939) and others stressed the impact of the subconscious and early life experiences; and in political economics, Karl Marx (1818-1883) highlighted the means of production as critical to human choices and behaviors.[42] All of these developments served to decenter the importance of the individual and to diminish confidence in personal, rational choices as determinative of human action.

This decentering of the modern self has left many adrift in the world without clear bearings or a satisfactory direction. This situation poses the pressing problem of reconceptualizing the nature of person-hood in terms that hold together individuality and community. Post-modernity is searching for an individuality beyond the empty construct of Western individualism and for a community greater than the social forces that influence it.

Pluralist Society

A persistent thread of concern in our current culture is the increased diversity that we encounter. Globalization is now leading to multiple ethnic cultures and racial traditions living together in the same neigh-borhoods. With increased immigration and migration to North America from all parts of the globe, more persons now come into direct contact with cultures, religions, and traditions other than their own. The intro-duction of media options such as cable and satellite television, as well as video rentals, contributes to fewer and fewer persons sharing com-mon experiences, even as they encounter similar images, icons, and story lines. Indeed, the introduction of other electronic technologies such as E-mail, Internet, and Worldwide Web has created a new sort of electronic community unfettered by the traditional limits of space (shared geographic location) or time (shared schedule). The social

41. Manicas, *History and Philosophy of the Social Sciences,* 133-36.
42. See R. F. Baum, *Doctors of Modernity: Darwin, Marx, and Freud* (Peru, Ill.: Sherwood Sugdon, 1988), respectively, 85-114, 49-84.

nature of life is still evident, but its foundation and forms have shifted significantly.

The function of community within the social order is changing. The context of modernity, with its philosophy of individualism and personal freedom, assumed that persons shared some sense of communal identity. This condition no longer exists for most people as a primary framework for understanding life. The structures that previously shaped such community have eroded. With this erosion, persons find themselves very alone. In this context, individualism is not so much a choice people make as a condition forced upon them.

We see these shifts in the areas of family, neighborhoods, and ideology. The form of community fostered through the extended family during earlier modernity gradually declined in importance as people moved into urban areas and social mobility accelerated in a capitalist economy. Even the nuclear family that replaced the extended family as a basic social unit has undergone significant change, with rising divorce rates, increases in the number of single-parent households, the prevalence of two-income families, busy lifestyles, and diverse definitions of what constitutes a family. The forms of community formerly based on geographic neighborhoods have been pressured to change by increased mobility, the socioeconomic and racial transition of communities, and expanding diversity among those living in proximity to one another. The declining influence of ideology for shaping identity and communal commitments has changed communities formed originally around a common set of beliefs and experiences, so-called voluntary societies. A retreat to ethnic tribalism can be viewed as one result of these shifts. Forms of national community fostered by sharing a common national story and set of values have come under stress as the once familiar metanarratives of the United States and Canadian stories have become pluralized.

New forms of community, shaped largely by media and consumer choices, are displacing many of the former structures of community. But they carry with them a major drawback: they often do not bring persons into face-to-face relationships. Many people today desperately search for a face-to-face community, "a place where everybody knows your name," as the theme song to the popular sitcom *Cheers* put it. Yet many remain alone, trapped in the individualism of the modern condition. Social and ethnic diversity represents a threat, not a resolution. The church itself is often also trapped in identities formed under the notions of modernity and the social structures pervasive in an earlier era.

Frequently it offers little more than an oasis of memory for forms of community assumed in a former age. Today's Generation Xers, the first postmodern generation, find little in the church that promises an answer to their quest for meaning and connection.

The Context and the Church

Our culture's ways of determining truth, defining the self, and shaping society present to the church both critical challenges and significant opportunities. The modern self, now in a postmodern condition, lives amid an array of social conditions and dynamics. This too is the context of the church's life in North America. In this situation the church is called into being and sent to participate in God's mission in the world. Several brief sketches help to fill out the picture of this context. They point to some of the more critical places where the context bears on the church's responsibility.

Spirituality. The postmodern openness to perceiving life in a variety of ways has contributed to the reemergence of spirituality as a viable and necessary part of the human struggle for meaning today. People are very secular, but they are often spiritual secularists. This spirituality tends to express itself in the United States through more activistic and emotional forms, while in Canada the expression of spirituality has a more private and reserved quality.[43]

National Identity. While the United States developed its story around notions of God's providence and divine destiny, Canadian identity developed more in terms of a modified establishment of the church. The postmodern condition is associated with the continued social fragmentation of the multiple ethnic stories within both countries. In Canada this challenge has been complicated by the increasing movement toward regionalism in recent decades, thereby straining the principle of confederation. In contrast, U.S. identity faces the complication of a continuing naïveté about how diverse persons can and should be incorporated into a common story and set of values, a melting pot. The church confronts the challenge of disengaging itself from the privileges of a previous church culture (United States) or semi-establishment (Canada), while

43. See the presentation of this secular spirituality in Douglas Coupland, *Life After God* (Toronto: Pocket Books, 1994).

rediscovering its own identity as a social community in the midst of a broader national community of communities.[44]

Multiple Cultures. Globalization and expanded immigration have brought increased ethnic and cultural diversity to both the United States and Canada. This diversity challenges the church to be a social community that creates true unity among different people, even as it affirms particular identity. Canada's immigration policy, more open than that of the United States, has led to a more substantial increase of its ethnic minority population, especially in Ontario and British Columbia. In addition, its bicultural history has made it more sensitive to the complexity of multicultural realities. Canada's current policy of multiculturalism, which attempts to adjudicate the historical deprivations of certain ethnic and social groups, creates real strains on the maintenance of national identity.[45] Many U.S. citizens often view the increase in ethnic minority populations as a threat to the once dominant Anglo culture. At the same time that national policy continues to shift away from race as a basis for guaranteeing social rights, many whites exhibit a rising racist militancy. In both countries, violence associated with immigration policies and ethnic relations continues to grow.[46] This situation makes it even more critical for the church to demonstrate the reconciling power of the gospel in multicultural communities.

Living in the Now. In the postmodern condition, whatever is "now" is privileged as the primary reality. With this dynamic comes an incessant need for persons to recreate themselves and a subsequent loss in value of any historical perspective. Persons think less in terms of the consequences associated with their choices. This condition affects notions of morality and accountability. On the other side, many experience a loss of future direction and a diminished sense of hope and purpose. Postmodern persons tend to live in the present, a present that thrives on surfaces, images, and experiences.[47] In this context, the church bears a gospel that is rooted in actual history, a gospel that takes seriously both consequence and contingency, and a gospel that offers a genuine hope for a real future.

44. Craig Van Gelder, "Defining the Center — Finding the Boundaries," in George R. Hunsberger and Craig Van Gelder, eds., *The Church Between Gospel and Culture* (Grand Rapids: Eerdmans, 1996), 29-30.

45. See discussion in Bibby, *Mosaic Madness.*

46. See James D. Hunter, *Cultural Wars: The Struggle to Define America* (New York: Basic Books, 1991).

47. Harvey, *Condition of Postmodernity,* 3-9.

Missional Challenge:
Understanding the Church in North America

The church exists in North America. It is a historical reality. Its rich diversity of traditions, beliefs, and experiences has accumulated over centuries, and there is no way to erase the board and start over. Any effort to develop a missional ecclesiology for the North American context needs to take seriously the church as it presently exists. Such an ecclesiology must address the new initiatives required to move the church forward. It must also identify the principles and processes required for rethinking churches' identities and renewing their lives.

In considering the church as it currently exists in North America, we will first give attention to the broader interaction of Christianity with the cultural context. In the process, we will discuss the unique form of a functional Christendom that emerged within the United States and Canadian settings. Then we will consider the distinctive structures that the church has adopted in these contexts, including both denominations and paralocal Christian organizations.

The Unique Version of Christendom Developed in North America

Anywhere City/Suburb in North America: Christendom —
How Seductive You Are!

Sally sat and reflected on the meeting she was attending. Because she had spoken out at her local church, the pastor had asked her to represent her congregation at this regional gathering. Area church leaders in the city were planning for the upcoming National Day of Prayer. A broad coalition of persons from diverse denominations and religious groups attended the meeting.

   Some from evangelical churches were advocating that the group make a sincere application of the 2 Chronicles' concept of national repentance. Others, especially from mainline denominations, wanted the day to focus attention on the problem of homelessness in the city. Several Roman Catholic sisters were asking that the issues of world peace and dismantling nuclear weapons be a main focus. Then there were those from the right-to-life crowd who insisted that the coalition accept their agenda up front. Of course, a significant number of representatives from various churches sharply protested this proposal.

   By this time in the meeting, the gathering had split into two separate groups, each making plans for different ways to honor the day of prayer. One group seemed to be made up mostly of evangelicals, representatives from parachurch organizations, and the right-to-life people. The other group appeared to be largely from mainline churches, while the Roman Catholics divided up and joined both groups in planning for the separate day's events.

   "What a collage," she thought, "and they all claim to represent God as they articulate their vision for the country." She pondered whether God really identified with any of these agendas. "After all, what was a 'national' day of prayer, anyway?"

The church's story in North America is deeply enmeshed within the story of modernity. Whether in its service of the United States' national aims or in its assumed contribution to Canadian national identity, the reality of religion must be reckoned with. It is part of the air we breathe.

   Sally's experience primarily reflects the U.S. context, but a similar mind-set is evident in Canada as well. The church's responsibility to serve as a guide for the broader society is assumed in both countries. This reality includes such dimensions as:

- specially designated privileges for the church in society
- expectations on the part of churches to address national policy or issues
- a broad range of agenda among diverse groups for influencing the public
- the process of building networks and coalitions to affect policy or bring about change
- the pattern of creating separate activities by coalitions of diverse groups
- an activistic agenda toward public policy pursued by numerous churches
- a view held by many that the church's role is primarily to offer spiritual guidance.

The word *Christendom* is often associated with the type of relationship that has developed between the church and the broader culture in North America. Technically this term is limited to a church that has an official ecclesiastical status through legal establishment. The state churches in Europe possessed this status (some still do), and it was out of such a long tradition of establishment that most early immigrants took up residence in the colonies of North America.

"Christendom" also describes the functional reality of what took place specifically in the North American setting. Various churches contributed to the formation of a dominant culture that bore the deep imprint of Christian values, language, and expectations regarding moral behaviors. Other terms like "Christian culture" or "churched culture" might be used to describe this Christian influence on the shape of the broader culture. The following section discusses the functional Christendom of North America, and how the stories of the U.S. and Canadian churched cultures differed somewhat.

The U.S. Version of a Functional Christendom as Churched Culture

In considering the influence of the Christian faith in the United States, it is helpful to distinguish between the terms *Constantinianism* and *Christendom*. Constantinianism is used to describe the legal establishment of the Christian church by the Emperor Constantine in the fourth century. This action made Christianity an official religion in the Roman

Empire. Christendom refers to the resulting impact of the Christian church on the empire's dominant culture. Taken together, these actions meant that the church held both a legally established position that privileged its existence, and a moral influence in shaping the society that privileged its life and work.

Although a Constantinian legal establishment of the church in America was only temporary in some colonies, the formal separation of church and state in the U.S. Constitution at the end of the colonial period still allowed what can only be described as a functional Christendom. The relationship between the church in the United States and its culture began with efforts to establish the church, but thereafter a series of cultural changes led gradually to the church's disestablishment. The initial quest to establish the church coincided with the founding of the American colonies. The progressive disestablishment of the church took over two hundred years to evolve and passed through three phases.

Efforts at Establishment. The North American colonies were founded during the seventeenth century at a time when tremendous changes were taking place within European state-churches and among various persecuted churches. The Puritans, in particular, influenced the U.S. story as they sought a more thorough reformation of the Church of England. Their persecution led many to immigrate to the newly developing colonies. They brought with them views about the church that can only be described as more radical. These settlers officially established the Congregational Church in the New England colonies, where they developed a church-centered society built around biblical principles and theocratic ideals.

By contrast, the southern colonies were shaped mostly by the Anglican Church, which functioned in an established manner, reflecting the English tradition. In between were the middle colonies, where immigrants arrived from numerous countries with diverse state-church traditions, like the Reformed from Holland, Lutherans from Germany, and Presbyterians from Scotland. Mixed into this milieu were various persecuted churches from Europe such as the Mennonites and Quakers, and indigenous groups that emerged in the New World but like the Baptists of Rhode Island patterned themselves after European models. Finally, overlaying this whole mix was a significant number of Roman Catholic immigrants. These new arrivals came from numerous countries and organized themselves along ethnic lines, while maintaining an allegiance to their common church.

This historical accident of multiple churches from diverse traditions occupying the same space created a dilemma for the church. While some colonies established a particular church within their boundaries, even these colonies eventually recognized that other churches were present in their midst. No one church could establish complete domain throughout the colonies. But how were these churches to understand themselves and relate to one another? The issue of pluralism had to be faced, especially in the middle colonies.[1] Part of the solution found for this dilemma was the new organizational structure, the denomination. This structure gradually took shape as diverse churches began to accept one another's legitimacy and forge working alliances where possible.

The formative period between the early seventeenth and late eighteenth centuries shaped a particular type of relationship between churches and the social order. The relationship was influenced most by the churches of the radical right, who conceived the church's role to be an "errand in the wilderness," carrying out a "divine destiny."[2] While no one church could establish preeminence in pursuing this destiny, almost all the churches took for granted their special place in shaping the social order. Similar in function to the emerging free market of capitalism, a type of religious economy developed in this context where the various denominations competed for adherents. The combination of expected privilege and religious competition translated into the formation of a functional Christendom and a churched culture. Such a culture placed the churches clearly at the center of public life, where they attempted to influence policy, morals, and institutions, while building a host of private institutions under their control.[3] This type of establishment fostered a unique version of church-state relations in the United States, and it is this establishment that has passed through several phases of being disestablished.

First Disestablishment: Separation of Church and State. A mixture of intellectual currents shaped the discussion of the relationship between

---

1. Fred J. Hood, "Evolution of the Denomination Among the Reformed of the Middle and Southern States, 1780-1840," in Russell E. Richey, ed., *Denominationalism* (Nashville: Abingdon, 1977), 139-60.

2. See discussion in Williston Walker, *The Creeds and Platforms of Congregationalism* (Philadelphia: Pilgrim, 1960).

3. Timothy L. Smith, "Congregation, State, and Denomination: The Forming of the American Religious Structures," in Richey, ed., *Denominationalism*, 47-67.

the church and the state within the American colonies in the mid-seventeenth century. These included Enlightenment theories promoting freedom from religion, establishment ideals representing state-church traditions, and free-church theories seeking the freedom of religion. The compromise solution finally rendered under Jefferson's influence was the separation of church and state as defined in the U.S. Constitution. By the nineteenth century, this solution would lead to what Martin Marty has called "controlled secularity."[4] The basic principle of separation of church and state insured that persons would have full rights to practice their religion without interference from the state.[5] This allowed a privileged position for the church, without the church being officially established. The founders clearly expected the church to play a primary role in shaping the social order, and this expectation fostered the formation of a functional Christendom.

The separation of church and state constituted the first disestablishment of the church. But it did not disrupt several assumptions deeply embedded in the expectations of denominational churches as they forged their own national identities after 1790. First, while these churches enjoyed a freedom from state interference, they clearly expected to have a major voice in forming public policy, morality, and institutions. Second, because these churches were predominantly Protestant, they shared a set of faith tenets and a commitment to the Bible's authority for carrying out their work. While significant diversity existed among these Protestant denominations, they generally accepted each other's legitimacy and entered into various coalitions.[6] One of the most significant of these coalitions was the Evangelical Alliance formed in 1867.

These churches considered it their responsibility to infuse society with the gospel and to plant congregations of their denominations throughout the expanding nation. This dual task of creating a churched culture and churching an expanding frontier consumed much of the churches' efforts during the nineteenth century. For this purpose, the church developed new methods, including revivals, camp meetings,

---

4. Martin E. Marty, *The Modern Schism: Three Paths to the Secular* (New York: Harper & Row, 1969), 9-17.

5. It is somewhat ironic that in the latter part of the twentieth century the focus has shifted to protecting the state from the practice of religion.

6. Sydney E. Mead, "Denominationalism: The Shape of Protestantism in America," in Richey, ed., *Denominationalism,* 70-105.

Christian schools and colleges, and morality movements such as temperance and abolition. Biblical language was shared in common by most everyone in society, whether they claimed to be Christian or not, and many believed that converted persons living morally as individuals would shape a moral Christian society.

The churches' capacity to inform the society was severely tested by the issue of slavery. Slavery fractured denominations along regional lines, and churches on both sides struggled to understand how to be the church without serving as a tool of the state or falling into bondage to a particular cultural practice. By the end of the nineteenth century, new developments forced changes in the relationship of the Protestant denominations to the cultural context. The limits of personal morality for creating a moral social order became increasingly evident as cities grew rapidly and the industrial revolution brought massive immigration.[7] These developments led to a further disestablishment of the church.

Second Disestablishment: Protestant, Catholic, and Jew. Unprecedented immigration in the late nineteenth and early twentieth centuries included fewer persons from northern Europe but many more from southern and eastern Europe. With this shift came increased numbers of Roman Catholic, Orthodox, and Jewish immigrants. They settled primarily in the growing urban areas in the Northeast, and their presence began to challenge the hegemony of the Protestant establishment. While the story unfolded over a number of decades, the trajectory of its plot was clearly evident by the turn of the century. The Protestant establishment would in time give way to a Judeo-Christian heritage shared by Protestants, Catholics, and Jews, and in this context the earlier pluralism among Protestant denominations was replaced by a pluralism of diverse religious traditions.

Along with the disestablishment of the Protestant empire of the nineteenth century came a marked change in understanding how the gospel functioned within society. Emphasis on personal morality in the midst of industrialization, urbanization, and immigration no longer seemed sufficient for shaping a Christian society. Churches continued to expect a privileged position in shaping their culture, but after 1900 different denominations pursued various strategies.[8]

7. Winthrop S. Hudson, *Religion in America* (New York: Charles Scribner's Sons, 1965), 291-324.
8. Ibid.

Some groups, especially Protestants, refocused their effort to develop a public morality around the specific issue of temperance. This nineteenth-century debate grew in popularity and culminated in the enactment of Prohibition in 1920. The repealing of this action in 1933 symbolized the waning influence of the Protestant establishment generally and of its rural and small-town constituencies in particular. Other groups, including both Protestants and Catholics, focused their attention on problems in the growing cities. The viability of personal morality shaping a moral society broke down, however, in the face of overwhelming suffering in the urban context. The complexity of urban society led some to think about the gospel in social, structural, and institutional terms. A social gospel movement attempted to address the more systemic nature of evil as it was lodged within society's institutional structures.[9]

After the turn of the century the discussion of the relationship between the churches and the social order became further complicated by theological debates over biblical authority that fractured a number of denominations. On the one hand, many conservatives, known as fundamentalists, turned inward and focused once more on faith in individual terms. Personal morality became privatized morality for most of these groups. On the other hand, those of a more liberal persuasion struggled to define a Christian approach beyond what they now viewed as the naïve optimism of the social gospel after its humbling in the face of the devastation of World War I. Many, however, turned to a new theological perspective known as neo-orthodoxy. Their focus remained on transforming culture, but the reality of evil and brokenness within society brought new awareness of the need for God's power to be present in the transformation process.[10]

The diverse religious traditions of Protestant, Catholic, and Jew, along with the various theological streams within these communions, gave birth to a complex and diverse relationship between the church and society. By mid-century, after two world wars, the focus shifted to what came to be described as the full development of a civil religion. This civil faith built on the earlier notions of divine destiny and God's providence as it formulated a renewed version of the coalescence of God, country, and democracy. By the mid-twentieth century, civil religion

9. Sydney E. Ahlstrom, *A Religious History of the American People,* 2 vols. (Garden City, N.Y.: Image, 1975), 2:250-73.
10. Ibid., 274-97.

found direct expression in the inclusion of the words "under God" in the Pledge of Allegiance and the institution of the phrase "In God We Trust" as the national motto (it had been on the nation's coins since 1865). Churches were divided over what approach to take in addressing the public sector, but they all continued to share the common expectation that society as a whole should reflect God's agenda. This version of churched culture would undergo a tumultuous transformation in the 1960s.

Third Disestablishment: The Individualization of Society. As we move further from the tempestuous 1960s, we continue to gain perspective on how these events dramatically transformed the lives of all U.S. citizens. The host of interrelated movements that swept through society at that time sounds like a litany of social ferment today: the civil rights movement demanded constitutional equality become a reality; the counterculture forged an alternative identity for a generation of baby boomers coming of age; the sexual revolution collapsed the sexual norms of the churched culture's morality; the women's movement redefined gender relationships and the role of women in society; the ecology movement insisted big business stop industrial pollution and ecological abuse; the Vietnam War and antiwar movement questioned the authority of institutions and the validity of civil religion; the black power movement replaced civil rights with economic empowerment; and the urban crisis sobered a whole nation by questioning whether the myth of the American dream worked for everyone.

As these diverse movements raged across the American landscape for over a decade, the relationship of churches to society went through significant changes as well. The most noteworthy was the collapse or substantial erosion of much of the churched culture that had been built up over a period of two hundred years. Notions of shared public morals gave way to personal decisions of expediency, pleasure, or private judgment. Expectations of privileged position gave way to irrelevance and marginalization. People no longer assumed that the church had anything relevant to say on matters beyond personal faith. Public policy became increasingly secularized, as public morals became increasingly personalized and privatized.[11]

Underlying much of this transition was a fundamental shift in the

11. Wade Clark Roof and William McKinney, *American Mainline Religion: Its Changing Shape and Future* (New Brunswick: Rutgers University Press, 1987), 11-39.

way society conceived truth to function. The intellectual grounds for this movement had been laid decades earlier as Enlightenment thinkers used instrumental reason and the scientific method to divorce objective truth — facts — from subjective feeling — values. The fuller implications of this divide manifested itself in U.S. society during the ferment of the 1960s. The shift undermined the idea that any commonly accepted external authority existed to direct our choices about values. Science provided facts about the physical world, but offered no authoritative help for our making value choices.[12] Moral truth became relativized, and society became individualized. This comprised the third disestablishment of the churches in the United States. For most people today, the hermeneutics of decision making involves "oneself" and "one's situation."[13] This is true, as well, for many who still participate in churches. We live increasingly in a post-Christian society, or what might better be labeled a post-churched culture. Either way, it is clear that the relationship of the churches to the social order has undergone profound change.

Canada's Version of a Functional Christendom as Churched Culture

The church was initially established in Canada both by the French in Quebec and by the English in the other provinces. The relationship between these churches and their cultures went through changes over time. But the concept of the church occupying an official place in society and having a primary responsibility for guiding the social order remained central to the Canadian understanding of the church up to the 1960s. To tell this story, we first review the formulation of the concept and then examine the three phases that it passed through as it was modified by new circumstances.

The Assumption of Establishment. Although the development of the Canadian church includes several themes that must be interwoven into a common story, the primary story line involves the influence of the British. The impact of the British was initially felt through the Hudson Bay Company, and later through the direct imposition of British rule within several provinces. Since the Anglican Church enjoyed exclusive

---

12. Lesslie Newbigin, *Foolishness to the Greeks: The Gospel and Western Culture* (Grand Rapids: Eerdmans, 1986), 1-20.
13. Roof and McKinney, *American Mainline Religion*, 40-71.

established status in England, it naturally became the established church within these emerging provinces. While the rights of other Protestant groups were protected, open hostility was often expressed toward Catholic residents. This practice paralleled the restrictions placed on Protestants by the Catholics in the colony of New France during the seventeenth and early eighteenth centuries.[14] The Catholic Church was fully established within this colony, and although civil magistrates governed society, the church's influence was woven into every aspect of public and private life. The rights of Protestants living there were severely restricted and carefully controlled.

These two church traditions found themselves in direct conflict during the war between the English and the French in the mid-eighteenth century. The English victory and the subsequent Treaty of Paris in 1763 brought the French colony under English control. But this did little to alter the Catholic Church's role within the colony. Both the Catholics who controlled Quebec and the Protestants who dominated the other provinces had to work out principles to protect the rights of persons of the other religion in their areas. Public schools and universities became the battleground for developing these principles.[15] The situation became even more complex when diverse immigrants from other church traditions settled in the various provinces, when denominations in the American colonies made connections with their counterparts in Canada, and especially when Tory sympathizers fled north in the aftermath of the Revolutionary War, bringing their denominations with them.

The commingling of these many traditions began to challenge the Anglican establishment by the early nineteenth century. The church's privileged position continued to erode as the Protestant groups became more diverse and as the Anglican Church failed to provide sufficient clergy to minister to the growing and shifting population. Discussions of confederation began in the mid-nineteenth century, and these discussions made clear that Anglicanism would have to relinquish its privileged position to a more general Protestantism in the provinces outside Quebec. Now Protestant Canadian churches in general could assume many of the privileges once enjoyed exclusively by the Anglican Church:

14. H. H. Walsh, *The Christian Church in Canada* (Toronto: Ryerson, 1956), 51-61.

15. Ibid., 186-200.

special provisions of state encouragement, some financial support in a few provinces in the case of public schools, and the expectation that these churches would help shape the public, moral behavior of the citizens. This pattern was the operational framework for churches at the time of confederation in 1867, and became formalized in the Act of 1875.[16]

Becoming a Nation with a Moral Society. The special relationship between the churches and the social order in both the English-speaking provinces and French-speaking Quebec gave the Canadian denominational churches a more formal responsibility than their counterparts in the United States. While the Canadian Protestant churches functioned on the similar principle of being voluntary associations, a different ethos shaped this association. Canadian churched culture sought to introduce English civility and certain biblical morals into Canadian public behaviors.

With regard to morality, four moral behaviors in particular became the responsibility of the church to inculcate into the social order. These were abstinence from alcohol, and the prohibition of gambling, dancing, and smoking. The Protestant churches made a concerted nationwide effort to infuse Canadian society with these moral commitments, with most churches cycling sermons on these topics through their church year.[17] This attempt to create a moral social order, one that focused primarily on external, moral behaviors, had serious consequences over time. Later, the logic of shared social norms began to erode. With this erosion, the shallow foundations for enforcing such morality became evident as many members shifted to inactive status in what has become a pervasive nominalism.

In addition to helping shape a moral society, the churches also built national, denominational structures following confederation. They patterned these structures after their U.S. counterparts, even though the ethos of a quasi-establishment gave them a somewhat different character. Consolidation within the same denominational structure among those who shared a similar theological tradition developed early.

These new, national, denominational structures took on the major responsibility for spreading Christianity and civilization throughout the

16. Ibid., 220-40.
17. John Webster Grant, *The Church in the Canadian Era: The First Century of Confederation* (Toronto: McGraw-Hill Ryerson, 1972), 78-82.

emerging nation of Canada. Missions within Rupert's Land, the former Hudson Bay Colony territory to the west, received primary attention. Although such missions' main goal was to win converts from the native populations, denominations also contributed to taming the West by bringing the church to new settlers on the frontier.[18] As additional immigrants continued to arrive, the churches took on the role of nurturing these persons into both church life and Canada's dominant culture. This meant introducing them to Canadian-English civility as part of making them active church members.[19] This mission helped forge a sense of national responsibility among the various denominations.

The Protestant Canadian version of Christendom included the two tasks of moral responsibility for society and a shared missions work. This type of churched culture was deeply woven into the cultural ethos of English society. In contrast, the Catholic version of Christendom in Quebec assumed a central role for the church in every aspect of life. Both forms, however, reflected characteristics of established church traditions.

Becoming a Nation with Social Responsibilities. Around the turn of the twentieth century, Canada followed a similar pattern to that occurring in the United States. Expanding industrial development stimulated the growth of large cities while attracting waves of new immigrants. Much of this immigration originated in central Europe, bringing with it the diverse religious traditions of the Orthodox, Jews, and Mennonites. Large segments of these immigrants initially chose to bypass the growing cities and to settle instead in religious communities on the central plains as these areas opened up after 1900. But similar to the pattern in the United States, none of the Canadian denominations ever established a strong presence in the western provinces. There a more secular tradition and spirit has always dominated.

In light of these developments, Canadian churches had to make some adjustments in order to build a churched culture. One involved the creation of a social gospel movement in order to meet the challenges of urbanization and industrialization. Although never as substantial as the one in the United States, the Canadian social gospel did not suffer

18. Ibid., 46-57.
19. Ramsay Cook, "The Triumph and Trials of Materialism (1900-1945)," in Craig Brown, ed., *The Illustrated History of Canada,* 2nd ed. (Toronto: Lester, 1991), 383-93.

from the theological split that greatly marginalized the U.S. version. In Canada the social gospel made the church aware of broader institutional realities that the gospel needed to address, but the churches' primary focus remained the formation of a Canadian society that reflected biblical morals and English civility.[20]

The formation of the United Church of Canada in 1925 represented a further major development during this period. The Congregationalists, Methodists, and Presbyterians merged to create a national church rivaling the Anglican Church in both size and prestige. Inherent within this merger of diverse bodies was the reality that their shared responsibility for shaping a moral society rather than maintaining theological consistency was more influential in forming organizational commitments.[21] This implicit priority reflects a key element of the functional Christendom of Canada's churched culture. By the tumultuous 1960s, this churched culture had little defense to stem the tide toward declining participation, or nominalism, among many members.

Members Becoming Nominal in Canadian Churches. Canada traversed the same series of tumultuous social revolutions during the 1960s as other Western nations. In the midst of these changes, active participation in churches rapidly eroded, both in Quebec during the Quiet Revolution and among the Protestant churches in the other provinces. The scope of the shift was staggering. Whereas 50-60 percent of Protestant members had been active in weekly attendance up to that time, participation rates dropped by almost two-thirds within twenty years. The decline of Catholic participation in Quebec was even more pronounced given the high rates that had been the rule. It dropped from 80 percent to under 40 percent during the same twenty-year period.[22] In the throes of this upheaval, many pastors and churches concentrated on maintaining the faith of their active members, and because of this focus a whole generation of youth and young adults was lost to the church. This situation proved especially characteristic of those churches that kept strong ties to the English tradition and secured significant numbers of their pastors from England.

What stands behind this rapid shift to member inactivity and nom-

20. Grant, *Church in the Canadian Era,* 121-24.
21. Ibid., 124-29.
22. Reginald W. Bibby, *Fragmented Gods: The Poverty and Potential of Religion in Canada* (Toronto: Irwin, 1987), 11-23.

inalism? It is clear at this point that the compelling logic that once supported regular church participation no longer held sway. While people still maintained their membership in the institutional church of their heritage, they simply stopped regular participation. Canadians have worn their church identities lightly for some time, however, because the church's formation was deeply rooted in establishment traditions. Even though a voluntary principle was eventually developed, this establishment heritage weakened the loyalty of church members to specific religious traditions. The historical development of Canadian institutions from the top down meant that individuals felt less obligated to participate actively once the value of such institutions no longer seemed relevant to their personal lives. While recent studies indicate that Canadians are quite spiritual, they now pursue their spirituality in personal ways outside the institutional church. Canadian churches also tended to focus too heavily on external moral behaviors in helping to shape a churched culture. When the shared social norms supporting these behaviors collapsed, the church's relevance imploded.[23]

The churches in both the United States and Canada have developed a type of functional Christendom in the form of a churched culture. Starting from somewhat different points, the processes within each country followed similar paths. Therefore today we find churches seeking a public voice but finding that they are no longer taken seriously. Their voice in the United States has been marginalized into a highly personalized and privatized practice of faith, while their voice in Canada has been silenced through the declining participation or nominalization of membership within the institutional churches. These results are related to the fact that North American Christianity has evolved and been organized as denominations and paralocal organizations.

23. Grant, *Church in the Canadian Era*, 184-206.

The Distinctive Shape and Character
of the North American Church

Anywhere City/Suburb in North America: Denominationalism — How Are We to Sort It Out?

Jim and Ruth were having a discussion about their church. It was a discussion that had taken place over several months. Jim's background was Episcopalian while Ruth's was Baptist. In a compromise decision made in the early years of their marriage, they had joined a Methodist church. This had worked fairly well for about ten years. Over the past several years, however, they had become interested in strengthening their personal spiritual lives, and each had become involved in a paralocal Christian organization. Ruth was now regularly attending a woman's Bible study known as Bible Study Fellowship, and Jim had become active in the local chapter of the Christian Businessmen's Association.

As a result of these involvements, three things had taken place. First, they had become increasingly restless with the ministry of their local church and the endless hours spent in committee meetings and activities. Second, they began to examine more closely some of the positions taken by their denomination on various social issues and were increasingly uncomfortable about their dollars supporting such causes. Third, their exposure to persons from other churches through their outside involvements made them realize that genuine Christian fellowship crossed many denominational boundaries.

One of the couples Jim and Ruth had recently gotten to know invited them to visit a large community church that had been started about seven years previously. In fact, this was the topic of their discussion that evening. After visiting this church several times, they felt strongly attracted to the biblical teaching and warm fellowship that they experienced there. The issue was whether they could or should make the move from the Methodist church they had been part of the past decade. Their daughter, Mary, who was in college, encouraged them to make the change. She had become involved in the ministry of Campus Crusade for Christ at her college and was enthusiastic about the ministry of the church that her parents were considering.

It was a real struggle. They had so many friends in their present church. What about their loyalty in supporting the denomination that had ministered to them for a decade? What about their concerns over denominational views and the endless activities of the local church? What was the "church," anyhow? How were they to decide?

The experience of Jim and Ruth is one that many Christians in North America share. They find in the church a vast array of structures and diverse organizations. Therefore, they are faced with making personal choices about what their own commitments should be. The challenges before them include the following realities:

- scores of denominations to choose from, shaped by different theological and historical traditions
- the organizational culture of church structures
- numerous individuals crossing denominational lines
- differences on key policy issues between local churches and national leaders
- specialized Christian organizations ministering to peoples' personal lives
- the growth of independent or community churches with strong teaching ministries
- people living out multiple church and organizational commitments for personal growth
- persons making individual choices without accountability to any Christian community.

In North America today it is not easy to live as a Christian or to understand the biblical intention that the church is the created body of Christ in the world. The organizational complexity of the church is overwhelming. This complexity consists of two forms: the denominational, organizational church and its counterpart, the paralocal Christian organization. These forms of church, developed over the past two hundred years, now represent a diverse mosaic of structures. While the particulars of the story have unique dimensions in the U.S. and Canadian contexts, the logic and functioning of denominations and paralocal organizations are similar within both countries.

The Historic Development of Denominations and Their Congregations

The transfer of Christianity into the North American context initially revolved primarily around particular congregations or ethnic communities with multiple congregations. It was not long, however, before efforts were begun to bring new patterns of organization to these diverse congregations that were populating the colonies. In the following discussion, we use the term *denomination* to describe the primary type of church structure that came into existence within the North American context in order to provide for the organized life of multiple congregations. This new type of structure became formalized during the eighteenth century. The number of these organizations has grown dramatically from about thirty-six in 1800 to over several hundred today.[24] While the vast majority of persons who are church members can be accounted for in the fifty largest denominations, this wide array of structures gives some indication of the capacity of denominations to reinforce group identity and cohesion. The collective of these church forms constitutes the distinctive North American organizational pattern called "denominationalism."

These denominational structures wove together into new organizational patterns literally hundreds of local congregations that existed within the various colonies. The rise, development, and structuring of these congregations parallel the story of denominationalism. For this reason, the various organizational and structural changes in congregations should not be overlooked as we consider similar changes in the denominational structures that framed and justified congregations' existence. Basically, congregations began by serving local, geographic communities. This factor provided a fundamental coherence to their social existence. Over time many have moved to being organized around lifestyles, value choices, and mission commitments, making social cohesion more difficult to develop and maintain.

The emergence of denominations in North America is something of an historical accident. The multiple streams of European Christianity commingled within the emerging colonies forced these churches into a new pattern for relating to one another. As Martin Marty has observed, the formation, legitimization, and expansion of this new form of church represented one of the most significant shifts in the life of the institutional church in over fourteen hundred years.[25] In some ways, these developments were inevitable. In other ways, they were intentional. Together they produced a fundamentally new way of thinking about the

24. Robert Wuthnow, *The Restructuring of American Religion* (Princeton: Princeton University Press, 1988), 20-25.
25. Martin E. Marty, *The Righteous Empire* (New York: Dial, 1970), 67-68.

church. Denominations became the reality of North American church life. But their shape did not remain static.

The church form we know as the "denomination" has undergone substantial change over time in the North American context. Russell Richey identifies five distinct phases through which denominations have gone in the past two hundred years.[26] These phases provide helpful perspective to understand the changing character of this church form. They also aid in understanding the patterns of change in local congregations.

Ethnic-Voluntarism Denominations and Ethnic-Village Congregations. The first phase of denominational formation occurred between the early seventeenth and late eighteenth centuries. It created denominations based on voluntarism and ethnicity; the technical term is *ethnic voluntarism.* Here the denominational form functioned as an organizational link for numerous congregations transplanted from European countries that shared a common church tradition and ethnic identity. The Scottish Presbyterians in the middle colonies pioneered this form. The congregations in these early ethnic denominations were essentially ethnic-village churches. They served as the focal point of life in an ethnic, family-related, intergenerational social community. In such congregations, the pastor was responsible for the religious and moral life of the whole community. The congregation met primarily for worship and usually constructed its church building in the center of the village. This location expressed the understanding of the central character of the church's role in the life of the community.

Purposive-Missionary Denominations and Purposive-Village Congregations. The second phase of denominational formation witnessed the rise of the purposive missionary association after the Revolutionary War. Ideally suited for churching the frontier, this form was created and used effectively by the Baptists, Methodists, and Disciples, who took aggressive steps toward achieving that goal. Most denominations had taken on this form by the 1830s and had developed internal boards and agencies to organize and carry out their mission work. This type of denomination proved effective in starting hundreds of new congregations on the expanding frontier. Its basic local structure remained the village church,

26. Russell E. Richey, "Denominations and Denominationalism: An American Morphology," in Robert B. Mullen and Russell E. Richey, eds., *Reimagining Denominationalism* (New York: Oxford University Press, 1994), 74-98.

but a shift was taking place. A large number of these village congregations continued to be populated by immigrant ethnic groups settling as social communities with the church as the center of the community. But increasingly village congregations served as mission vehicles for the more evangelistic denominations seeking to create new churches of diverse persons. These village congregations often had several ethnic backgrounds represented, which diversity led them to form a new type of social community. The location of the community was still geographic in character. The bonds holding members together were support of a common mission, commitment to a particular theology, and familiarity with specific denominational practices.

Churchly Denominations and Institutional Congregations. The third phase of denominational formation took place during the latter half of the nineteenth century, when the denomination assumed the shape of a churchly movement. As denominations grew in size, they built vast institutional systems of ministry for their members that carried them from the cradle to the grave. These elaborate systems devoted increasing attention to promoting a standardized, organizational program in all their congregations. This allowed many denominations to begin the process of bringing the church from the villages to the emerging cities. Rather than living as a social community in a common geographic area, more and more individuals moved into a variety of growing urban neighborhoods. Here congregations developed a logic for building their identity around the shared structures and programs that shaped their church life. Increasingly, denominations fed this development with standardized sets of local church ministries, usually delivered through specialized programs for different age and gender groups.

Corporate Denominations and Organizational Congregations. After the turn of the century, as the science of organizational management began to develop, denominations adapted these insights by shaping themselves as corporate organizations. What had grown up as an ad hoc arrangement of diverse boards and agencies within most denominations was now consolidated into a modern management system organized around key functions and managed by administrative committees. The size of denominational staffs mushroomed during this time as did the professionalization of their roles. Complementing these developments within denominations, congregations increasingly adopted an organizational identity as well. This change meant that the point of reference for persons joining such congregations became a denominational loyalty that was rooted in a common structure and theological tradition, and was administered through a shared set of organizational programs.

This new glue bound the church together for a number of decades and allowed for the rapid expansion of congregations into the growing suburbs following World War II. The suburban church became a denominational, organizational congregation that had a set of standardized programs and ministries coordinated through a structure of administrative communities under the leadership of a professional minister. Even with rapid mobility and transience of membership, these structures functioned as social communities with a sense of continuity and coherence in purpose and identity. They were only able to function as such, however, because the broader churched culture still tended to reinforce church values, moral choices, and member participation.

Regulatory Denominations and Lifestyle Congregations. The fifth phase of development in denominational forms has occurred since the 1960s in the aftermath of increased internal diversity, stagnation or decline of membership growth, and the loss of prestige in the broader culture. In this form of the denomination, the model of the regulatory agency became dominant. The regulatory denomination pays attention to administering rules and securing compliance from member congregations. This shift to a regulatory posture begins to make sense when viewed against the backdrop of the rapid erosion of churched culture in the past several decades. In the face of this erosion, many congregations have had to become much more intentional about forming their identity and shaping their ministry.

Rather than serving primarily as local franchises of a denominational program, congregations now increasingly organize themselves around a set of distinctive lifestyle choices. The lifestyle congregation is more intentional about its purpose for existence. Most of these congregations develop some type of mission or vision statement. The lifestyle congregation also concentrates on carrying out its local ministry, usually by operating out of a strategic ministries plan. Often much more diverse in its membership, it draws people from a variety of church traditions and geographic locations through the ministry and programs that it offers. Such a lifestyle congregation represents a new type of constructed social community, one reflecting some of the characteristics of the emerging postmodern condition.

Assessment of Denominations. The dynamic character of both the denominational and congregational forms is evident in these phases of development. Apparent as well is the fundamental organizational character that these forms have taken on over time. Also evident, however, are the tremendous accomplishments achieved through these structures. This review of their history is not intended to diminish the contributions they have made to North American church life, but rather to bring further understanding to how they function in shaping our understanding of the church, and, even more important, how they function relative to the perspective of a missional ecclesiology.

Today most people in North America take denominations and denominationalism, along with the unique congregational structures they have formed, for granted. These organizational arrangements are so familiar to us that most of us assume they are prescribed somewhere in Scripture. While the concept of local congregations is certainly biblical, the particular organizational forms that we have developed in North America are in need of some substantial critique. The following chapters develop this critique. In doing so, they focus on local congregations as particular missional communities.

The validity of denominations is not readily apparent in the biblical materials, although these materials clearly support the development of local congregations. It is clear that there were connectional structures between congregations in the New Testament world, but how these relate to our present-day denominations is not always evident. It is important to reflect carefully on the character of denominations and denominationalism if we are to address the church's nature, ministry, and organization from a biblical, historical, and contextual perspective. There are several different ways to understand the character of denominations and the principle of denominationalism. These perspectives can be found woven into the rationale for the existence of different denominational churches and the congregations they support.

Understanding Denominations and the Principle of Denominationalism

This brief survey of the denominational church in North American indicates that the capacity of the church to create new organizational forms seems almost limitless. All of these church structures profess, in some manner, a biblical rationale for their existence. Some bolster their biblical claims with historical arguments. Others consider it a value to think ahistorically and operate as if they were a direct application of what the New Testament intended the church to be. The question requiring an answer is not so much, Do denominations have a right to exist? but rather, How are we going to explain this church form? This collage of church forms needs to be sorted out if we wish to develop a missional ecclesiology for North America. Such an ecclesiology should provide criteria and direction in assisting these diverse forms to express more fully God's design for the church in our context.

A Biblical-Theological Perspective. Most denominations take a biblical-theological position as the starting point for explaining their existence. The Independents in England, who originated the rationale for this type of church organization, sought to establish biblical grounds for its legitimacy over against the established, Anglican state-church. They defined the essential New Testament principles for what constituted valid local churches.[27] Many denominations have followed this approach by arguing that their organization is patterned after the New Testament ideal.

Other denominations representing historical traditions usually provide some biblical principles for their existence but rely on a confessional statement as the primary rationale for their legitimacy. Most of these denominations tie themselves to the ecclesiological developments flowing out of the Protestant Reformation. They typically employ some formulation of the criteria for the "true" church in order to justify their claims for legitimacy, and then use these criteria as a test for the viability of other denominations.

Biblical-theological approaches to justifying the legitimacy of denominations have problems. A missiological reading of the New Testament makes clear that no one church form existed in that context. The early church was developmental in character and found expression in a number of different organizational arrangements. The effort by any denomination to justify its existence as representative of the New Testament ideal of the church is simply misdirected. No one such ideal exists.

Establishing legitimacy for the church on a confessional statement has a similar problem, especially when the particular confessional statement used was developed to define that church over against a false church. It is most critical for the church to develop a confessional un-

---

27. Winthrop S. Hudson, "Denominationalism as a Basis for Ecumenicity: A Seventeenth Century Conception," in Richey, ed., *Denominationalism,* 21-42.

derstanding of all that God intends for his church, and for the church within this understanding to define itself over against a fallen world.

The approach needed, however, is one that starts with the biblical intent God has for the church and then reflects on how organizations might be designed to carry out that intent. Applying biblical and confessional rationales to denominations after they already exist is not sufficient to establish legitimacy. Denominations may have legitimacy, but they must be evaluated critically in order to assess the extent to which they represent all that God intends the church to be. A missional ecclesiology requires the church to start with biblical and theological foundations before proceeding to designing organizations or assessing the viability of our present denominations.

An Historical Perspective. Denominations exist. They now represent the primary form of the church in North America and, in many ways, in large parts of the church throughout the world. We have already pointed out in this chapter that the emergence of denominations in North America represents something of an historical accident.[28] The historical reality of particular denominations has often been turned into sacred history by its adherents. This transformation occurs when key events in a denomination's story are declared providential, and key leaders given legendary status. These events and figures then become part of the rationale for the denomination and often function as an authoritative guide for interpreting its true essence. A denominational ethos is transmitted through the retelling of the story in these terms. These stories usually function as important interpretations or applications of a denomination's formal ecclesiology and polity.[29] Those denominations with less formal ecclesiologies and polities usually rely more heavily on such event and leader histories to reinforce their legitimacy. But the practice appears common to all denominations.

Since denominations exist as our historical reality, we cannot go back and rewrite the script. We must start where we are in North America and try to develop a holistic understanding of the church in light of the present reality. A missional ecclesiology takes the context seriously, as it explores how God's Spirit forms and sends the mission community in a particular setting. It is important, then, to reflect care-

---

28. See Hood, "Evolution of the Denomination," 139-60.
29. Henry Warner Bowden, "The Death and Rebirth of Denominational History," in Mullen and Richey, eds., *Reimagining*, 17-30.

fully on the formation of denominations from a biblical perspective and to draw out lessons from that study for translating the gospel into the current context of the church in North America. This process will inevitably involve a critique of present organizations and a search for ways to further their development toward missional faithfulness. Thus the missional ecclesiology that we seek will not only be biblical and historical but also developmental in character.

A Sociological Perspective. Another perspective used to understand the formation and development of denominations examines the sociological factors that shape their membership and ministries. This perspective provides the important insight that most denominations tend to organize themselves around particular social characteristics such as ethnicity, race, social class, shared traditions, discrete cultural characteristics, and even gender and age. There is more at work in shaping a denomination than just shared biblical commitments and a common history.[30] Shared social features powerfully galvanize group identity and cohesion.

It is important for the church to understand the social forces in its midst because of the church's dual nature: social and spiritual. The church is a social community. Moreover, churches function in society as carriers and translators of culture, just as do many other social institutions. From a biblical perspective, however, it is critical that the church be not just a vehicle for people to associate with others who are socially the same. The church is called to be God's divine presence on earth, and as such, it lives by an eschatological set of values that brings people with different social characteristics together through the common bond of mission under Jesus Christ.

A missional ecclesiology challenges the church to be intentional about its unique social potential. Congregations should reflect the full social mix of the communities they serve, if they are truly contextual. In like manner, denominations as larger communions of congregations should seek to reflect the broad social reality of the North American population. Taking this approach will require substantial changes on the part of many congregations and most denominations. But it is in taking such an approach that congregations and denominations will rediscover what it means that the church is "sent" into a particular context. If the

30. See discussion of this approach in the classic work by H. Richard Niebuhr, *The Social Sources of Denominationalism* (1929; repr. Cleveland: World, 1957).

North American church is to regain a public voice for the gospel, it must address this issue.

An Organizational Perspective. The denomination is a voluntary association. As such, it is a collection of self-selecting individuals who make a commitment to participate. Through their commitment, persons bear responsibility to contribute to the whole, but they also receive membership rights that are constitutionally guaranteed. Implicit in the nature of the denomination, then, is the freedom of every individual to make or break their commitments.[31] Since the implications of this freedom for denominational church life have been enormous, a missional ecclesiology must address the denominations' voluntary character. Personal freedom is important, but it needs always to be framed for Christians by the biblical perspective of the covenantal community of God's people sharing an inherent unity. This inherent unity critiques as inadequate the assumptions of Western individualism and the current practice of voluntarism in organizations.

The denomination is also an organization. It provides a shared structure for the orderly management of numerous congregations by offering a common purpose and identity. This naturally focuses the denomination on the tasks of planning, organizing, structuring, and managing.[32] But while these tasks are all essential to give order to the church, the church itself is more than its organization. One of the interesting features of Christianity in recent decades has been the formation of a host of large independent or community churches. These congregations carry the principles of "member as volunteer" and "church as organization" to their logical conclusion. While these congregations may ally with other churches on occasion, they function for the most part as self-contained church communities. A missional ecclesiology will examine critically the powerful role of organizational factors in defining such megachurches.

A missional ecclesiology will always include organizational forms, but one should not see these as the essence of the church. Organization needs to serve, not determine the nature of the church with its duality

31. David W. Hall, "The Pastoral and Theological Significance of Church Government," in David W. Hall and Joseph H. Hall, eds., *Paradigms in Polity* (Grand Rapids: Eerdmans, 1994), 12-34.

32. Elwyn A. Smith, "The Forming of a Modern American Denomination," in Richey, ed., *Denominationalism,* 108-36.

of being both divine and human. It also needs to serve the ministry of the church with all of its diverse functions. We must establish clearly the church's nature and ministry before we proceed to design organizational forms to concretize both in a specific cultural context. Unless we do so, we may fall subject to the illusion that managing the organization is equivalent to being the church. This illusion already plagues many denominations and their local congregations.

Significant Recent Developments in the North American Church

Because the church is missionary by its nature, it always seeks engagement with its context. Clearly the church has engaged in such mission in North America, but the various ecclesiologies undergirding this work have not worked out of a thoroughgoing missiological perspective. A number of significant ecclesiologies, however, have guided the ministry of the church. It is helpful to review each of these briefly in order to gain further perspective on the task before us of developing a missional ecclesiology.

Denomination Building. The first of these significant ecclesiologies is illustrated well in the five phases of the church's development discussed above. Moving always toward consolidating and strengthening the denomination, this ecclesiology assumed that what was best for the denomination was best for the member congregations. Following this logic, member congregations were expected to support the denomination's mission efforts with dollars, volunteer time, and its sons and daughters, because this support reinforced their own self-interest. This assumption has fallen on hard times amid the changes of the last few decades. Consequently, denominations are now constantly implementing new strategies in order to shore up denominational support. What is overlooked in this process is a fundamental rethinking of the nature and purpose of the denomination as a *form* of church.

Church Renewal. Another movement in the development of many North American churches centered around the theme of renewing existing forms for a more relevant ministry. This theme became influential in the church during the 1950s and 1960s when a new generation of members, the postwar generation, raised fundamental questions about the viability of existing church forms that were the result of denomination building. Like its predecessor, this movement focused on the internal organizational configuration of the church. While it prompted helpful changes in various churches, especially in the area of worship renewal, it failed to address the more systemic problem. Though it still persists, this movement appeared to run out of steam in the 1970s as the culture began to fragment. By then the church was reeling before a much larger set of problems that could not be addressed merely by updating obsolete forms.

Church Growth. Approaching the work of the church from a very different perspective, this movement focused on reaching persons outside the church to incorporate them into the church. To do so, it intentionally planted congregations within given social boundaries so that persons could meet Christ without having to cross cultural barriers. It accepted social homogeneity as a necessary condition for congregational formation. The church growth movement has profoundly influenced the North American church, but it has failed to address adequately a number of issues. One was anthropology: the church growth movement tended to assume the neutrality of culture and accept the brokenness of the world as normative. Another issue was sociology: it often treated culture as something beyond us that we could consider a commodity, target, and reach. A third was ecclesiology: church growth tended to view the church primarily as a social organization that could be planted, marketed, and managed. The first phase of this movement peaked by the late 1980s as a more complex understanding of the organizational makeup of the church took hold.

Various Movements Toward Effectiveness. Since the 1980s, a number of movements have been at work in the North American church, all associated with the concept of effectiveness. Although somewhat diverse in emphasis, each nevertheless represents some new directions beyond church renewal and church growth. All these movements currently attempt to refocus the life and ministry of the church in a fundamentally changed context. Most treat the whole of church life as a complex organizational system. They further assume that the church must be embedded within as well as interactive with its context. This assumption has contributed to a more comprehensive approach to managing the church. But often they tend to end up offering just more versions of organized management, albeit very sophisticated versions in comparison to those proposed by earlier movements. They still do not address fully the nature, ministry, and organization of the church. This requires a more holistic approach, a missional ecclesiology.

Understanding the Mission and Purpose of Paralocal Organizations

Beyond its host of denominational forms, the church in North America finds expression through literally hundreds of Christian organizations that are by definition not traditional denominations. Over eight hundred such entities in America qualified as religious nonprofit organizations by 1985.[33] These paralocal or parachurch organizations are described in a number of ways, including mission societies, faith missions, and special-purpose organizations. They share in common a self-understanding that they are not local congregations, or particular missional communities. Their purpose lies outside the ministry and organization of the local church. For this reason, we describe them in this book as "paralocal," that is, "next to the local congregation or particular mission community." It is important to reflect on the nature of these ministry organizations when we approach the development of a missional ecclesiology for North America.

These organizations exist primarily for a specific religious activity or function, often defined as a biblical purpose in the form of a specialized ministry role. Sometimes these organizations develop a particular ministry role over against the local church, by picking up a ministry that is underdeveloped within congregations or neglected in denominational programs. Specialized youth ministries beyond the local church, such as Young Life and Youth for Christ, follow this pattern. In other cases, such organizations develop their particular ministry role as an extension of the local church's work. A cross-cultural mission organization, such as Wycliffe Bible Translators, illustrates this pattern, as well as various evangelistic organizations that seek to direct their converts into local congregations.

Historically, paralocal structures have tried to carry out a circumscribed piece of the church's mission through a specialized organizational structure. They emphasize their own calling and spiritual gifting for their particular activities. Paralocal structures have usually viewed themselves as interdenominational. The parochial character of denominations and their control over their internal mission structures through delegated assemblies have helped foster this perspective. Paralocal ministry structures are, in general, a reflection of deficiencies inherent within the

33. Wuthnow, *Restructuring*, 108.

understanding of the church's nature, ministry, and organization as defined in denominational ecclesiologies.

Paralocal structures find precedents for their existence in the local and mobile expressions of ministry in the New Testament.[34] In the Scriptures one discovers congregations along with specialized ministries for extending the church and strengthening all congregations. The itinerant apostolic missionary teams would be one example of such a ministry that was not bound to a congregation. As the church embodies the gospel within the context of its many cultural locales, it will often shape its ministries using these two types of structures. The complex history and development of the religious orders through the Middle Ages are the most obvious example of this duality of local and paralocal structures. The Reformation movements rejected the orders, and the emerging Protestant denominations did not generally build such structures into their organizational designs. From the seventeenth century forward, however, they emerged in a variety of ways, including the Pietistic movements within the churches, the mission societies alongside the churches, and the faith missions and specialized missions outside the churches.

A missional ecclesiology takes seriously the organizational life of the church both in its expressions of local missional congregations and in paralocal missional structures. Developing such an ecclesiology in North America will require a careful evaluation of the diverse paralocal organizations that now exist, and how they fit into a more holistic understanding of the biblical character of missional structures generally. The church's nature as both one *and* catholic means that these structures must exist in a symbiotic relationship with local congregations and their denominational structures. The apostolic character of the church implies a variety of ways in which its mission is carried out, and thus a variety of structures that a missional ecclesiology must address.

The historic transformations and current existence of the church in North America form a complex reality that we must deal with in considering the development of a missional ecclesiology. In chapters two and three, we have examined this distinctive North American context. The culture of modernity defines the self and shapes the way North

34. Ralph Winter described this duality as the "modality" and the "sodality" of the church; see "The Two Structures of God's Redemptive Mission," *Missiology* 2, no. 1 (1974), 121-39.

Americans hear the gospel in particular ways that the missional church must understand. The development of North American denomination-alism in both its U.S. and Canadian forms frames the organizational setting in which the missional church must function today. We do not believe, however, that the context itself defines the mission and message of God's people. Rather, we understand the investigation of the cultural context to be one necessary part of the equipping of the church for its missional vocation. The critical doorway into the discussion of this complexity is the biblical message of the formation of the church as the sign, foretaste, firstfruits, and agent of the reign of God that Jesus an-nounced and inaugurated. We turn now to the basic themes of this gospel and the formation of God's missionary people.

· 4 ·

Missional Vocation:
Called and Sent to Represent the Reign of God

The last two chapters have traced the cultural currents in North America and the forms of life taken on by the churches in that setting. Changes associated with the move from a modern to an increasingly postmodern condition have created a cultural crisis. But the churches face a crisis of their own. They manifest an increasing dis-ease with their heritage of a functional Christendom and forms of church life shaped by modern notions of voluntary association and rational organization.

This is a time for a dramatically new vision. The current predicament of churches in North America requires more than a mere tinkering with long-assumed notions about the identity and mission of the church. Instead, as many knowledgeable observers have noted, there is a need for reinventing or rediscovering the church in this new kind of world.[1]

---

1. In the current discussion, one finds phrases like "once and future church," transition from "churched-culture local congregations to mission outposts," or visions of a phoenix-like church rising from the ashes in new forms of church that will grow "up from the grassroots." See Peter C. Hodgson, *Revisioning the Church: Ecclesial Freedom in the New Paradigm* (Philadelphia: Fortress, 1988); Lynne and Bill Hybels, *Rediscovering Church: The Story and Vision of Willow Creek Community Church* (Grand Rapids: Zondervan, 1995); Loren B. Mead, *The Once and Future Church: Reinventing the Congregation for a New Mission Frontier* (Bethesda: Alban Institute, 1991); Kennon L. Callahan, *Effective Church Leadership: Building on the Twelve Keys* (San Francisco: Harper & Row, 1990); E. Dixon Junkin, "Up from the Grassroots: The Church in Transition," in George R. Hunsberger and Craig Van Gelder, eds., *The Church Between Gospel and Culture: The Emerging Mission in North America* (Grand Rapids: Eerdmans, 1996), 308-18.

Two things have become quite clear to those who care about the church and its mission. On the one hand, the churches of North America have been dislocated from their prior social role of chaplain to the culture and society and have lost their once privileged positions of influence. Religious life in general and the churches in particular have increasingly been relegated to the private spheres of life. Too readily, the churches have accepted this as their proper place.[2] At the same time, the churches have become so accommodated to the American way of life that they are now domesticated, and it is no longer obvious what justifies their existence as particular communities. The religious loyalties that churches seem to claim and the social functions that they actually perform are at odds with each other. Discipleship has been absorbed into citizenship.[3]

The churches have a great opportunity in these circumstances, however. The same pressures that threaten the continued survival of some churches, disturb the confidence of others, and devalue the meaning of them all can actually be helpful in providing an opening for new possibilities. Emerging into view on the far side of the church's long experience of Christendom is a wide vista of potential for the people of God in the postmodern and post-Christian world of North America. The present is a wildly opportune moment for churches to find themselves and to put on the garments of their calling, their vocation.

The Chinese character for signifying the idea of "crisis" combines two other characters, the one for "danger" and the other for "opportunity." Crisis is made of both, and so too is the current situation of the church. Dangers lurk on all sides for churches, but probably the greatest dangers lie within. Long-established routines and long-held notions have a strong hold on any community, and a church is no exception. These routines and notions constitute a way of seeing what the church is and what it is for and in turn inform how a church operates from day to day. Such assumed patterns are brought into question, however, when the church recognizes that it has been demoted from its prior social importance and may have accommodated away something of its soul. The church must then ask, Are our structures and our assumptions about the church's nature and purpose

2. See Lesslie Newbigin, *Foolishness to the Greeks: The Gospel and Western Culture* (Grand Rapids: Eerdmans, 1986); Walter Brueggemann, *Disciplines of Readiness* (Louisville: Theology and Worship Unit, Presbyterian Church [U.S.A.], n.d.).

3. Stanley Hauerwas and William H. Willimon, *Resident Aliens: Life in the Christian Colony* (Nashville: Abingdon, 1989).

no longer suited to the time and place in which we currently live? Might it be that both our organization and presuppositions have been dislodged from their moorings in the biblical message?

These are difficult questions for the church of any age and place because they involve the complicated calling of the church to both relevance and faithfulness. The church may fit well into its social environment, but unwarranted accommodation may cause it to lose touch with its biblical warrant. Or the church may adhere too strictly to scriptural forms of expressing its faith that were intelligible to the cultures of biblical times, and in the process neglect to translate the biblical warrant into an incarnation relevant to the church's current time and place. The struggle to be both faithful and relevant is constant for every church. It is the church's calling to embody the gospel's "challenging relevance."[4]

How is the church to give relevant expression and faithful embodiment to the gospel? The present crisis over the church's identity and mission is wrapped up in that question.

A Place? or a People?

One way to illustrate and pose this question for the church today is to contrast the church's notion of itself in terms dictated by a functional Christendom with newer biblical and theological rumblings in this century concerning the church's nature. In lectures in 1991, shortly before his untimely death, mission theologian David Bosch of South Africa put it this way.[5] The churches shaped by the Reformation were left with a view of the church that was not directly intended by the Reformers, but nevertheless resulted from the way that they spoke about the church. Those churches came to conceive the church as "a place where certain things happen." The Reformers emphasized as the "marks of the true church" that such a church exists wherever the gospel is rightly preached, the sacraments rightly administered, and (they sometimes added) church

---

4. See Lesslie Newbigin, "Christ and the Cultures," *Scottish Journal of Theology* 31 (1978): 1-22; and *The Open Secret: Sketches for a Missionary Theology*, rev. ed. (Grand Rapids: Eerdmans, 1995), chap. 9.

5. These six lectures were given by Bosch in April of 1991 at Western Theological Seminary in Holland, Michigan. There are audio and videotapes of the lectures in the seminary's library collection.

discipline exercised. In their time, these emphases may have been profoundly missional since they asserted the authority of the Bible for the church's life and proclamation as well as the importance of making that proclamation accessible to all people. But over time, these "marks" narrowed the church's definition of itself toward a "place where" idea. This understanding was not so much articulated as presumed. It was never officially stated in a formal creed but was so ingrained in the churches' practice that it became dominant in the churches' self-understanding.

This perception of the church gives little attention to the church as a communal entity or presence, and it stresses even less the community's role as the bearer of missional responsibility throughout the world, both near and far away. "Church" is conceived in this view as *the place where* a Christianized civilization gathers for worship, and *the place where* the Christian character of the society is cultivated. Increasingly, this view of the church as a "place where certain things happen" located the church's self-identity in its organizational forms and its professional class, the clergy who perform the church's authoritative activities. Popular grammar captures it well: you "go to church" much the same way you might go to a store. You "attend" a church, the way you attend a school or theater. You "belong to a church" as you would a service club with its programs and activities.

This view corresponds well to the basic notion of mission that has existed under Christendom. On the one hand, the Reformers and their immediate successors believed that the commission Jesus left with the apostles — to disciple the nations — was fulfilled in the first century. Therefore it was no longer required of the church. The colonial expansion of European nations raised new questions about this belief as the churches of Europe encountered peoples who had never heard the gospel. When the question of evangelizing these peoples began to press itself, another strongly held belief of the time came into question as well. In Christendom Europe, civil magistrates were obligated to ensure the spiritual well-being of all citizens of their realm, so it was natural to assume that they would bear the same role vis-à-vis the new peoples brought under their dominion. This arrangement began to break down when voluntary missionary societies emerged. Many of those societies were ultimately adopted into the life of the churches, but mission continued to be conceived as something that happens at a great physical or social distance. The missionary movement throughout the nineteenth century altered little the western churches' self-conception as a place where certain things happened.

In the twentieth century, Bosch went on to say, this self-perception gave way to a new understanding of the church as *a body of people sent on a mission.* Unlike the previous notion of the church as an entity located in a facility or in an institutional organization and its activities, the church is being reconceived as a community, a gathered people, brought together by a common calling and vocation to be a *sent people.* This understanding arose out of global reflections on the church's nature particularly in the light of the worldwide missionary movements of the previous several centuries and the fruit of that work in the existence of new churches throughout the world. From the mid-twentieth century on, biblical and theological foundations for such a communal and missional view of the church have blossomed.

Reflections among numerous missionary agencies and denominational mission boards following World War II underscored this perspective. During the middle of the twentieth century, the colonial worlds of the European nations were dismantled, and newly independent nations arose throughout the so-called Third World. Those churches previously called "younger churches" now pressed toward their own independence from the missions and churches of the West. A now global church recognized that the church of any place bears missional calling and responsibility for its own place as well as for distant places. The church of every place, it realized, is a mission-sending church, and the place of every church is a mission-receiving place.

As a result of these developments, a shift from an *ecclesiocentric* (church-centered) view of mission to a *theocentric* (God-centered) one took place. Mission as a church-centered enterprise characterized mission thinking earlier in the twentieth century. Mission had been considered to be activities arising out of the church with an aim to extend the church or plant it in new places. The church sent the mission out and defined its character. The expansion of the church into new locales was thought to be its guiding goal. In many respects this shift represented an advance for the church because it acknowledged a global sense of mission. But this approach tended to reinforce the dichotomy between the churches of the West and the so-called younger churches planted in other parts of the world.

By mid-century, the emphasis in mission thought shifted toward a *theocentric* approach that, in contrast, stressed the mission of God *(missio Dei)* as the foundation for the mission of the church. The church became redefined as the community spawned by the mission of God and gathered up into that mission. The church was coming to understand that in any place it is a community sent by God. "Mission" is not something the church does, a part of its total program. No, the church's essence is missional, for the calling and sending action of God forms its identity. Mission is founded on the mission of God in the world, rather than the church's effort to extend itself.

Theocentric mission theology recovered the trinitarian character of mission. As Lesslie Newbigin indicated at the time, missionary practice must be grounded in the person and work of Christ, seeded by "trust in the reality and power of the Holy Spirit" and rooted in a practical faith that discerns "God's fatherly rule in the events of secular history, . . . in the revolutionary changes which are everywhere taking place in the life of the world."[6]

Recent theology has made a similar rediscovery by bringing to light the implications of the Trinity for ecclesiology. It has recognized that the *perichoresis,* or interpenetration, among the persons of the Trinity reveals that "the nature of God is communion." From this point of view, the church is learning that it is called to be a "finite echo or bodying forth of the divine personal dynamics," "a temporal echo of the eternal community that God is."[7]

What is not yet fully developed in these fresh approaches to trinitarian doctrines is the missional implication for ecclesiology. What does it mean that the church bears the stamp of the "eternal community" that God is *and* reflects the eternal mutual "sending" that characterizes that divine communion? Nowhere is the latter characteristic of the church so fully evident as in the biblical account of Jesus Christ. Jesus can and does say he will send his disciples the Advocate, the Spirit of truth (John 15:26), but it was that very same Spirit who baptized Jesus, led him in the wilderness while he was facing temptation, and filled him with power when he began his itinerant preaching (Luke 3:22; 4:1, 14). Jesus proclaimed that this Spirit rested on him and anointed him to preach good news (Luke 4:17-21). This mutuality in sending or "interprocession," if we may call it that, marks the divine

---

6. Lesslie Newbigin, *Trinitarian Faith and Today's Mission* (Richmond: John Knox, 1964), 77.

7. Colin E. Gunton, *The Promise of Trinitarian Theology* (Edinburgh: T. & T. Clark, 1991), quotations from 72, 74, and 79, respectively; see also Leonardo Boff, *Trinity and Society,* tr. Paul Burns (Maryknoll, N.Y.: Orbis, 1988), esp. 232-42.

communion as a communion of mission, and this in turn leaves its mark on the church.[8]

One more point of theological recovery that is particularly relevant to this discussion involves the importance of the fourth of the *notae,* or characteristics, of the church mentioned in the Nicene-Constantinopolitan Creed (AD 381). This creed affirms belief in "one, holy, catholic, and apostolic church." The last-mentioned distinctive of the church, "apostolic," asserts the church's missional vocation. As Jürgen Moltmann has put it, "The historical church must be called 'apostolic' in a double sense: its gospel and its doctrine are founded on the testimony of the first apostles, the eyewitnesses of the risen Christ, and it exists in the carrying out of the apostolic proclamation, the missionary charge. The expression 'apostolic' therefore denotes both the church's foundation and its commission."[9] In a recent and important study of the understanding of the word *apostolic* within the early church, Robert Scudieri concludes the same: "The church is apostolic not just because it represents the apostles' teaching, but because it re-presents Christ."[10]

A People Sent or a Vendor of Religion?

This rethinking of the nature of God, church, and mission would appear to be a promising development if it were in fact evident in the operative style of today's churches or in the conceptions that govern them. But it is not. Indeed, the grammar commonly used to refer to or ask about the church still carries the heavy baggage of being a "place where certain things happen." We ask, for instance, "Where do you go to church?" "Where is your church?" "Did you go to church last Sunday?" Indeed, even when not referring to a tangible building, we tend to relate "church" to a meeting or activity, a set of programs, or

---

8. See also Colin E. Gunton, *The One, the Three and the Many: God, Creation and the Culture of Modernity* (Cambridge: Cambridge University Press, 1993); Catherine Mowry LaCugna, *God for Us: The Trinity and Christian Life* (San Francisco: HarperSanFrancisco, 1991); Jürgen Moltmann, *The Trinity and the Kingdom: The Doctrine of God,* tr. Margaret Kohl (San Francisco: Harper & Row, 1981).

9. Jürgen Moltmann, *The Church in the Power of the Spirit: A Contribution to Messianic Ecclesiology,* tr. Margaret Kohl (New York: Harper & Row, 1977), 358.

10. Robert J. Scudieri, *The Apostolic Church: One, Holy, Catholic and Missionary* (Fort Wayne: Lutheran Society for Missiology, 1995), 28.

an organizational structure. Only with awkwardness would one talk about being "part of a church."

In North America, this "place where" orientation manifests itself in a particular form. Both members and those outside the church expect the church to be *a vendor of religious services and goods*.

It is not hard to see how this expectation arose in North American life, particularly after considering what previous chapters recounted. As we have said, the social order in modern societies was defined by the fact that freely choosing, autonomous individuals decided out of rational self-interest to enter into a social contract to construct a progressive society. Also defined in this way were the various social entities within society, including the church. The church as one such voluntary association lives off the willingness of its members to remain in it. Gaining the loyalty of members and retaining that loyalty takes priority in a voluntary association. The development of rational social organization in modern societies added another element to this characteristic of social life. Models of order, efficiency, progress, and growth were increasingly applied to the social order, and with this application, the orderly management of social organizations by rational technique became the rule. This naturally focused attention on the division of labor around the tasks of planning, organizing, structuring, and managing in a social entity conceived to be a machinelike, rational whole. In such an organizational configuration the individual was both manipulable part and capable master, and managing the organization became the equivalent of being the church.

Parallel with the rise of the "member as volunteer" and the "church as organization" was the impact of economic developments. Recent scholarship in the sociology of religion has brought to light how this aspect shaped the church's life. In *The Churching of America, 1776-1990: Winners and Losers in Our Religious Economy,* Roger Finke and Rodney Stark argue that the choice made early on in the United States not to have an established religion meant that an economic understanding of religious life and practice was inevitable. They contend that "where religious affiliation is a matter of choice, religious organizations must compete for members and . . . the 'invisible hand' of the marketplace is as unforgiving of ineffective religious firms as it is of their commercial counterparts. . . . Religious economies are like commercial economies in that they consist of a market made up of a set of current and potential customers and a set of firms seeking to serve that market." Indeed, they suggest that it is appropriate to use "economic concepts such as markets, firms, market penetration, and segmented markets to analyze the success and failure of religious bodies." In their view, then, the clergy are the church's sales representatives, religious doctrines its products, and evangelization practices its marketing techniques.[11]

This model has a ring of truth about it. It describes only too well assumptions about membership, program, structure, success, and purpose that give shape to today's church culture, "the way we do things around here." It certainly illumines the current circumstance in which the churches live, a pervasive religious consumerism driven by the quest to meet personally defined religious needs. It also explains the heavy concentration of church efforts to produce and promote programs, and it corresponds with the emphasis in one stream of literature flowing out of the church growth movement. That stream has accepted the commercial image without question by commending strategies for effectively and successfully "marketing your church."[12]

But here is the rub. Does this image of church correspond to the cluster of images found for the church in the New Testament? Does it correlate with New Testament speech about the nature and purposes of the church? At the very least, this producer-consumer model separates its notion of church (a religious firm producing and marketing religious products and services) from its members (potential and hopefully committed customers consuming those products and services). Members are ultimately distanced in this model from their own communal calling to be a body of people sent on a mission. The gap between these two notions is great, and it is in the transformation from the one to the other that the present challenge before the churches finds focus.

11. Roger Finke and Rodney Stark, *The Churching of America, 1776-1990: Winners and Losers in Our Religious Economy* (New Brunswick: Rutgers University Press, 1992), 17. These authors represent a "new paradigm" for the analysis of religious behavior in North America. They posit a "rational-choice" theory of religion by applying economic theories in a "market perspective" to religious phenomena. The work cited is typical of this approach.

12. E.g., George Barna, *A Step-By-Step Guide to Church Marketing: Breaking Ground for the Harvest* (Ventura, Calif.: Regal, 1992).

Rehearing the Gospel

Questions about the church's life that are this fundamental require a fresh hearing of the gospel. They demand that we return to the biblical rendering of the gospel and contemplate its vision of the church against the backdrop of recent social and cultural trends like those surveyed in the last two chapters. A fresh hearing of the gospel is an effort to get back to roots in order to be clear about the essence of what it means to be the church. Hans Küng contends that the essence is in the church's "origins in the gospel." It is in the good news told in the New Testament, news that is continually spawning the church in every time and place. The church's essence, he points out, is always embodied in some tangible, visible form that is shaped by its particular time in history and its place in some specific human society. This is why we should not be surprised that the church's forms are diverse and variable across time and space. But what explains the church — what makes it the *church* — is that its life is birthed by the Holy Spirit as the Spirit gives hearing and response to the gospel.[13]

To say that the church's essence is found in its origins in the gospel is not, however, to say we only look back to the church's historical beginnings. The gospel, centered profoundly for Jesus in the announcement that the reign of God is at hand, is eschatological in character. It pulls back the veil on the coming reign of God, thereby revealing the horizon of the world's future. The gospel portrays the coming of Jesus, and particularly his death and resurrection, as the decisive, truly eschatological event in the world's history. Therefore a community with origins in the gospel is "an eschatological community of salvation." As such, it "comes from the preaching of the reign of God — the reign of God is its beginning and its foundation. And it moves towards the revealed consummation of the reign of God — the reign of God is its goal, its limitation, its judgment." The church is defined by its origins in a gospel that casts a vision of its destiny that always draws it forward.[14]

This definition suggests for the church a lifestyle of continual conversion as it hears and responds to the gospel over and over again.[15]

13. Hans Küng, *The Church* (Garden City, N.Y.: Image, 1967), 22-24.
14. Ibid., 116-33, quotations from 116 and 133, respectively.
15. For a full treatment of this important theme, see Darrell L. Guder, *The Continuing Conversion of the Church: Evangelization as the Heart of Ministry* (Grand Rapids: Eerdmans, forthcoming).

The church is constantly being reevangelized, and by virtue of that it is always being constituted and formed as the church. The essence of what it means to be the church arises perpetually from the church's origins in the gospel: it is in every moment being *originated* by the Holy Spirit as it hears the gospel and is *oriented* by "the present reign of Christ in which the coming completed reign of God ... is revealed and becomes effective in the present."[16] This is true whatever the time or place, but it becomes especially crucial at times of great social and cultural shifts, both those involving the church's own social position and those in the surrounding context itself. Such transformations raise questions about how the church will fit in its altered setting, and these questions lead ultimately to queries about whether the church's forms reflect an authentic hearing of the gospel and a genuine sharing in its vision.

What exactly is the gospel, then? Identifying the gospel is both simple and challenging. No culture-free expression of the gospel exists, nor could it. The church's message, the gospel, is inevitably articulated in linguistic and cultural forms particular to its own place and time. Thus a rehearing of the gospel can be vulnerable to the "gospels" that we may tend to read back into the New Testament renderings of it. The first tellings of the gospel in Scripture themselves have a richly varied quality. They are as culturally particular as our own. Nevertheless, they are the root narrative of God's action in Jesus Christ for the salvation of the world, and as such, the church's originating message. It is of the essence of the church to root itself in what those first tellings portray of the character, actions, and purposes of God.

Good News: The Reign of God Is at Hand

The gospel is Jesus himself. The New Testament's Gospels narrate the life, death, and resurrection of Jesus as the action of God that both reveals God's passion for the world and achieves God's purpose for that world. Other depictions of the gospel in the New Testament affirm the same thing, whether in Luke's reports in Acts of the early churches' communication of the gospel, or in the letters and literature that constitute the churches' reflections on its significance. Long anticipated in the Old Testament's portraits of the saving and covenanting urges of the God

16. Küng, *Church*, 126.

who made the world and all that is in it, Jesus is recognized throughout the New Testament as the incarnate Son of God, the anointed Redeemer ("Messiah" from the Hebrew, "Christ" from the Greek), and the Ruler and Judge of the world.

If this is true, however, we must also hear what Jesus himself said, what he himself called the "good news." The churches of the New Testament proclaimed Jesus as the Christ, the reigning Lord, by virtue of his crucifixion and resurrection. In this sense their gospel was *about* Jesus. But whatever they proclaimed about Jesus was in concert with the spirit and substance of Jesus' teaching and preaching. Their gospel was not only *about* Jesus — it was also the gospel *of* Jesus, the gospel that he preached. This was so because the Jesus whom they announced as the risen Christ of God, the living Lord of the nations, embodied the message spoken from his lips. Jesus' good news that the reign of God is at hand is clothed with meaning by his continuing presence as the risen, reigning, and glorified Lord. Believing *in* Jesus Christ also means believing Jesus Christ about the reign of God.

Proclaiming a gospel about Christ that is not shaped by the gospel Jesus preached distorts the gospel by proclaiming only part of its meaning. The absence of the gospel Jesus preached in the gospel the church has preached has woefully impoverished the church's sense of missional identity. A rehearing of the gospel at this time in the history of the North American churches requires special attention to Jesus' own announcement of the good news.

What did this one who is the good news have to say when he announced the good news? What was the gospel he preached? What was the message in his evangelizing? The answer is not hard to find. It comes in quick succession from the pages of the biblical Gospels. The earliest one, Mark, sets the stage in its opening lines: the theme will be "the beginning of the good news of Jesus Christ, the Son of God" (1:1). Thereafter, in the briefest of introductions, John the Baptist offers a trumpetlike fanfare for Jesus, a descending dove (the Spirit) anoints him for his mission, and a voice from heaven validates him. Then Jesus is heard in tones that would permeate all his preaching and teaching: "Jesus came to Galilee, proclaiming the good news of God, and saying, 'The time is fulfilled, and the kingdom of God has come near; repent, and believe in the good news'" (1:14-15). For Mark, as for Matthew and Luke after him, this fundamental announcement was emblematic of all Jesus taught. Here lies the central and guiding theme of the message he was

88

compelled to announce. One New Testament scholar has said what scholarship in general has accepted:

> The central aspect of the teaching of Jesus was that concerning the Kingdom of God. Of this there can be no doubt. . . . Jesus appeared as one who proclaimed the Kingdom; all else in his message and ministry serves a function in relation to that proclamation and derives its meaning from it. The challenge to discipleship, the ethical teaching, the disputes about oral tradition or ceremonial law, even the pronouncement of forgiveness of sins and the welcoming of the outcast in the name of God — all these are to be understood in the context of the Kingdom proclamation or they are not to be understood at all.[17]

It is important to note here that this central theme shaped for Jesus the sense of his mission as well as the mantle of that mission that he passed to his followers. Luke, who reports the beginning of Jesus' preaching by describing his maiden sermon in his hometown synagogue in Nazareth, notices the hold this theme has on Jesus' mind. The Nazareth incident itself involves the Isaiah text about the anticipated "year of the Lord's favor" and a messianic appointment by the Spirit of one who will proclaim its arrival: good news to the poor, release to the captives, sight to the blind, freedom to the oppressed. Surely this is a portrait of the reign of God coming! About this Isaiah text, Jesus said simply, "Today this scripture has been fulfilled in your hearing" (4:21). As the narrative of Jesus' ministry unfolds, the intent of that ministry is clearly identified. Healings among the people of Capernaum lead them to cling to Jesus and urge him to remain with them. "But he said to them, 'I must proclaim the good news of the kingdom of God to the other cities also; for I was sent for this purpose'" (4:43). Jesus' commitment to do and say only what his Father had assigned him, so in evidence elsewhere in the Gospels, focused his mission on this announcement of the good news that the reign of God is at hand.

It was this message that Jesus placed on the lips of disciples whom he sent out to share in the fulfillment of his mission. "As you go, proclaim the good news, 'The kingdom of heaven has come near'" (Matt. 10:7). The same was also embedded in his forecast of the mission that the whole church would inherit: "And this good news of the kingdom will

17. Norman Perrin, *Rediscovering the Teaching of Jesus* (New York: Harper & Row, 1967), 54.

be proclaimed throughout the world, as a testimony to all the nations; and then the end will come" (Matt. 24:14).

The language and emphasis of John's Gospel move in directions different from those of the Synoptic Gospels. But his Gospel nevertheless corresponds with the portraits of the other three by showing Jesus' mission as centered on the presence of the reign of God. As Albert Curry Winn has noted, John portrays Jesus as one who possessed a "sense of having been sent." His will is not his own, but God's. His words are not his own, but God's. His works are not his own, but God's. His very life depends on the Sender.[18] Jesus declares to Pilate, "My kingdom is not from this world. . . . My kingdom is not from here" (John 18:36). Throughout the Gospel of John, what is at stake is whether one believes, and belief or lack of it is linked with whether one can "see" or "enter" the kingdom of God (3:3, 5). What is announced is that "God so loved the world that he gave his only Son" and that God sent the Son "in order that the world might be saved through him" (3:16-17). The kingdom of God and the world are at odds in the portrait offered by John's Gospel. John's use of the term *world* refers, for the most part, to "human society as it is structured in opposition to Christ and to the followers of Christ," just as it is also "opposed to God" and God's rightful authority.[19]

What Is This Reign of God?

Exactly what is this reign of God, then, that Jesus so routinely announces? All the Synoptic Gospels convey the sense that the reign of God has a certain indefinable quality in Jesus' own teaching. Always a mystery yet an open secret, it was best passed on by way of parables, whose intent was to reveal and to hide in the same breath.

A definitive answer to the question, What is the reign of God? cannot be given. But we can at least sketch some of its contours by listening to the Old Testament's prophetic forecasts of the coming day of God and the prophets' expectations of God's intended future for the world. In lectures given in the early 1980s, philosopher Arthur Holmes summarized that prophetic vision as *shalom*. It envisions a world charac-

18. Albert Curry Winn, *A Sense of Mission: Guidance from the Gospel of John* (Philadelphia: Westminster, 1981), 30-34.
19. Ibid., 69-70.

terized by peace, justice, and celebration. *Shalom,* the overarching vision of the future, means "peace," but not merely peace as the cessation of hostilities. Instead, shalom envisions the full prosperity of a people of God living under the covenant of God's demanding care and compassionate rule. In the prophetic vision, peace such as this comes hand in hand with justice. Without justice, there can be no real peace, and without peace, no real justice. Indeed, only in a social world full of a peace grounded in justice can there come the full expression of joy and celebration.[20]

It is striking to note, in this light, Paul's brief passing notes about the character of the reign of God. During an extended conversation about diverse opinions on dietary practices, he comments, "For the kingdom of God is not food and drink, but righteousness [justice] and peace and joy in the Holy Spirit" (Rom. 14:17). The prophetic vision is there, joined now to the presence of the Holy Spirit, who enables it.

The reign of God most certainly arises as God's mission to reconcile the creation accomplished in the death and resurrection of Jesus. "In Christ, God was reconciling the world to himself" (2 Cor. 5:19). "If anyone is in Christ, there is a new creation" (2 Cor. 5:17). "But each in his own order: Christ the first fruits, then at his coming those who belong to Christ. Then comes the end, when he hands over the kingdom to God the Father, after he has destroyed every ruler and every authority and power" (1 Cor. 15:23-24). Ruling by way of a cross and a resurrection, God thwarts the powers of sin and death that distort the creation once good at its beginning. The future rule of God breaks in ahead of time as a harbinger of the world's future to be fully and finally reconciled to God.

Where Did We Lose It?

It is hotly debated just when and how the church lost its sense of this gospel of the reign of God, with the result that its message ceased to orient the church's own life and witness. Some say it was quite early because the church's formation itself was a reversal of the kingdom. This view is hard to sustain, especially since it was the earliest, emergent church that remembered and subsequently put into writing the gospel

20. Arthur Holmes, the Staley Lectures, Belhaven College, Jackson, Mississippi.

of Jesus, the proclaimer of the reign of God. Luke's account of the early church and the spread of its witness emphasizes how centered it was on this core announcement. Philip "was proclaiming the good news about the kingdom of God and the name of Jesus Christ" (Acts 8:12). Paul and Barnabas encouraged new disciples to continue in the faith: "It is through many persecutions that we must enter the kingdom of God" (14:22). Paul entered the synagogue in Ephesus and "spoke out boldly and argued persuasively about the kingdom of God" (19:8). His memoir would assert that there in Ephesus he had gone about "proclaiming the kingdom" (20:25). While under house arrest in Rome, he entertained visitors, both Jews and Gentiles, among whom he was "proclaiming the kingdom of God and teaching about the Lord Jesus Christ with all boldness and without hindrance" (28:23, 31). These comments and others show how central this announcement was in the early church's missional identity and message.

But it is not hard to see that at many times in the church's history this central affirmation of good news has suffered a pattern of omission or "eclipse," as Mortimer Arias has described it.[21] Two tendencies in the long history of Christendom help to explain this troublesome pattern. First, the church has tended to separate the news of the reign of God from God's provision for humanity's salvation. This separation has made salvation a private event by dividing "my personal salvation" from the advent of God's healing reign over all the world. Second, the church has also tended to envision itself in a variety of ways unconnected to what must be fundamental for it — its relation to the reign of God. If it was Jesus' announcement of the reign of God that first gathered the fledgling church into community, and if that church grew and matured around the way that reign found meaning and hope in his death and resurrection,

---

21. Mortimer Arias, *Announcing the Reign of God: Evangelization and the Subversive Memory of Jesus* (Philadelphia: Fortress, 1984), 55-67. Arias argues that the "eclipse" is not adequately explained simply by noting that in place of the good news of the reign of God the church has proclaimed Jesus as King. These are not opposed to each other but are complementary. As one Latin American theologian has put it: "Kingdom of God and person of Jesus (in the Lukan conception) explain and fulfill each other, in such a way that we cannot speak of kingdom of God without Christ, or Christ without *basileia* (kingdom). . . . Christology is always oriented towards its frame of reference in the *basileia*" (Augustin del Agua Perez, "El Cumplimento del Reino de Dios en la Mision de Jesus," *Estudios Biblicos* 38 [1979-80]: 292, quoted in translation by Arias, *Announcing the Reign of God*, 60).

then the church must always seek its definition with the reign of God in Christ as its crucial reference point.

The Reign of God as Missional Perspective

A significant recovery of "reign of God" or "kingdom of God" language has been evident within the field of biblical scholarship. To some extent, the same is true of church conversations about mission. But even when that is so, the use of such language in common church parlance tends not to be thought out very well. Typical Christian conversation on this subject speaks of "building" or "extending" the reign of God. These two ways of talking represent dominant and sometimes opposing ideologies in the North American churches. In both cases, the images of building or extending arise from the combined effects of a Christendom heritage of power and privilege, the Enlightenment's confidence in reason and social progress, and modern culture's dependence on managing life with pragmatic technique.

Those who imagine the church's role as "building" the reign of God may also use words like "establish," "fashion," or "bring about." The reign of God in this view is perceived as a social project. The church is sent out by God to achieve that project, to create it. This view tends to place the reign out there somewhere, where we go to construct it as its architects, contractors, carpenters, or day laborers.

Others say the church is sent to "extend" the reign of God. They speak in terms of "spreading," "growing," or "expanding" the reign of God. This treats the church's mission as a sales project. The church attempts to provide an expanded place where the reign of God may reside. Functionally, the church becomes the CEOs, promoters, or sales force for the reign of God.

But the grammar by which the New Testament depicts the reign of God cuts across the grain of these North American culture-bound ways of seeing things. The verbs *to build* and *to extend* are not found in the New Testament's grammar for the reign of God. The announcement of God's reign nowhere includes an invitation to go out and build it, nor to extend it. These are not New Testament ways of speaking about the reign of God.

The words most often used evoke quite a different spirit and, therefore, a very different missional identity and engagement. The New

93

Testament employs the words *receive* and *enter*. They come at times intertwined in the text. "Truly I tell you, whoever does not receive the kingdom of God as a child will never enter it" (Luke 18:17).[22] In that same context Jesus notes how hard it is for those who have riches to *enter* the reign of God (vv. 24-25), and he assures the disciples that there is no one who has left mother or father, houses or land, for the gospel's sake, who will not *receive* one hundredfold (vv. 29-30).

These two verbs represent dominant image clusters embedded throughout the New Testament's discussion of the relationship between the people of God and the reign of God. Taken together they indicate the appropriate way for a community to live when it has been captured by the presence of God's reign.

For example, the reign of God is, first of all, a gift one receives. The reign of God is something taken to oneself. It is a gift of God's making, freely given. It calls for the simple, trusting act of receiving.

The reign of God is something that *has been* given. "Do not be afraid, little flock," says Jesus, "for it is your Father's good pleasure to *give* you the kingdom" (Luke 12:32). It is something, then, that one can possess now. "Blessed are you who are poor, for yours *is* the kingdom of God" (6:20). "Let the children come to me; do not stop them; for it is to such as these that the kingdom of God *belongs*" (Mark 10:14; cf. Luke 18:16).

While God's reign can "belong" to the children, as something already possessed, it is also described as a gift that awaits our possessing. It *will be inherited*. On the final day of judgment the Son of Man will say, "Come, you that are blessed of my Father, inherit the kingdom prepared for you from the foundation of the world" (Matt. 25:34). James refers to

---

22. Here, as throughout, direct biblical quotations are from the New Revised Standard Version. That translation consistently uses "kingdom" to render the Greek word *basileia*, and so that word will appear within direct quotations of the Bible. But we have chosen to use "reign" throughout this text because it better captures, in our judgment, the dynamic meaning of *basileia*, which refers to the reigning itself and thus secondarily the realm incorporated under such reigning. "Kingdom," we believe, is too static, political, and archaic a word in our contemporary usage to do justice to the term, and it too easily identifies the *basileia* with a temporal entity like Christendom or particular structures of the church. As we will emphasize, the *basileia* and the church must never be divorced, but they also must never be equated. Similarly, the reign must never be separated from the One who reigns, the *basileos* at the heart of the *basileia*.

the poor as the "heirs of the kingdom" (2:5). The meek, Jesus said, "will inherit the earth" (Matt. 5:5). Paul in turn speaks of those who "will not inherit the kingdom of God" (1 Cor. 6:9-10; 15:50; Gal. 5:20; Eph. 5:5).

In addition to being a gift, the reign of God is equally a realm one enters. Here the imagery is quite different, for the reign of God is cast as a domain into which one moves. It meets everyone with God's welcome and Jesus' invitation.

The reign of God is a realm — a space, an arena, a zone — that may be inhabited. Hence the biblical grammar for this reign uses the spatial preposition *in*. In the Sermon on the Mount, Jesus declares that some "will be called least *in* the kingdom of heaven" and others "called great *in* the kingdom of heaven" (Matt. 5:19). Likewise, Colossians 1:13 tells us that Jesus "has rescued us from the power of darkness and transferred us *into* the kingdom of his beloved Son."

This realm of the reign of God into which we are welcomed to enter is never equated with a particular human political regime. It is always, after all, the realm of the regime of God. But on the horizon lies the cosmic specter of the reign of God fulfilled. So the grammar of "inhabiting" the reign of God includes the prospect of a future destiny. The reign of God is an inhabiting for which we are destined. The question raised by many of the parables concerns who, in the end, shall enter. At the end time, the Lord's word to some will be, "Enter into the joy of your master" (Matt. 25:21, 23). Yet "not everyone who says to me, 'Lord, Lord,' will enter the kingdom of heaven, but only the one who does the will of my Father in heaven" (Matt. 7:21). Second Peter 1:11 affirms: "Entry into the eternal kingdom of our Lord and Savior Jesus Christ will be richly provided for you."[23]

Taking seriously these two images of the reign of God as a gift one receives and a realm one enters restrains our cultural instincts to think of the reign of God as something we achieve or enlarge. The biblical images of gift and realm are not without their own dangers, certainly. The former can lead to the presumptuous claim of owning

---

23. Also in terms of this spatial image cluster, Jesus says to some, "You are not far from the kingdom of God" (Mark 12:34). Of others he says, "How hard it will be for those who have wealth to enter the kingdom of God" (10:23; cf. vv. 24-25; Luke 18:24-25; Matt. 19:23-24). Indeed, he says of some, "I tell you, unless your righteousness exceeds that of the scribes and Pharisees, you will never enter the kingdom of heaven" (Matt. 5:20).

the reign of God, and the latter to the prideful assertion of knowing ourselves to be "in" it. But if we follow faithfully the Bible's own use of these two images, we will discover that the images themselves provide the sharpest warnings against both presumption and pride. Jesus signals a great reversal in the imagery of giving and receiving, and welcoming and entering: "Therefore I tell you, the kingdom of God will be *taken away* from you and *given* to a people that produces the fruits of the kingdom" (Matt. 21:43). And to those who assumed themselves rightfully first in line for entering God's reign, he warned: "Truly I tell you, the tax collectors and the prostitutes are going into the kingdom of God ahead of you" (21:31).

To summarize what we have learned, then, the reign of God is *given.* God's gift and welcome are its most striking and critical features. Biblical language about the reign of God also embraces the eschatological tension of God's reign being a present fact and an anticipated future. It suggests the need as well for decisive action now. The call to receive warns against the consequence of rejecting the gift. The invitation to enter casts a shadow on hesitation at the door.

Inherent within the two biblical images of gift and realm are the further issues of repentance and faith. Receiving and entering are actions that mark a turning from other hopes and loyalties that we may accumulate to a singular hope in the one true God. They mark a turning in faith from sinful rejections of God's rule as well as carefree disdain for God's mercy and care. Receiving and entering the reign of God are the ways we "turn to God from idols" (1 Thess. 1:9). This movement indicates that we are involved in an ongoing dynamic relationship with the divine reign and that we must distinguish between the reign of God and its responsive community, between God's reign and the church.

It is in these findings that any biblically rooted and contextually relevant sense of the calling of the church in North America must begin. Here is a far more dynamic sense of the church's identity and its mission in the world. This sense stands in bold contrast to the merely functional or activist notions of building or extending that have so prepossessed the church in North America. In this beginning place, one finds a more humble starting point for mission. It leads to the fresh insight that the first mission is always the internal mission: the church evangelized by the Holy Spirit again and again in the echoing word of Jesus inviting us to receive the reign of God and to enter it.

Here is also found a more dynamic image for every Christian's personal calling and discipleship. Daily life becomes a discipline of asking how one may move more squarely into the realm of God's reign and how one may welcome and receive it into the fabric of one's life this day more than ever before. Here as well one can find a more focused way of living together as the community of Christ. This point is especially crucial for churches that have suffered the loss of focus, the loss of a sense of what lies at the center, the loss of their soul.

Here, moreover, is a far more welcoming framework for evangelism. Evangelism would move from an act of recruiting or co-opting those outside the church to an invitation of companionship. The church would witness that its members, like others, hunger for the hope that there is a God who reigns in love and intends the good of the whole earth. The community of the church would testify that they have heard the announcement that such a reign is coming, and indeed is already breaking into the world. They would confirm that they have heard the open welcome and received it daily, and they would invite others to join them as those who also have been extended God's welcome. To those invited, the church would offer itself to assist their entrance into the reign of God and to travel with them as co-pilgrims. Here lies a path for the renewal of the heart of the church and its evangelism.[24]

The Church and the Reign of God

It is obvious from all that has been said thus far that in Scripture and in the present the divine reign is distinguishable from *us*. It is something we can be in and something we can possess. But it is ultimately something other than who or what we are, and it can never be captive and owned by us in the sense of being controlled by us.

One of the two points where Matthew's Gospel mentions "church" *(ekklesia)* underscores this distinction and begins to establish the interrelationship between the reign of God and the church: "on this rock I will build my church," and then "I will give you the keys of the kingdom" (Matt. 16:18-19). Here it is clear that the church *(ekklesia)* and the reign

---

24. See William J. Abraham, *The Logic of Evangelism* (Grand Rapids: Eerdmans, 1989), for a compelling development of a theology of evangelistic ministry as "initiation into the kingdom."

of God *(basileia)* are separate conceptions, but also that the two are intimately bound together.

A clue to their relationship is present three chapters earlier amid the parables of the divine reign. In the interpretation Jesus gave to the parable of the weeds in the field, he says, "The field is the world, and the good seed are the children of the kingdom" (Matt. 13:38). At the end of the age, he goes on, "the Son of Man will send his angels, and they will collect out of his kingdom all causes of sin and all evildoers. . . . Then the righteous will shine like the sun in the kingdom of their Father" (vv. 41, 43). The messianic community is here construed to be the children of the divine reign, on the way to shining like the sun in that reign which is coming. In other words, the church is the offspring of the divine reign. It is its fruit, and therefore its evidence.

The church must not be equated with the reign of God. The church as a messianic community is both spawned by the reign of God and directed toward it. This is a different relationship from what at times has captured the church's thinking. The church has often presumed that the reign of God is within the church. The two have been regarded as synonyms. In this view, the church totally encompasses the divine reign. Therefore church extension or church growth is the equivalent of kingdom extension or kingdom growth, and the reign of God is coterminous with the people who embrace it through faith and gather together as the church. This view leads easily to the affirmation that there is no salvation outside the church. The church then sees itself as the fortress and guardian of salvation, perhaps even its author and benefactor, rather than its grateful recipient and guest.

The biblical portrait of the divine reign and the church does not allow such conclusions. The church always stands in a position of dependence on and humble service to the divine reign. The Dutch Reformed scholar Herman Ridderbos has stressed this point in *The Coming of the Kingdom:*

> The *basileia* [reign, kingdom] *is the great divine work of salvation in its fulfillment and consummation in Christ; the ekklesia* [church] *is the people elected and called by God and sharing in the bliss of the basileia.* Logically, the *basileia* ranks first, and not the *ekklesia.* . . . [The *basileia*] represents the all-embracing perspective, it denotes the consummation of all history, brings both grace and judgment, has cosmic dimensions, fills time and eternity. The *ekklesia* in all this is the people who in this great

drama have been placed on the side of God in Christ by virtue of the divine election and covenant.[25]

But at the same time we must say with equal force that the reign of God must not be divorced from the church. The church is constituted by those who are entering and receiving the reign of God. It is where the children of the reign corporately manifest the presence and characteristic features of God's reign. The divine reign expresses itself in a unique, though not exhaustive or exclusive, fashion in the church.

The desire to distinguish between the two has sometimes led to views that ultimately divorce them. Such was the case in some ecumenical circles during the 1950s and 1960s when it was affirmed that "the church goes out into the reign of God." This trend of thought began with people like Hans Hoekendijk who were concerned that the church had for too long centered mission on the church itself, as though the church were both the initiator of the mission and the goal of it. Hoekendijk rightly insisted:

> The church cannot be more than a sign. She points away from herself to the Kingdom; she lets herself be used for and through the Kingdom in the oikoumene [the whole inhabited earth]. There is nothing that the church can demand for herself and can possess for herself (not an ecclesiology either). God has placed her in a living relationship to the Kingdom and to the oikoumene. The church exists only *in actu*, in the execution of the apostolate, i.e., in the proclamation of the gospel of the Kingdom to the world.[26]

As this view matured and was carried forward by Hoekendijk and others, however, it pictured the divine reign as essentially, if not totally, "out there" in the world. Consequently, the church was to go out to meet God. This vision of the church and its mission was most forcefully expressed by the report of a World Council of Churches study program entitled *The Church for Others* (1967). Lesslie Newbigin has summarized the thrust of that document:

25. Herman N. Ridderbos, *The Coming of the Kingdom*, ed. Raymond O. Zorn, tr. H. deJongste (Philadelphia: Presbyterian & Reformed, 1962), 354.
26. J. C. Hoekendijk, *The Church Inside Out*, ed. L. A. Hoedemaker and Pieter Tijmes, tr. Isaac C. Rottenberg (Philadelphia: Westminster, 1966), 43.

"Thinking about the Church should always begin by defining it as part of the world" (17). It is the world, not the Church, which "writes the agenda" (20-23), and the Church is not to be concerned about increasing its own membership (19). "Participation in God's mission is entering into partnership with God in history, because our knowledge of God in Christ compels us to affirm that God is working out his purpose in the midst of the world and its historical processes" (14). So "What else can the Churches do than recognize and proclaim what God is doing in the world" — in the emancipation of coloured races, the humanization of industrial relations, and so on?[27]

The instinct here to include the larger world within the scope of God's mission and reign is a good one. But the position stated here implies that the church is ultimately irrelevant to the mission of God or at least peripheral to it, since the reign of God is entirely located in the world. What is lost in this view is the church's reason for being a particular community, both distinct from the divine reign and yet spawned by it as its intended fruit and servant.

In contrast, Newbigin has affirmed a perspective that seeks to maintain the distinction between God's reign and the church but not break their connection:

The . . . danger to be avoided is the separation of the Kingdom from the church. It is clear that they cannot and must not be confused, certainly not identified. But they must also not be separated. From the beginning the announcement of the Kingdom led to a summons to follow and so to the formation of a community. It is the community which has begun to taste (even only in foretaste) the reality of the Kingdom which can alone provide the hermeneutic of the message.[28]

When we ask then what positive model or understanding of the church would do justice to these two negative affirmations, we are led to capture the biblical sense of the church's calling and vocation this way: *the church represents the reign of God.* This is another way of rendering the fundamental New Testament notion of witness, but promises a fresh and holistic approach to viewing all of the church's life missionally. The

27. Lesslie Newbigin, "Recent Thinking on Christian Beliefs: VIII. Mission and Missions," *Expository Times* 88, no. 9 (1977): 261.

28. Lesslie Newbigin, *Sign of the Kingdom* (Grand Rapids: Eerdmans, 1980), 19.

word *represent* can carry two different senses, a passive one and an active one. The passive meaning indicates that one thing stands for another. When you have seen the one, you have known the other. An example of this form of representation would be the sentence, "The paper submitted to the professor represents the student's best effort." In contrast, the active meaning of *represent* indicates the way a person may be given authority to act on another's behalf or to care for another's interests, such as, "A lawyer represents her client," or "The secretary of state represents the president in this meeting." Both the passive and active meanings of "represent" are intended when it is said of the church that it represents the reign of God, and each adds particular force to the missional calling of the church.

The church represents the divine reign as its *sign and foretaste*. Themes woven into the fabric of the book of Ephesians illustrate this intended meaning. When the author speaks of the breaking down of the barriers between Jews and Gentiles (2:11ff.) that has resulted from the expansion of the gospel mission to the Gentile world, he states that this profound social change within the small community of Christians represents God's purpose for the world: "that he might create in himself one new humanity in place of the two, thus making peace" (2:15). The emerging multicultural church is here a foretaste of God's redeeming purpose for the world, which is the mystery now revealed: "that is, the Gentiles have become fellow heirs, members of the same body, and sharers in the promise in Christ Jesus through the gospel" (3:6). This point is even more explicit when the church is described as the sign of God's wisdom for the cosmos: "so that through the church the wisdom of God in its rich variety might now be made known to the rulers and authorities in the heavenly places" (3:10). As a sign represents something else and as a foretaste represents something yet to come, the church points away from itself to what God is going to complete. In this sense, the divine reign's otherness is guarded. The church must affirm that it is not identical with God's reign.

But the church also represents the divine reign as its *agent and instrument*. Here it represents that reign in an active sense. The church bears the divine reign's authority (the authority of the "keys," Matt. 16:19; and the authority of "forgiveness," as indicated in John 20:19-23). It engages in the divine reign's action (living in terms of the lordship of Jesus over all creation). For this reason, Paul may address Christians as "co-workers for the kingdom of God" (Col. 4:11) and consider them to

101

be "suffering" for the reign of God (2 Thess. 1:5). The church is representative in the sense of an embassy ("ambassadors for Christ," 2 Cor. 5:20) of the divine reign.

By its very existence, then, the church brings what is hidden into view as sign and into experience as foretaste. At the same time, it also represents to the world the divine reign's character, claims, demands, and gracious gifts as its agent and instrument.

The Mission to Represent the Reign of God

In what forms should this representation take place? Just how does a community of people go about representing the reign of God among its neighbors near and far? The most likely location for an answer to these questions is the mission of Jesus. His mission, after all, represents the most direct and complete expression of God's mission in the world. Therefore the church's own mission must take its cues from the way God's mission unfolded in the sending of Jesus into the world for its salvation. In Jesus' way of carrying out God's mission, we discover that the church is to represent God's reign as its community, its servant, and its messenger.[29]

---

29. This triad, which emerges from Scripture, has constantly surfaced in the church's recent thinking about its mission. This was particularly the case in the 1950s when the experience of the modern missionary movement led Hans Hoekendijk and Hendrik Kraemer to articulate their threefold sense of the church's mission as *kerygma, diakonia,* and *koinonia.* The 1961 New Delhi Assembly of the World Council of Churches used the themes of witness, service, and unity to signal the three strands that had converged in the formulation of the Council (International Missionary Council, Life and Work, and Faith and Order). The Vatican II document *Lumen Gentium* portrays the church using the images of prophet, king, and priest. In *The Mustard Seed Conspiracy* (Waco: Word, 1981), Tom Sine speaks of the mission as words of love, deeds of love, and life of love. The book *Who in the World?* ed. Clifford Christians, Earl J. Schipper, and Wesley Smedes (Grand Rapids: Eerdmans, 1972), presented a report of a Christian Reformed Church conference that organized the church's mission around the truth (message), the life (community), and the way (servant). Darrell L. Guder talks about being the witness, doing the witness, and saying the witness in *Be My Witnesses: The Church's Mission, Message, and Messengers* (Grand Rapids: Eerdmans, 1985).

Representing the Reign of God as Its Community

Jesus believed it was his mission to embody the reign of God by living under its authority. He was the willing subject of God's reign. His baptism by John and anointing by the Spirit placed him under covenant obligations and promises. He claimed the role of fulfilling all righteousness. Therefore he bore the same covenant obligations Israel had borne, but fulfilled them as Israel never had.

This is the point of Jesus' temptations in the wilderness. It is not by accident that Jesus responds to each temptation presented by Satan with words from the Deuteronomic recapitulation of the covenant. In effect he was saying, "Here are the rules under which I am to live. I will abide by them." The test was whether he would keep covenant, whether he would live in ultimate trust and dependence on God, and whether he would give ultimate loyalty and obedience to God. The reign of God was present in a radically new way in Jesus because he lived trustingly and loyally under the gracious rule of his Father as none had lived before.

The church shares this calling with Jesus. In the church's case, though, its vocation is corporate, not individual. Jesus, the one who represented Israel, is now represented by the new Israel, the church. Like Jesus, the church is to embody the reign of God by living under its authority. We live as the covenant community, a distinctive community spawned by God's reign to show forth its tangible character in human, social form.

Before the church is called to do or say anything, it is called and sent to be the unique community of those who live under the reign of God. The church displays the firstfruits of the forgiven and forgiving people of God who are brought together across the rubble of dividing walls that have crumbled under the weight of the cross. It is the harbinger of the new humanity that lives in genuine community, a form of companionship and wholeness that humanity craves.

What the church identifies as true about itself because of Christ, it also knows to be far from true about itself in its present experience. Yet it is precisely this affirmation made by Christ concerning who the church is that moves it to actualize in practice what it believes true.[30]

---

30. Küng comments that while the church is a historical phenomenon, it is always more than it appears; this is what he calls the "invisible aspect" of the church (*Church*, 59-65).

Believing itself to be one in the "unity of the Spirit" (Eph. 4:3), the church knows God has sent it into the pursuit of the "unity of the faith" (4:13).

Of course, God delights in having a people who are one in love, and God's people enjoy the freedom of being that particular people. But there is another reason for this mission of being the community of the reign of God. "You are the light of the world," Jesus said (Matt. 5:14). We are a noticed and watched people. The genuineness of our identification as the disciples of Jesus is observed only in our love for each other (John 13:35). Jesus seeks our oneness with one another "so that the world may believe" that he indeed has been sent by his Father (17:21). The church's love and unity holds ultimate significance for the world as the visible basis of the gospel's power and legitimacy. In fact, the church is itself the promise of the gospel. The universal invitation to believe the gospel includes the invitation to enter the reign-of-God-produced community of the new humanity. Just as Jesus exhibited his union with his Father in obedient submission to God's rule and thus could say, "Whoever has seen me has seen the Father" (14:9), so too God has designed it so that when people have seen God's "peculiar" people, they have in a real sense caught a view of God. "As the Father has sent me, so I send you" (20:21).

Representing the Reign of God as Its Servant

Jesus further believed it to be his mission to exhibit the signs of the presence of the reign of God by exercising its authority over brokenness, domination, oppression, and alienation. By virtue of his faithfulness, he was to be given a name and dominion above every other in the future. But even during his earthly ministry, he demonstrated his authority over disease and nature, over people and their social structures, and over spirit forces that bind and distort. This authority must be carefully understood as an authority derived from being "under authority."

Perhaps the most interesting clue regarding the relationship between these first two facets of Jesus' mission comes from the most unlikely source. Luke reports how a centurion approached Jesus to request healing for his servant (7:1-10). He sent word to Jesus that Jesus need not come but only say the word, and his servant would be healed. He added, "For I also am a man set under authority, with soldiers under me; and I say to one, 'Go,' and he goes, and to another, 'Come,' and he comes, and to my slave, 'Do this,' and the slave does it." Jesus' immediate commendation of the centurion's faith affirms how the man understood authority — his own and that which Jesus possessed. One exercises authority only insofar as one is under authority. The source of Jesus' authority lay not in the powers he had as divine. His authority sprang from his own faithful trust and loyalty, his living under authority. In later chapters we shall see that there is a lesson here for contemporary Christian leadership who hunger for authority and power.

Jesus' healings, exorcisms, calming of storms, feeding of the multitudes, and raising the dead to life were all signs. These signs revealed that in Jesus' life under the authority of God the reign of God was at hand. The deeds themselves were simply doing what ought to be done under God's reign. They also point to what God intends the world to be like when God's reign comes. They represent what God fully intends to bring about at the world's consummation, when all that creation was envisioned and imagined to be is made finally true. The actions of Jesus show forth the horizon of the coming world of shalom — peace, justice, and joy in the Holy Spirit.

The church shares that horizon, and with it the impulse to respond to the whole range of need in humanity and in the creation. Thus the church represents the reign of God by its deeds as the servant to God's passion for the world's life. Like Jesus, it exhibits by numerous signs the reign of God, thereby exercising its authority.

To use Jesus' imagery, as the church is light to the world, so also it is salt. Going to all the earth, the church bears the mission to *do* all that Christ commanded just as it is to *teach* others to do the same (cf. Matt. 28:18-20). The fruits of repentance and the Holy Spirit's gifts of conversion bring about deeds arising from genuine discipleship. As we live under God's reign, our involvements with the world are repatterned.

The design for that repatterning is Jesus himself. Throughout his earthly ministry we sense the heartbeat of his action: compassionate response to human need. He was predisposed to be interrupted, even from his focal task of preaching, whenever hunger, sickness, demonic oppression, the grip of sin, social ostracism, or death crossed his path (Mark 1:35-45). Tears paved the road he traveled in order to bring good news. Such a predisposition was the theme of his keynote address in Nazareth (Luke 4:16-20) and the proof of his messianic appointment, as he indicated to John the Baptist (Matt. 11:1-6).

Far from being a distraction from his preaching in all the towns and villages, Jesus' compassionate responses to human need were an integral part of the message he preached. They were signposts raised to public view.

The church carries Jesus' mantle as the people of God "under authority." Our responses of compassion and service, like our actions for peace and justice, are deeds of authority and therefore signs that the reign of God is present now in our world and is on the way as its future. Our responses may be small and personal: a cup of cold water, a warm blanket, or a visit with cookies and cakes. They may be bold: "Rise up and walk," or the expulsion of evil spirits in the name of Jesus. They may engage the complexities of corporate modern living: pressuring governments and corporations for the sake of the disadvantaged or the ravaged earth, lobbying for just laws, solidarity with oppressed peoples, initiatives to cease hostilities among nations, care for marginalized peoples and the creation, or compassionate remolding of socioeconomic structures. Whatever our responses may be, they bring wholeness and dignity to the world and thereby provide a taste of a future in the reign of God under the rule and authority of Christ's lordship. These are signs that invite people to "enter and taste more, to eat and be full." They cultivate the hunger to pray the petition, Give us today the bread of tomorrow's heavenly feast. This eschatological rendering of the phrase from the Lord's Prayer is in keeping with the whole emphasis of the prayer as well as the meaning of the Greek text. When the church prays this way, the reign of God intrudes on the life of the world.

Representing the Reign of God as Its Messenger

Finally, Jesus believed it to be his mission to announce the presence of the reign of God and its implications and call. It was his mission to put into words what was true about his presence and his deeds. "Whoever has seen me has seen the Father" (John 14:9). "But if it is by the finger of God that I cast out the demons, then the kingdom of God has come to you" (Luke 11:20). Preaching and teaching with illuminating parable-puzzles and penetrating responses to situations in teachable moments were required to interpret what was seen and experienced. If his own presence was a *sign* of the reign of God, and his deeds were *signposts* pointing to it, his verbal proclamation of the meaning of his presence and deeds added the *signature*. Jesus is saying with his speech, "These things you see and hear mean that the reign of God has come among you. Receive it. Enter it."

The church shares this missional role as well. It identifies the reign of God by announcing its authority. The church's being and doing are irretrievably tied to its proclaiming. Its verbal interpretation of all that is lived and done makes clear where the real issues of life lie: "The reign of God is at hand!" The declaration of the message entrusted to the church gives substantial content and definition to what its being and doing signify. It affirms the character of what the world sees it being and experiences it doing. Jesus not only exhibited his oneness with the Father but also put it into words: "If you have seen me. . . ." He not only displayed the signs of the divine reign's presence, he labeled them: "If it is by the finger of God that I cast out demons. . . ." To proclaim the divine reign is to add the signature of Jesus; to refrain from proclamation leaves all else anonymous, ambiguous, and subject to misreading the situation. Such vocal signing makes explicit what is implicit in the other signs. Verbalizing the gospel of Jesus removes the ambiguity. It also renders the reign of God accessible. By it, the reign of God is opened to the participation of the whole world. Our words become the way to say of it all, "It's free! This community is open! You are welcome!"

Announcing the reign of God comes as a spontaneous expression of gratitude, humility, and joy when it occurs in the context of being the forgiven community that embodies the divine reign and signals its character in actions of compassion, justice, and peace. It is the simple response of the otherwise insignificant and lowly of the earth who have come into the freedom of a new identity in God's re-creation, an identity that was really true of humanity from the beginning. In proclamation we simply and profoundly name ourselves, and that is the place where ultimate power and authority lie. No repressive government, no oppressive social structure, none of the principalities and powers, not even death, can strip us of that power. "To all who received him, who believed in his name, he gave power to become children of God" (John 1:12). Our witness to the reign of God speaks in the voice of that God-granted right.

Proclamation is inevitable if our being and doing signify anything at all about the presence of God's reign. If in our being the church, the world *sees* God's reign, and by our doing justice, the world *tastes* its gracious effect, then the call to all on the earth to receive and acknowledge that reign begs to be expressed. That is why Jesus said it is necessary that his followers preach repentance and the forgiveness of sins in Christ's name to all the nations, so that all the nations may hear (Luke 24:47; cf. Rom. 10:14-17).

In summary, the church in mission may be characterized as the sign of Messiah's coming. Our being, doing, and speaking are signs that his coming is "already" and "not yet." He is here already or the signs would not be present. He is coming still or the signs would not be muted. Broken though they may be, the signs persist in the world by the Spirit's insistence, and they spell hope for the renewal of the human community in the final reconciliation of all things to God through the Lord Christ. In this respect, the church is the preview community, the foretaste and harbinger of the coming reign of God.

Further, it is important to hold these three facets of the church's mission together in synoptic vision, to look, as it were, through all three lenses at once in order to see mission whole. Synergy, not competition for primacy, exists among the three in the mission of the church. Wherever the Bible evidences a priority for one or another of these three aspects of representing the reign of God, we are quickly reminded how each implicates its two counterparts.

Finally, the three facets of mission illuminated by this vision directly answer the most fundamental questions and challenges for the contemporary church. They signal three basic priorities for the church's recovery of its missional soul.

First, in a free world of the autonomous and decentered self, and with a gospel of reconciliation in Christ, the churches must revive what it means to be communities of the reign of God. Churches are called to be bodies of people sent on a mission rather than the storefronts for vendors of religious services and goods in North American culture. We must surrender the self-conception of the church as a voluntary association of individuals and live by the recognition that we are a communal body of Christ's followers, mutually committed and responsible to one another and to the mission Jesus set us upon at his resurrection.

Second, in a secular world of privatized religious faith and with a gospel of Christ's reign over all things, the churches must discover what it means to act faithfully on behalf of the reign of God within the public life of their society. Because we live in a plural world that no longer gives us privileged place and power, we have the choice to confine our business to the private realm of the self and its leisure choices or to find new patterns for faithful public deeds. The calling to seek first the reign of God and God's justice means orienting our public deeds away from imposing our moral will onto the social fabric and toward giving tangible experience of the reign of God that intrudes as an alternative to the public principles and loyalties.

Third, in a plural world of relativized perspectives and loyalties, and with a gospel of the knowledge of God through the incarnate Christ, the churches must learn to speak in post-Christendom accents as confident yet humble messengers of the reign of God. A postmodern world is a wildly exciting arena for learning to speak boldly, often, and in fresh ways. The church speaks not to recruit members into an organization through an individualized version of the gospel, easily understood by an equally individualistic culture. It speaks boldly and often so that the signs of the reign of God in the Scriptures, in the world's history, and in the present may be clearly seen. It speaks so that the signposts to the reign of God evidenced in the church's own deeds will not be misunderstood.

The calling of the church to be missional — to be a sent community — leads the church to step beyond the given cultural forms that carry dubious assumptions about what the church is, what its public role should be, and what its voice should sound like. Testing and revising our assumptions and practices against a vision of the reign of God promises the deep renewal of the missional soul of the church that we need. By daily receiving and entering the reign of God, through corporate praying for its coming, and longing for its appearance, and in public living under its mantle, this missional character of the church will be nourished and revived.

5

Missional Witness:
The Church as Apostle to the World

When the church in North America discards the Christendom mind-set, it can become truly apostolic. To be apostolic is, literally, to be sent out. This implies a distinction between the church and that to which it is sent. The church exists as community, servant, and messenger of the reign of God in the midst of other kingdoms, communities, and powers that attempt to shape our understanding of reality. The world of those kingdoms, communities, and powers often opposes, ignores, or has other priorities than the reign of God. To that world, the missional church is apostle — sent out on behalf of the reign of God.

In, but Not of, the World

Principalities and Powers

The Bible sometimes describes the missional church as being in the world but not of the world. That is, the church is in the midst of the world, both geographically and culturally, but it is not of the world. It does not have the same values as the world, the same behaviors, or the same allegiances. The missional church differs from the world because it looks for its cues from the One who has sent it out, rather than from the powers that appear to run the world.

In the New Testament, the world is not only the human beings whom God loves and the place in which God acts. The world is also the arena in which the powers act. These "powers," "principalities," "governments," "thrones," "authorities," "angels," or "elemental spirits of the universe" have both material and spiritual form. For example, a "throne" represents an actual chair and the person who sits on it and rules, as well as the authority that person possesses by virtue of office, the customary ways of ruling in that jurisdiction, and the spirit that guides that rule. School spirit, for another example, is a "power" that shows itself in concrete behaviors at pep rallies or student council meetings, but it is also an atmosphere or an accepted way of doing things that exists beyond the particular students or teachers attending the school at any one time. A company may have a corporate culture that continues, even when all the original owners and employees are gone. These powers, principalities, and spirits pervade all human culture, governments, societies, and institutions.

In themselves, the powers are neither wholly good nor wholly bad. God has created them; they have roles ordained by God. For instance, human governments have been instituted by God to control societal evil (Rom. 13:1-5). God ordains that there be human governments. God does not ordain, however, any particular regime or any particular system of government, although governments like other powers have a tendency to set themselves up as ultimate authorities, in the place of God. When this occurs, the powers become idolatrous. Colossians 2:15 speaks of Christ, through his cross and resurrection, triumphing over the powers, who tend to turn away from God. Through Christ the powers have been unmasked, and believers can see them for what they really are. Romans 8:38-39 testifies that none of these powers, not even death, can separate us from the love of God in Christ Jesus our Lord. The Gospels, as well, portray Jesus as having authority over the unclean spirits. Yet the powers can be instruments of evil, as they are in racism, sexism, systems of violence, and so on. The evil of racism goes beyond individual acts of racial discrimination; racism is also manifested in systems of white privilege and is indeed one of the powers.[1]

---

1. For a more detailed description of the powers in the Bible, see H. Berkhof, *Christ and the Powers,* tr. John Howard Yoder (Scottdale, Penn.: Herald, 1962); D. Schroeder, "Die Haustafeln des Neuen Testaments: Ihre Herkunft und ihr theologischer Sinn" (diss., University of Hamburg, 1959); John Howard Yoder, *The Politics of Jesus,* 2nd ed. (Grand Rapids: Eerdmans, 1994), chap. 8; and Walter Wink, *Naming the Powers: The Language of Power in the New Testament* (Philadelphia: Fortress,

No powers, governments, institutions, spirits, or established ways of doing things are absolute, according to the New Testament. They are intended to serve God. Ultimately, Jesus Christ is the ruler of the kings of the earth (Rev. 1:5), and in the age to come all rulers and powers will acknowledge God's sovereignty.

Bill, whom we met in chapter two, experiences modernity as a particular set of powers: technology, urbanization, bureaucracy, and professionalism. Although Bill has choices, they are heavily shaped by these powers. It would be difficult for Bill to decide to do his work outside the framework of bureaucracy and professionalism, for example.

Likewise, Jim and Ruth's church experiences, recounted in chapter three, have been influenced by the "power" of individualism. The pervasiveness of individualism in North America's dominant culture reaches into the church as well. Church becomes defined apart from community, in terms of individual choice, individual morality, individual self-actualization, and individual decisions about where to obtain the best spiritual goods and services. All too typical is the woman who, after attending worship and disliking the sermon, asked her visiting friend, "Now tell me, what did you get out of that worship service?" The woman was taken aback when the friend replied, "That's not a question I ask myself. I ask myself, 'Did this community of God's people worship God today?'" It never occurs to many people to define worship in terms other than meeting individual needs, or to put God rather than personal satisfaction at the center of worship. This situation is the result not just of people's individual perversity, but of the pervasiveness of the power of individualism that tries to determine not only the answers but also the way one shapes the question.

Because the church has assumed the forms of a functional Christendom in North America, much of the church has lost its ability to critique the powers. Although no denomination is officially established in the United States or Canada, most churches nevertheless act out of an establishment mind-set. They behave as if the churches' goals and the goals of the nation-state were entirely compatible. They sometimes put national flags in sanctuaries or honor those who have served in the military by placing their names on engraved plaques under stained-glass

1984); idem, *Unmasking the Powers: The Invisible Forces That Determine Human Existence* (Philadelphia: Fortress, 1986); idem, *Engaging the Powers: Discernment and Resistance in a World of Domination* (Minneapolis: Fortress, 1992).

windows. The church has grown to expect privilege from governments — tax breaks, laws that support Christian morality, prayer at civic events. In a similar fashion, economic powers tend to captivate the church through its adoption of a market mentality in its evangelism or a dependence on investments for its future survival.

Whenever the church has a vested interest in the status quo — politically, economically, socially — it can easily be captivated by the powers, the institutions, the spirits, and the authorities of the world. And whenever the church becomes captivated by the powers, it loses the ability to identify and name evil.

In general, the modern world's Enlightenment mentality has no place for evil. As in Platonic thought, Enlightenment thought believes that evil has no reality in itself. Evil is simply the absence of good, as darkness is the absence of light. In popular understandings, this has often translated into the claim that everything that happens, no matter how tragic, is the will of God. Or it has meant a denial of death, a desire to look only on the positive and deny the negative.

Without an acknowledgment of evil, the church has little basis for evaluating and judging the powers, whether they have turned toward God or toward evil. Without an understanding of evil and of God's ultimate victory over evil in the age to come, it is difficult for the church to have any sense of urgency about its participation in the mission of God's reign in and to the world. If the church is truly apostolic, it must see itself as participating in God's victory over evil.

Church, Culture, and the Powers

Culture is related to the powers. Many of the aspects of culture (customs, tradition, language, all those things that give a people a distinctive identity) are themselves powers that can work for good or evil.

Everyone lives in the context of a culture or cultures. Even the most radical individualist lives within a culture, a set of social understandings and practices. Culture is often related to national identity or ethnicity. But most people in North America are surrounded by many cultures and ethnicities. Those from minority cultures and ethnicities usually function biculturally, that is, both in their primary culture and in the dominant culture. Commonly, only those who are squarely within the dominant culture believe that there is some neutral place to stand outside all cultures. They are like participants in a seminar who were asked to write their ethnicity on a piece of newsprint hanging on the wall. African-Americans knew their ethnicity. Jews knew their ethnicity. But most of the white people from the dominant culture in the United States were either puzzled as to what to write or wrote such things as, "I have no ethnicity," or "I am a world citizen." The dominant culture gave them the illusion that it was neutral. But there is no such neutrality of culture. All culture is particular.

The church always lives in and among a culture or group of cultures. The vast majority of the church's particular communities share with their neighbors a primary culture or cultures, which include their language, food, perhaps styles of dress, and other customs. But they are called to point beyond that culture to the culture of God's new community.[2]

This does not mean that the church or the gospel it preaches is somehow outside culture. There is no cultureless gospel. Jesus himself preached, taught, and healed within a specific cultural context. Nor is it the case that the gospel can be reduced to a set of cultureless principles. The message of the reign of God, the gospel, is always communicated with the thought constructs and practices prevalent within the cultural setting of the church in a specific time and place. But when truly shaped by the Holy Spirit, this message also points beyond its present culture's thought forms and customs to the distinctive culture of God's reign proclaimed by Jesus. For this reason, the church is always bicultural, conversant in the language and customs of the surrounding culture and living toward the language and ethics of the gospel. One of the tasks of the church is to translate the gospel so that the surrounding culture can understand it, yet help those believers who have been in that culture move toward living according to the behaviors and communal identity of God's missional people — in the language of the New Testament, God's *ethnos* (see 1 Pet. 2:9).

This is one of the ways the church lives in but not of the world. The church's particular communities live in the context of the surrounding culture, engage with the culture, but are not controlled by the culture. The faithful church critiques its cultural environment, particularly the dominant culture; affirms those aspects of culture that do not contradict the gospel; speaks the languages of the surrounding cultures and of the gospel; constantly tries to communicate the gospel in the surrounding

2. For a fuller discussion of the cultivation of the Christian culture, see the discussion of practices of the church in the next chapter.

cultures; and is cultivating and forming the culture of God's new community, a culture not of the world. To do so is part of its being apostolic, sent into the world.

This understanding of the church and culture is quite different from the understanding of H. Richard Niebuhr in *Christ and Culture*.[3] There he outlines five possible relationships between Christ and culture: Christ against culture, the Christ of culture, Christ above culture, Christ and culture in paradox, and, his favorite, Christ the transformer of culture. Though influential in many church communions and read in most mainline seminaries in North America, his analysis is inadequate for the church to find its way among the cultures surrounding it.

To begin with, "Christ" and "culture" are not parallel concepts. "Christ" (from Greek = "messiah," from Hebrew) usually refers to the church's title for the specific person Jesus of Nazareth and his continuing relationship with the church. By contrast, "culture" is a very general term. It involves an ongoing aspect of human society in every time and place. Moreover, the use of the singular term *culture* does not recognize the multiplicity and diversity of cultures that commonly exist in any one space and time. To compare "Christ" and "culture" is like comparing apples and organization.

Further, Niebuhr's analysis has no real place for the church. His primary actor is the individual Christian, who must make choices concerning Christ and culture. By implication, the church is simply a collection of individual Christians. The church as a social reality, a community that affirms or dissents from culture based on its following Jesus Christ, is lost when the primary categories are "Christ" and "culture." The "Christ transforming culture" model, in particular, does allow for both affirmation and dissent. It assumes, however, that the real arena of God's action is in the surrounding culture, not in and through the church.

All but one of Niebuhr's options take for granted a Christendom or Constantinian model of the church as well. Not only the "Christ of culture" option but also most of the others assume that Christians have a common identity with the surrounding culture, so that the church and the culture mutually support each other; if there are problems in the culture, Christians are responsible to fix them. Moreover, responsibility is always defined in terms of service to the culture, rather than

3. H. Richard Niebuhr, *Christ and Culture* (New York: Harper & Row, 1951).

in terms of Christians' covenant responsibility to God in the context of the church.

Finally, the only non-Christendom model, "Christ against culture," Niebuhr claims to be flawed because in it Christians are said to withdraw from the world, to reject any responsibility for it, and to be no longer "in the world." This model, however, is a straw figure set up to be knocked down easily. The possibility of living human beings not being "in the world" or withdrawing completely from "the culture" does not exist. Even those churches that have dissented from many aspects of the dominant culture still participate in it in many ways — through sharing its language, through involvement in its economic system, through social interaction of various kinds. Niebuhr further criticizes this model of Christian life by calling it inconsistent wherever it does participate in the dominant culture. Yet Niebuhr ignores the possibility that the most transforming activity of the church in relationship to the culture might not be to try to wield power in the dominant culture, but instead to demonstrate by the church's own life together the renewing and healing power of God's new community.

In North America many churches have an uncritical view of culture, even when they have wished for change. Those on the political left have tended to think that the main arena of God's action is in Congress or Parliament or in service projects for the improvement of society, and they consider mission to be something one goes out and does away from the gatherings of the church. Meanwhile, those on the political right, who have traditionally placed the main arena of God's action in the privacy of the human heart, have also attempted more recently to influence government and to enforce Christian moral codes through secular law. These efforts on the part of many churches traditionally categorized as "free churches" are a new form of functional Christendom, heading toward erasing the distinction between the church and the world.

Nonconformity to the World

In Romans 12:2 Paul instructs believers: "Do not be conformed to this world, but be transformed by the renewing of your minds, so that you may discern what is the will of God — what is good and acceptable and perfect." Then he provides a partial list of what it means to be transformed in accordance with the will of God rather than conformed to the world: not thinking of yourself more highly than you ought to think, valuing the gifts of others in the body of Christ, loving one another with mutual affection, being ardent in spirit, being patient in suffering, praying, extending hospitality to strangers, blessing persecutors, associating with the lowly, not repaying evil for evil, living peaceably, and overcoming evil with good.

These instructions are not the common wisdom of the dominant culture in North America at the end of the twentieth century. Those who follow them will not always be in sync with, or understood by, their neighbors. This way of behaving is not necessarily possible outside a relationship with Jesus Christ and his church. Indeed, Paul defines this life as a process of becoming transformed into the image of Christ (2 Cor. 3:18). Jesus himself told his disciples, "If any want to become my followers, let them deny themselves and take up their cross and follow me" (Mark 8:34).

The church is called to be this community, not controlled by the idolatrous powers, not conformed to the common sense of the surrounding culture, but shaping its life and ministry around Jesus Christ, his life, his death, and his resurrected power, and living now according to the pattern of the resurrected life in the age to come. The nature of the church's witness to the world is this nonconformed engagement with the world. This engagement happens both through specific words and deeds performed in the world and through the witness of being a presence in the world, different from the world, inviting questions, challenging assumptions, and demonstrating a life not of the world.

This nonconformity to the world — and conformity to Christ — is part of what the New Testament means by the church's being "holy." To be holy is to be set apart, separated on behalf of God. The church must have as its direction to be holy as God is holy.

The Missional Church in the World Is a Holy Nation among the Nations

In contrast to contemporary understandings of the church as voluntary association, chaplain to society, or vendor of religious goods and services, one of the most important understandings of the church in the New Testament is a political one: the church as holy nation.

The New Testament's Political Language for the Church

This key image in the New Testament is explicitly invoked for the church in 1 Peter 2:9. This passage itself paraphrases Exodus 19:5-6, which is the Jewish self-understanding (see, e.g., Luke 23:2; John 18:35; Acts 10:22). The Christian church took for itself the idea of nationhood but opened it up more radically than had the Jewish proselytizers to include Gentiles as well as Jews.

A word just as political but more frequently used in the New Testament is *kingdom*—in Matthew "kingdom of heaven," elsewhere "kingdom of God." As we have shown in the last chapter, the center of Jesus' message was the reign or kingdom of God.[4] His preaching of the reign of God was continued by the early church: Philip (Acts 8:12), Paul and Barnabas (14:22), Paul alone (19:8; 20:25), the writer of Hebrews (1:8; 12:28), James (2:5), the second letter of Peter (1:11), and John (Rev. 1:9; 12:10). Jesus is given the title "King" or "King of kings" and in Revelation the saints are called "kings" as well (King James Version, 1:6; 5:10). Even the title "Lord" for Jesus is a political title, since in the first-century Roman Empire it was expected that one would call Caesar "lord." Like the rulers of the world, God is seen as Judge (2 Thess. 1:5; Heb. 12:23; Rev. 18:8), and the title is applied to Jesus as well (Acts 10:42).

Even the word *church* has a political connotation. While the Greek word for "church," *ekklesia,* can mean any assembly, it often refers to an assembly gathered for decision making, a town meeting. Thus the church is that gathering of the reign of God assembled to be a sign of that reign, to proclaim the reign of God in word and deed, to make decisions, and to give allegiance to their Ruler. Participants in this gathering are citizens of heaven (Phil. 3:20). They are no longer strangers and aliens, but citizens with the saints, those who are holy (Eph. 2:19).

The New Testament also claims that, in Jesus' death and resurrection, Christ has defeated the "rulers and authorities," or the "principalities and powers," as the King James Version translates it. Colossians 2:9-15 declares that Christ has disarmed the rulers and authorities and made a public example of them, leading them as hostages in triumphal victory procession. Indeed, Christ is now not only head of the church but head of every ruler and authority (see also Eph. 1:20-23). Part of the

---

4. See Mark 1:15; the discussion in chap. 4 is on pp. 87ff.

task of the church is to make known the wisdom of God to the rulers and authorities (Eph. 3:10).

Such language is a dramatic challenge to the powers, governments, authorities, and institutions of the world. These political claims for Christ and for the church as the people of God demand that people make a choice, a choice of allegiance. The "holy" people will be those who have been set apart for Christ's service. They are the people different from those around them, different because they have given their ultimate allegiance to God through Jesus as Lord.

Worship as a Political Act

The community, the church, is called to have a different political identity from the people around it. The symbol of the church's alternative political identity is worship. In its most concrete origins, the Hebrew word for *worship* denotes the physical act of falling on one's face on the ground in homage before one's ruler. Thus God the Ruler is at the center of the church's worship. The praise and prayer of worship, the reading and preaching of Scripture, the fellowship around the table, and the washing of baptism that initiates new citizens of heaven — all these define an alternative community with an alternative allegiance.

The church's allegiance grows out of its covenant with God through Christ. As 1 Peter 2:10 quotes Hosea 2:23, "Once you were not a people, but now you are God's people." This new people is not a community in isolation from the world. It is, instead, a community engaged with the world in order to proclaim the mighty acts of the One who has called them out of darkness into God's marvelous light (1 Pet. 2:9).

Alternative Culture

In every cultural context, no matter how benevolent or hostile the governments and societies around it may be, the church is called to demonstrate an alternative culture. If Christian faith makes any difference in behavior, then the church in conformity with Christ is called to an alternative set of behaviors, an alternative ethic, an alternative kind of relationships, in dialogue with the surrounding cultures. Its differentness is itself a witness to the gospel. The church may be different from the world at only a few key points, but that is enough to make a powerful witness. Moreover, as its cultural setting is constantly changing, the church itself must discern where its allegiance to the reign of God requires nonconformity.

The *Letter to Diognetus* (possibly from the 2nd century) provides an early example of the church seeking to discern at what points it may conform and when it must not conform if it is to be faithful to the gospel:

> Christians are not differentiated from other people by country, language or customs; you see, they do not live in cities of their own, or speak some strange dialect, or have some peculiar lifestyle. (5.1-2)
>
> They live in both Greek and foreign cities, wherever chance has put them. They follow local customs in clothing, food and the other aspects of life. But at the same time, they demonstrate to us the wonderful and certainly unusual form of their own citizenship. (5.4)
>
> They live in their own native lands, but as aliens; as citizens, they share all things with others; but like aliens suffer all things. Every foreign country is to them as their native country, and every native land as a foreign country. (5.5)
>
> They are treated outrageously and behave respectfully to others. When they do good, they are punished as evildoers; when punished, they rejoice as if being given new life. They are attacked by Jews as aliens, and are persecuted by Greeks; yet those who hate them cannot give any reason for their hostility. (5.15-16)
>
> To put it simply — the soul is to the body as Christians are to the world. The soul is spread through all parts of the body and Christians through all the cities of the world. The soul is in the body but is not of the body; Christians are in the world but not of the world. (6.1-3)[5]

The church's alternative allegiance may express itself culturally in a variety of ways. For example, the church usually has an alternative vocabulary, an alternative economics, and an alternative understanding of power.

Christians share the languages of the cultures that surround them, but they speak with a distinctive vocabulary that expresses realities that they experience and are now able to identify through the agency of the

5. Quoted in Tim Dowley, et al., eds., *Eerdmans' Handbook to the History of Christianity* (Grand Rapids: Eerdmans, 1977), 69.

Holy Spirit. This different vocabulary is not confined to technical theological terms employed by the church as a verbal shorthand for complex Christian experience. It also includes simple words like *sin, grace,* and *holiness,* words reflecting equally complex realities but seldom used in everyday speech in North America.

God's "sent people" certainly do not use this distinctive vocabulary in order to keep secrets from the world. This motive would be contrary to their mission in and to the reign of God. But distinctive words are needed to signal the new and different life Christians find themselves living in communion with God's holy nation and in allegiance to God's present and future reign. For the same reason, Christian apologetics is necessarily bilingual. Such efforts try to express the Christian faith in the language of the surrounding society in order to communicate with those who do not believe. Yet the Christian apologist knows that such borrowed language is ultimately inadequate, first, because the experience of the Spirit in the community of God's reign cannot be captured by any language, and second, because the meanings behind the words that the church shares with its culture have forever been changed for those found, renewed, and now sent by the vision of the reign of God.

The alternative community is called to an alternative economics as well. In the biblical worldview, economic justice is built on each person receiving what he or she needs, so that right relationships are maintained or restored. This view contrasts boldly to the Aristotelian understanding of justice, on which Western jurisprudence is built. In the latter view, each person should theoretically receive what he or she deserves, and yet free market economics in the West has tended less and less to provide people what they deserve, and more and more has favored the survival of the economically fittest.

Hebrew law gave special attention to the needs of those without a Hebrew male head of household. These included the widow, the orphan, and the alien. The law of Jubilee even allowed a leveling of economics every fifty years by commanding the restoration of family homesteads lost by debt (Lev. 25).

It is likely that the early church in Jerusalem was adapting Jubilee law to an urban setting when it instituted the practice of sharing all goods in common (Acts 2:44-45; 4:32-35). Even where the early church did not hold all goods together, it still practiced economic sharing. Paul collected money from the church in Macedonia for the needs of the church in Jerusalem. In numerous places, the Epistles urge Christians to share with

121

the needy (e.g., Rom. 12:13; Eph. 4:28). Indeed, they even suggest that it is impossible for God's love to be in anyone who has the world's goods, sees a brother or sister in need, and yet refuses to help (1 John 3:17).

This practice of mutual aid, as it has been termed in the twentieth century, has manifested itself in the formation of intentional communities and voluntary service units, as well as in various formal and informal means of meeting economic needs within congregations. The alternative economics of the church has also spread beyond its members to various programs of helping the poor, establishing hospitals and mental health institutions, building homes, and sharing food. The church is called to an alternative economics that puts needs ahead of wants.

The church as holy nation also has an alternative understanding of power. The church takes its cues for the exercise of power from Jesus. For Jesus, power was first of all from God. The power of God flowed through Jesus (Luke 5:17; Mark 5:30). It could be seen especially in Jesus' healing of many people, but it was evident as well in his teaching "with authority." Jesus did "mighty works" both out of compassion for those who were suffering and as signs of the reign of God.

In choosing these uses of power, Jesus rejected other uses. During his temptations in the wilderness, Jesus rejected the use of power for selfish reasons (feeding himself alone), for self-aggrandizement (being saved dramatically from the consequences of throwing himself down from the pinnacle of the temple), or for the ways of the "kingdoms of the world," which in Matthew 4:8-10 Satan claims are his to offer. What is it about the kingdoms of the world that puts them in the domain of Satan? Elsewhere Jesus described these kingdoms as realms in which rulers lord it over others (Mark 10:42) and people use violence against their enemies (John 18:36). These uses of power Jesus rejected.

Jesus taught his disciples quite differently. In the Sermon on the Mount, blessings are granted to those who are poor in spirit (who know that they don't have it altogether), to the meek (the gentle, the nonviolent, who leave vengeance up to God; see Ps. 37), to those who desire justice and righteousness, to those who show mercy and forgive, to peacemakers, and to those who are persecuted for the sake of righteousness and justice. These are the ones whose light will shine before all the world. They are the ones who will be like God in loving those who do not love them in return, who love and pray for their enemies, and who do not resist their oppressors with violence (Matt. 5:38-48).

Jesus himself practiced this nonviolent way of power. When Judas led the soldiers to arrest him, Jesus did not resist violently. He even called Judas "friend" and told Peter to put away his sword (Matt. 26:50, 52). Then, on the cross, he asked God to forgive his executioners (Luke 23:34). Jesus met death by putting himself completely into the hands of God (Luke 23:46). God responded with a remarkable display of power — by raising Jesus from the dead on the third day. By this resurrection, the New Testament writers assert, the powers of death, destruction, and violence were disarmed, and salvation from sin and from enemies was offered to everyone who would believe (Col. 2:13-15).

The early Christians applied this rejection of violent power to their lives in the church. Paul instructed believers not to repay anyone evil for evil, but instead to overcome evil with good (Rom. 12:14-21). First Peter gives Christ as an example of suffering without abusing or threatening in return (2:19-24). The early church applied this rejection of violence not only to murder and other such crimes, but also to state-sanctioned violence, including military service. According to the New Testament writers, real power comes from the Holy Spirit, who gives the ability to witness boldly in spite of persecution and who continues the mighty works of healing. Even the "sword" of the Spirit is the nonviolent, powerful Word (see Rev. 1:16; Eph. 6:17). Loving power rather than violent power will win out in the end, in that day of a new heaven and a new earth where justice and love triumph and when the righteous are resurrected to a new life with God.

The church today is likewise called to practice Jesus' kind of power. This power is not based on "might makes right." It is the power of love, of forgiveness, of working for right relationships. It is power that does not force anyone into the church. Instead, the church claims to be a people made up of those from around the world who have chosen to follow Christ. As such a nation, the church has no geographical boundaries to defend, and therefore no need to use violent power to defend them.

This rejection of violent power is based primarily on Jesus' example and teaching. It understands that one cannot get to a peaceful goal by violent means. Violence does not overcome violence; it only turns us into violent people. Indeed, the only way out of violence and hate is through forgiveness and love. Only these have the power to transform enemies into friends. Only these have the power to keep us from becoming what we hate.[6] Only good can overcome evil.

6. See Wink, *Engaging the Powers*, 195-207.

Thus the church is a people that relies on the power of God's love, both now (in a provisional way) and in the end (as the fulfillment of God's promises). The church expects miracles. It depends on resurrection. As a people of the resurrection, the church practices what the New Testament often calls "patient endurance" (Rom. 12:12; Gal. 5:22; Eph. 4:2; Col. 3:12; Rev. 1:9; 2:3; 3:10; 14:12). Sometimes translated simply "patience," this is a kind of steadfast gentleness, even in spite of provocation. Even in the midst of suffering, Christians are called to practice loving, nonviolent power, confident that God will vindicate the way of peace and gentleness.[7]

The Radical Challenge of the Alternative Church

Understanding the church as an alternative culture for the sake of its missional faithfulness goes against the grain of the dominant Western culture with its legacy of Christendom. It inevitably raises questions across the spectrum of theological traditions, whether liberal or conservative, mainline or evangelical. Advocates of a radically alternative church can point, with historical justification, to the common Christendom mind-set that underlies these objections. In our view, however, the contemporary voices of the Radical Reformation have an important contribution to make to the formation of a missional ecclesiology in a post-Christendom context. They have grappled for centuries with the tensions that result from their theological decision not to support automatically the dominant culture with its principalities and powers. That witness should instruct the church today as it recognizes its own cultural captivity in functional Christendom.

One of the frequent criticisms of alternative understandings of the church's witness, especially when the question of violence and nonviolence emerges, is the charge of irresponsibility. Virtually every Christian public ethic justifying behavior that runs counter to the example and teaching of Jesus does it on the grounds of responsibility. In many cases, the critics admit that following Jesus would mean something quite

---

7. John Milbank argues persuasively that the church is the only possible nonviolent social order; see *Theology and Social Theory: Beyond Secular Reason* (Cambridge, Mass.: Blackwell, 1991).

different from what they are proposing. But Jesus' example is deemed irrelevant or irresponsible.[8]

If an action is not responsible, then, these critics imply, one must of course not do it. If sharing of money is not responsible, then Christians should behave economically according to society's standards. If being nonviolent is not always responsible, then Christians should defend themselves with violent power or take up arms whenever the government calls, so the argument goes.

The best rejoinder to such arguments is, Responsible to whom? Is Christians' primary responsibility to the dominant society or to the government or to cultural expectations? Or is Christians' primary responsibility to God and to the distinctive mission for which God calls and forms a missionary people? If one's primary commitment and allegiance is to God and to following Jesus, then responsibility is defined by the covenant between God and the people of God. Allegiance to God as Ruler and a commitment to following Jesus may at times require Christians to act according to understandings of responsibility that are different from those of the surrounding society. If the church does not let itself be held captive to the dominant culture, it will take most seriously its responsibilities to the reign of God, present and future.

Another frequently voiced criticism of the church as alternative community emphasizes the problem of so-called sectarianism. This critique is stated in a variety of ways. Some critics claim that the church wants to isolate itself from the surrounding society. Others fear that such an alternative church will renege on its Christian responsibility for the whole of society.

The term *sect* arose in Europe, where over centuries a church system evolved in which there was one established church in every region or political unit, supported (and sometimes imposed) in a variety of ways by the state. Any Christian movement that "cut itself off" from the established church was, by definition, "sectarian." Of course, on those terms all the churches of the United States and Canada are sects, since none of them is established by law. The concept "sect" acquired a

---

8. Cf. David Bosch's comment in discussing the Sermon on the Mount: "Indeed, this sermon expresses, like no other New Testament passage, the essence of the ethics of Jesus. Through the ages, however, Christians have usually found ways around the clear meaning of the Sermon on the Mount" (*Transforming Mission: Paradigm Shift in Mission Theology* [Maryknoll, N.Y.: Orbis, 1991], 69).

technical, sociological meaning in the work of Max Weber and Ernst Troeltsch, who contrasted it with "church." In their theoretical approach "church" denoted an established religious organization that claimed universality, accepted the secular order, and allowed itself to function within the dominant culture to serve general social and even political ends. The concept is clearly rooted in Constantinian Christendom. But Troeltsch saw in the sects, most of which were among the lower classes, an important role in religious renewal. "It is the lower classes which do the really creative work, forming communities on a genuine religious basis. They alone unite imagination and simplicity of feeling with a non-reflective habit of mind, a primitive energy, and an urgent sense of need." Without this, "no religious movement can live."[9] Although Troeltsch considered the church type superior, the sect also had an essential transformative function in the life of the total religious community.

Many of those who use the term *sect* pejoratively are not thinking in terms of these traditional definitions. They simply mean a church that does not bless the dominant culture, that does not accept the dominant culture on its own terms, and that attempts to live according to other-than-Enlightenment assumptions. As John Milbank has recently noted, the charge of sectarianism can be understood as a policing of Christianity. The church should participate in public life, but only on terms set by the currently dominant polity and culture. In North America, after several stages of disestablishment, this principle has come to mean that Christian symbols, language, and practice should be kept outside the public sphere. The liberal society (in our modern Western context) and its self-understanding define the norm for Christian social responsibility. Ironically, the effect is the marginalization and privatization of Christian faith and practice, rather than supporting the church as a transformative agent in society.[10]

The charge of sectarianism has become bound up in commitments to a particular form of social life, in a Christendom understanding of the church, and in certain political assumptions about the relation of the church to the state. However, the Christian community does not have to let these critics reserve the term *church* only for the churches embedded in the

9. Ernst Troeltsch, *The Social Teaching of the Christian Churches,* tr. Olive Wyon, 2 vols. (London: Allen & Unwin, 1931), 1:44, 45, quoted in Arne Rasmusson, *The Church as "Polis"* (Notre Dame, Ind.: University of Notre Dame Press, 1995), 235.

10. Milbank, *Theology and Social Theory,* 109; summarized in Rasmusson, *Church as "Polis,"* 240-41.

dominant culture. At least in North America, arguments that reserve the term *church* for some ecclesial movements and not others are problematic.

An additional charge against this understanding of the church as "holy nation" is that of inconsistency. The argument usually goes thus: If the church wants to be different from the world, or separate from the world, that means isolation from the rest of society. If, then, people in such a church participate at all in the broader society (e.g., its economic system), that is inconsistent.

The Amish are the most frequently cited North American example of this separation from the world. Although they shun electricity and automobiles, have their own educational system, and are conscientiously opposed to any use of violence, many of them do have steam-powered tools, eat commercially canned soup, work in non-Amish factories, and ride on trains. Is that inconsistent? Or have they simply decided at what crucial points to dissent from the dominant culture?

As we have consistently emphasized, it is impossible for any group of people to be completely isolated from the world, short of total geographic separation. Every social grouping within North America participates in the broader society in some way, whether through exchange of goods and services or social contacts. Total nonparticipation in the broader society is not only impossible but also unnecessary in order for the group to have an authentic witness to an alternative way of life. Total nonparticipation is not the answer to the charge of inconsistency. Alternative churches throughout history that have practiced radical separation from their environment have usually done so because of persecution from the outside, rather than solely from their own choice.

The church as an alternative community can make a powerful witness when it chooses to live differently from the dominant society even at just a few key points. An important task of the church is to discern what are those key points at which to be different from the evil of the world. For some, the key point will be authentic community in the face of the individualism of the dominant culture. For others, that point will be community of goods in the face of the power of the profit motive. For others, that point will be a reminder of God's redeeming love for all, no matter what crimes they have committed, in the face of calls for the death penalty. The communions that emerged from the Radical Reformation have much to say to the entire church about the importance and implications of such witness.

To discern those points of dissent is to be a missional church.

Indeed, given cultures' tendency to demand ultimate allegiance to one or more of their powers, some kind of dissent is required if the church is to be genuinely missionary to the dominant culture. The church must be different from its surroundings in order to make visible and witness faithfully to the inbreaking reign of God.

Community as Mission

The Alternative Community in North America as City on a Hill

Key images of God's alternative community, the missional church, are found in the Gospels' descriptions of the people of God as "the salt of the earth," a "light of the world," and a "city set on a hill." These images suggest that mission is not just what the church *does;* it is what the church *is.* Saltiness is not an action; it is the very character of salt. Similarly, light or a city on a hill need not do anything in order to be seen. So too it is with God's "people sent." The visible, taste-able nature of their community is their missional purpose: by encountering that "holy nation," others "may see your good works and give glory to your Father in heaven" (Matt. 5:16). Who the community is and how it lives points to God and is an invitation to join the community in praising God. The church by its life together shows others the nature of the reign of God. The church is a preview of life under the rule of God in the age to come, a forerunner of the new Jerusalem, a foretaste of the heavenly banquet, a sign of the reign of God.

In North America, what might it mean for the church to be such a city on a hill? to be salt? to be a light to the world? It means, first of all, that the inner, communal life of the church matters for mission. Instead of separating the work of particular congregational communities or the church in general into mission and nurture, the total life of the "people sent" makes a difference to its apostolic witness. How Christians behave toward one another, the testimony that their relationships make in the public square, and the character of their life together as a whole community are integral to their apostolic mission.

Such witness means that the woman who has been part of the small urban congregation for three or four years can say to her pastor, "One of the things I have learned here is that you can disagree and you don't have to leave." Such witness also means that one's seatmate in an airplane, after learning your church affiliation, will exclaim, "Oh, I've heard of

128

you! You're the people who are always there to clean up after tornadoes and floods."

The more accurately the church locates the key points of difference between its surrounding culture and that culture called for by the reign of God, the more faithfully the church lives a distinctively holy life in its place. And the more the church lives such distinctive faithfulness, the more visible the reign of God will be for all to see. The church that preaches equality with most of the other institutions in a society may be faithful to the gospel message but hardly visible. But if particular communities of the church demonstrate by their life together that different races and genders can, in fact, be brothers and sisters in Christ sharing leadership and responsibility, then they will be not only a faithful but a visible city on a hill. In like manner, churches that listen to sermons deploring crime may be faithful in attending to God's call for right relationships among humanity. But the church that sets up victim-offender reconciliation programs and promotes equitable economic opportunities for communities where crime is the main escape route from financial despair is not only faithful but a remarkable light to the world, a city on a hill.

Being the Missional Church as Sharing in the Death and Resurrection of Jesus

A frequent image for the church in the New Testament Epistles is "body of Christ." Sometimes this image describes how the different members of the body can have different functions yet work together in the unity of the same Spirit (as in 1 Cor. 12). But more broadly the church is the body of Christ, or participates "in Christ," because it shares in the sufferings of Christ (e.g., Phil. 1:20-21, 29; 3:10-11; Col. 1:24; 2 Tim. 2:11-13). Jesus invites his disciples to "take up their cross and follow me" (Mark 8:34 and parallels), and 1 Peter 4:12-19 cautions the church against surprise when persecution comes. As the epistle observes, they, the church, are sharing Christ's sufferings and therefore will be able to shout for joy when Christ's glory is revealed.

"Do not be surprised at the fiery ordeal" (1 Pet. 4:12). The church that is holy, set apart, nonconformed, different from the dominant culture, will often be hated by some and marginalized by others. One of the most difficult human tasks is to be different from another and yet to stay in relationship. In the North American context, churches that do not

129

follow the Christendom model seldom face outright persecution. More often, mainstream churches and others speak of alternative communities in derogatory terms, and legal barriers are raised. In some cities, for instance, zoning laws have been used to prevent churches from meeting in members' homes. In the 1970s the U.S. Internal Revenue Service generally refused to give new communal religious groups the tax status of the traditional religious orders, even though the new communities could demonstrate that they followed virtually identical financial patterns. In a few cases where special tax status was granted, it was revoked within a few years. During World War I, before exemptions were granted to conscientious objectors to military service on religious grounds, many young men from peace churches who refused to wear the military uniform were placed in military prison. Two such Hutterite young men from South Dakota died in Leavenworth prison from maltreatment and exposure to the cold.

It can be risky for the church to be different. The dominant culture has little tolerance for those who do not play by its rules. Jesus cautioned the Twelve about this risk when he sent them out on their first missionary journey, forewarning them that their witness could get them hauled into court and into conflict with their own families (Matt. 10:1–11:6). John 15:19 offers a similar message, explaining, "If you belonged to the world, the world would love you as its own. Because you do not belong to the world, but I have chosen you out of the world — therefore the world hates you."

"You are sharing Christ's sufferings" (1 Pet. 4:13). The church as holy nation lives according to the way of the cross. The Christendom-style church, whether liberal or conservative, has often employed theology to avoid living the way of the cross. In North America this view usually translates into a core doctrine that Jesus died on the cross so that people's sins could be forgiven, that whoever believes on him will be saved. In this case "believing" usually means thinking the right things about Jesus, or agreeing that what he said and did is true. Once you believe, then discipleship supposedly follows, but acting like Jesus is commonly seen as secondary to believing or changing one's attitude.

But this aspect is only half the gospel. Believing is also a matter of doing.[11] Believing is trusting that Jesus' way of living is the right way, and trusting it enough that one is willing to live that way — and die that

11. In Greek, the same verb can be translated "to believe," "to have faith," or "to be faithful"; see, e.g., Rom. 1:16; 4:3; 1 Tim. 1:12, 19; 4:10; James 1:22-25.

way. Alternative Christian communities in the Middle Ages and in the Reformation era often phrased it in a way similar to the Anabaptist leader Hans Denck: "The medium is Christ, whom no one can truly know unless he follow him in his life, and no one may follow him unless he has first known him."[12] Another Anabaptist, Leonhard Schiemer, wrote, "It is true, Christ's suffering destroys sin but only if he suffers in [a person]. For as the water does not quench my thirst unless I drink it, and as the bread does not drive away my hunger unless I eat it, even so Christ's suffering does not prevent me from sinning until he suffers in me."[13] In the twentieth century, Dietrich Bonhoeffer made Christian suffering after the example of Christ into the central theme of *The Cost of Discipleship:* "Jesus must therefore make it clear beyond all doubt that the 'must' of suffering applies to his disciples no less than to himself. Just as Christ is Christ only in virtue of his suffering and rejection, so the disciple is a disciple only in so far as he shares his Lord's suffering and rejection and crucifixion. Discipleship means adherence to the person of Jesus, and therefore submission to the law of Christ which is the law of the cross."[14]

In the New Testament, this believing that includes knowing and doing is often expressed in terms of sharing the sufferings of Christ. Those who follow Jesus will also take up their own crosses. To be willing to suffer or even die in the cause of Christ means a total commitment to the way of Jesus. It means to have the attitude of Jesus on the cross when he put himself completely into the hands of God. First Peter 4:19 expresses this attitude thus: "Therefore, let those suffering in accordance with God's will entrust themselves to a faithful Creator, while continuing to do good."

This willingness to suffer for the cause of Christ is missional. The Greek word for "witness" is *martyria*. The martyrs of the early church were the faithful witnesses. Because of the testimony of the martyrs, new persons were converted and came into the church. To share Christ's sufferings may or may not mean physical martyrdom. But it certainly means the attitude and action of putting oneself completely into the

12. Quoted from "The Contention that Scripture Says" (1526), in Walter Klaassen, ed., *Anabaptism in Outline: Selected Primary Sources* (Scottdale, Penn.: Herald, 1981), 87

13. "A Letter to the Church at Rattenberg," 1527, quoted in *Anabaptism in Outline,* 90-91.

14. Dietrich Bonhoeffer, *The Cost of Discipleship,* tr. Reginald H. Fuller, rev. ed. (New York: Macmillan, 1959), 77; cf. 76-83, the discussion of Mark 8:31-38.

hands of God. It means taking the risk that acting like Jesus may bring the same fate it brought Jesus. It means being willing to trust Jesus' way, all the way — rather than resorting to some other way (hate, violence, deception, etc.) in an effort to prevent ill consequences or to protect one's own life.

"So that you may also be glad and shout for joy when his glory is revealed" (1 Pet. 4:13). Suffering with Christ makes sense only if you know who wins at the end of the story. When one knows that God will have the final victory, then suffering along the way is put into a larger perspective. Sharing Christ's suffering comes as a package with sharing Christ's resurrection glory.

A significant theological shift that coincided with the rise of the church of Christendom involved the church's eschatology. The eschatology of the early church focused on the future, radical inbreaking of God into history. The age to come would be a time of setting right all injustices and the fulfillment of the reign of God in a new heaven and a new earth. But the church's thinking about end things began to change. In the fourth century Augustine was an important architect of this move. Although he kept a general resurrection at the end of this age, his eschatology (and that of the medieval church) focused primarily on whether the disembodied souls of individuals went to heaven or hell after their deaths. The emphasis was not on the new heaven and new earth, but on transportation from earth to heaven. This eschatological shift has continued in most North American churches. Many churches are reluctant to talk about eschatology at all. Those who do, focus almost entirely on the destination of the soul immediately after death.

The New Testament speaks rather infrequently about the state of persons between the time of their deaths and the resurrection. But the New Testament has much to say about the judgment at the end of this present age, God's final victory over the powers (including those that persecute the church), and the reign of the saints with Christ.

Risky witness depends on resurrection faith and faithfulness. It depends on God's rearranging things at the end of the age so that God's justice and God's peace prevail and so that the new community, the new Jerusalem, is fully established. Thus the church that lives in the way of the Christ is, in its being, a sign of the reign of God.

Continuing the Work of Jesus:
Preaching, Teaching, and Healing

Sharing the Work of Jesus

As we emphasized in the last chapter, the church is apostolic in its being and in its doing when it embodies Jesus' mission and patterns its actions after his. The Synoptic Gospels identify three main tasks of Jesus before his crucifixion: preaching, teaching, and healing. Many of the Gospel writers' summary statements name all three of these activities (e.g., Matt. 4:23; 9:35), and other passages include two of the three (Mark 1:39; Matt. 4:24–5:2; Luke 6:6-11, 17-19). Jesus' preaching, teaching, and healing are the net with which he fishes for people. These activities draw people to Jesus. They may accept or reject him, but preaching, teaching, and healing function to gather in people for the reign of God. Through miracles or "signs" (as in the Gospel of John), people are invited to see the power of God at work through Jesus and to enter the reign of God.

These activities — preaching, teaching, and healing — are also the vocation of Jesus' disciples. When Jesus sent out the Twelve and the Seventy, he gave them authority over unclean spirits and commissioned the disciples to preach and to heal (Matt. 10:5-8; Luke 9:1-2; 10:1-9). After his resurrection, in the so-called Great Commission, Jesus commissioned the disciples to teach as well. Repeatedly, Jesus told the disciples that his work was also their work. "As the Father has sent me, so I send you" (John 20:21). "Follow me" (Matt. 4:19). The book of Acts is testimony to the fact that Jesus' followers did indeed continue his work of preaching, teaching, and healing. That apostolic work still belongs to the church two thousand years later.

Healing

The apostolic work of healing is intended to draw people into the reign of God by a demonstration of God's love and compassion. "If it is by the finger of God that I cast out the demons, then the kingdom of God has come to you," Jesus said (Luke 11:20).[15] The Gospel of John portrays Jesus' healings as "signs" that God is at work in Jesus, signs that will

15. See chap. 4, pp. 104-6 above.

draw people to Jesus. Likewise, in our time, healing is one of the characteristics of the missional church.[16]

It is right to see healing in its broad sense — healing of the emotions, forgiveness of sin, peace, reconciliation, freedom, and restoration of justice and right relationships, as well as physical healing. But it is important to realize that healing in the missional church will go against the grain of many expectations in the dominant culture.

With its Enlightenment expectations that all truth can be perceived through the five senses and reason, the dominant culture is generally skeptical of spiritual healing, particularly healing of the physical body. Such healing is not always observable, repeatable, and verifiable by the scientific method. It simply does not fit the Enlightenment categories, because the Enlightenment mind-set does not factor God into the equation. Nonetheless, the missional church believes that God continues to act in the world, for the healing of the world.

Numerous theologies about healing are, however, defective. It is not true, for example, that the more faith one has, then the more healing one will receive. This idea is contrary to Jesus' promise that if one has even the slightest bit of faith, no bigger than a mustard seed, it is enough to move mountains. Neither should one put physical healing and long life at the top of one's list of priorities. Although healing is good, it is not the ultimate goal in the Christian life. Being in the love of God, life in the Spirit, and living in the grace of Christ are all far more important. The psalmist phrases it this way: "Your steadfast love is better than life" (Ps. 63:3). For Christians, dying for Christ's sake may be more important than simply extending life.

But the fact that some people have wrong ideas about healing is no reason to reject right thinking about healing. Healing was not only part of the New Testament church but also continued to be reported throughout the early centuries of the church. The Roman Catholic Church still tends to confer sainthood on persons through whom some healing miracle has taken place, and the powerful witness of Pentecostal and charismatic churches is certainly due in part to their practice of healing.

Healing — of mind, body, and spirit — is a sign of the work of God in the world, a sign that the reign of God is near, a sign of the love and

16. See Gerhard Lohfink, *Jesus and Community: The Social Dimension of Christian Faith*, tr. J. P. Galvin (Philadelphia: Fortress, 1984), 12ff., 152ff.

the power of God. The missional church points to these signs as it gathers people into the reign of God.

Healing the communal body, or societal healing, is one such sign. But its purpose is not to make the dominant culture run better, or to make good people who can go out and do the work of the dominant culture in beneficial ways. The first healing task of the church is to become a reconciled and reconciling community itself. It is a kind of demonstration project, a sign that kingdom living is possible. From that base, the missional church works in the world to show God's love and compassion to others outside the church. God's love is too great to be kept only within the church; it has to be shared.

Such social service or work for peace and justice is to be done out of the conviction that, one day, the whole world will acknowledge Jesus Christ as Lord, and even the rebellious powers will bow before Christ. Thus every way in which healing happens in the world becomes a sign of the complete reconciliation in the age to come.

Moreover, the missional church that works for healing among races, classes, and groups like "tax collectors and sinners" and others on the margins will often be an affront to the dominant culture. That culture has a vested interest in the status quo. The missional church is called not only to demonstrate healing among its own members but also to be a peacemaker and justice-maker in the world. The church is called to promote peace to those near and to those far off (Eph. 2:17 together with 2 Cor. 5:18-20). Where such healing happens, it is a sign of the nearness of the reign of God and an invitation into that reign.

Announcing the Reign of God

"Preaching" has also come to mean something quite different from the New Testament definition of the word. In many North American churches, preaching is practiced only within the church, to the faithful, on Sunday morning. Such preaching probably bears more resemblance to the New Testament concept of "teaching" than to its concept of "preaching."

The New Testament word for "preaching" is a rather political word. It means "to announce" or "to proclaim publicly." It was sometimes used in a political context when an official runner came into town ahead of the ruler with the message, "The king is coming!" To preach, then, is to announce good news, public good news for the community.

135

Jesus' public good news is summarized in Mark 1:15: "The time is fulfilled, and the kingdom of God has come near; repent, and believe in the good news." Paul and the early church continued this proclamation of the reign of God (cf. Acts 28:31).

While the proclamation could be the catalyst for dramatic conversions of individuals, its focus was not on the fate of the individual soul or on self-actualization, but on God. In 1 Peter 2:9 the purpose of God's calling a people together, to be a holy nation, is in order that they may proclaim the mighty acts of the One who has called them out of darkness into God's marvelous light.

Making public announcements about the actions of God and the reign of God is an apostolic task of the church. This preaching in public involves far more than attempting to influence Washington and Ottawa to enact the right legislation. Instead, the real center of power is in the reign of God, and in the church as its representative. Ephesians 3:10 claims that it is through the church that the wisdom of God is to be made known to the rulers and authorities.

The church publicly announces the reign of God because it is an embassy full of ambassadors of the reign of God (2 Cor. 5:20). To extend the image of the church as holy nation, the way one nation peacefully relates to another is through its ambassadors. Ambassadors are fully engaged with representatives of the country to which they are sent, but they are clear about their loyalties to the nation from which they have come and about the mission on which they have been sent. According to 2 Corinthians 5:18-20, that mission is to promote reconciliation with God and among peoples.

When preaching reconciliation to governments and other public institutions, the church should be under no illusion that any of those institutions will become Christian or take the place of the church as the intentional sign of the reign of God. What we can expect of governments and other institutions is that they will move a little closer toward the reign of God or will act a little more in accordance with God's purposes. For a government involved in intense persecution of the church, that may mean an end to killing or penalizing Christians. For a more benevolent government, that may mean legislation that benefits the poor or the marginalized. For a bank, it might mean granting loans in formerly redlined neighborhoods. For a public school, it might mean instituting peer mediation training among students.

Announcing the reign of God in public will have an impact on individuals. Jesus' message was not only corporate, "The kingdom of God is at hand," but also personal, "Repent and believe in the good news" (Mark 1:15). Public announcements of God's actions in the world are a call to conversion, to turning around, to giving up idolatries, and to placing one's loyalty in the one true God and God's reign.

The church's task of announcing the reign of God will mean moving beyond the four walls of the church building, out of the safe group of people who know and love each other, into the public square. The missional church will be in the world with good news.

Teaching for Citizenship in the Reign of God

Those who hear the good news and want to become citizens of the reign of God will need teaching. The church as holy nation has a culture, an accepted way of doing things, a specialized vocabulary to talk about life under the reign of God. The church should not expect new people in its midst to know these things automatically. Becoming a citizen of the reign of God does not come naturally. It is different from just being civil or being a good person. It requires a new loyalty to a new ruler. It demands that we acquire the new habits of a new culture. New people need to become "naturalized" citizens of the reign of God, and teaching is part of the naturalization process.

The Sermon on the Mount (Matt. 5–7) contains a summary of Jesus' teaching for the reign of God, the new practices that differ from the accepted wisdom ("You have heard that it was said . . . ; but I say to you . . ."). It is the constitution of the reign of God, or the manifesto for life under God's government. Within the Sermon on the Mount, the Beatitudes (5:1-12) provide a summary within a summary of the behavior that belongs to the reign of God.

Far from being platitudes, the Beatitudes bless behavior that differs greatly from that of the dominant culture. The dominant culture says, "How fortunate you are if you have your life under control and do not need anyone else." Jesus said, "Blessed are the poor in spirit," those who have the spirit of the poor, who know that they do not have their lives under control and need other people in order to make it. These are the people who know they need God. The poor in spirit know that they must depend on God. The rich are tempted to think that they do it all on their own without God's help. It is the poor in spirit who belong to the reign of God.

The dominant culture says, "You will be happy if you avoid any situation that exposes you to other people's suffering or that causes you yourself to suffer or mourn or sacrifice." This is the world of happy-face stickers and "Have a nice day." On the contrary, Jesus pronounced blessing on those who mourn. God will comfort those who sorrow over the state of the world, injustices, oppression, their own sin, the sin of others, and the situations in which evil seems to have the upper hand. Those who grieve over oppression, who do not turn away from seeing it, will find comfort because God is going to do something about it, either now or, certainly, in the age to come.

The dominant culture says, "You will be happy if you can get back at those who are hurting you, no matter how you do it." Jesus blessed those who are meek. The word *meek* here would be better translated "gentle" or "noncoercive." In the Gospels it does not mean being a doormat for someone else or never saying what one needs. Jesus describes himself with this term in Matthew 11:29, and Matthew uses it of Jesus in 21:5; but Jesus certainly did not wilt before the Pharisees or in the face of death. Psalm 37:11 is the closest Old Testament parallel to this beatitude: "But the meek will inherit the land and enjoy great peace."[17] This psalm encourages us not to fret or take revenge when evil people succeed, but to trust in God and wait patiently for God to set things right. This is not a call to be passive but to remain nonviolent, to be gentle and to trust in God's way of deliverance from the wicked. Jesus was saying that the earth really belongs to those who practice nonviolence, not to those who try to coerce others into doing things their way. Gentleness is the way to the land that God promises.

The dominant culture says that it is proper to hunger and thirst after material things: the latest car, the brightest toothpaste, the newest color scheme, the most financial security. Jesus says that the proper thing to hunger and thirst after is righteousness. Throughout the Bible, *righteousness* is a legal term. Its context is a covenant or contract between two parties. One is righteous if one is living in accordance with the terms of the covenant or agreement. The Hebrew and Greek words translated "righteousness" are sometimes translated "justice." In other words, justice is present when the covenant is being followed. One is righteous or just toward another person when one is doing what one has promised

17. The author's translation; the NRSV translates *shalom* with "prosperity," whereas "peace" should be the emphasis.

and is in right relationship with that person. One's relationship with God is righteous when one is living up to the covenant with God.[18] Those who hunger and thirst for righteousness are those who seek to live in right relationship with God and with others, and Jesus promises them God's blessing. They receive the promise of Isaiah 49:10 that, in the day of salvation, they will neither hunger nor thirst, but God will lead them beside springs of water. To live as part of God's nation means that one learns to desire righteousness and justice above all else.

The dominant culture teaches that good relationships depend on performance ("I will love you if . . ."). In the Beatitudes Jesus praises those who are merciful, who give others better than what they deserve. Mercy is one of God's attributes throughout the Bible. Mercy is often connected with showing favor, being compassionate, being gracious, or demonstrating kindness. God practices mercy by saving people from enemies, rescuing them from trouble, and forgiving their sins. People are also to show mercy, as the parable of the unmerciful servant teaches (Matt. 18:21-35). In Hebrew and Greek, the concept is connected especially with showing mercy to the poor and needy and giving alms. The biblical practice of mercy always means that the one who shows mercy has something to give to another who is unable to pay it back. You ask a creditor to show mercy when you cannot pay what you owe (Matt. 18:26-27). A blind man asks Jesus for mercy through healing, when there is no way for the blind man to return the favor (Luke 18:35-43). The psalmist asks God for mercy when he is totally undeserving of God's favors (Ps. 51:1-4). In Luke 6:36 Jesus asks the disciples to be merciful as God is merciful by loving one's enemies, those who do not love in return.

The dominant culture today hardly ever uses the word *pure*, except in a chemical sense. In fact, most people today do not see personal purity as a possible or even a desirable goal, everyone is tainted somehow. The beatitude speaks of being "pure" or "clean" in heart. Jewish law described being clean or pure as physical cleanliness (washing hands, being free of disease), ritual cleanliness (washing ceremonies and sacrifices), and practicing justice and mercy toward one's neighbors. The prophets saw ritual cleanliness as of no value if one were not also practicing justice. In Isaiah

---

18. For a full discussion of biblical justice and righteousness as covenant language, see Lois Barrett, *Doing What Is Right: What the Bible Says about Covenant and Justice* (Scottdale: Herald Press, 1987).

1:10-20 the prophet says that God will not listen to the prayers and sacrifices of those who are doing wrong. But forgiveness, becoming clean, is possible for those who seek justice, encourage the oppressed, and defend the orphan and the widow. Thus, in one sense, to be pure in heart is to act justly, to forgive, not to carry resentments, to be in right relationships with others. Such people will also be in right relationship with God. There is also a sense in which to be pure in heart means to be single-minded, not to be sullied by the worship of idols but to worship only God.

The dominant culture says, "You will be happiest if you stay out of conflicts and let other people fight it out." Jesus said, "Blessed are the peacemakers, for they will be called children of God." In the Bible, peace or shalom is much more than the absence of war. It is wholeness, health, economic prosperity, right relationships, and justice. Peace in the Old Testament is one of the gifts that God will bring in the day of salvation (Ps. 85:8-11). The peacemakers Jesus means are those who are actively working to see shalom come about. They go beyond simply being gentle or nonviolent. They practice justice and help restore right relationships rather than sit back and avoid controversy.

The dominant culture says, "You will be happy if everybody likes you all the time. By the same token, it is terrible if someone does something bad to you, especially something you in no way deserve." Jesus pronounces blessing on those persecuted for the sake of righteousness and justice, on those who are falsely accused, and on those about whom people say bad things. Not only are these people blessed, they are instructed to rejoice and be glad, because they are in good company, the company of the prophets — and, as the gospel story discloses, they are in the company of Jesus, who was crucified without just cause.

These Beatitudes are obviously not for the timid. Not everyone wants to rejoice when they are falsely accused. To do the Beatitudes requires commitment and practice in the context of the Christian community. This requires acts of the will empowered by the Holy Spirit. Acting in these ways is part of the culture of the community of disciples who are learning to follow Jesus and to live as he lived. They are the focus of the ecclesial practices that are the theme of the next chapter.

Such teaching is not only for those who are at the initial stages of entering the church, but also for the continuing formation of Jesus' disciples within the church. Disciples, like ambassadors, sometimes become captive to the dominant culture into which Christ sends them.

This result is only natural since they are asked to become fluent in the ways of the culture in which they reside so that they may translate their mission in an intelligible manner. But the disciple or ambassador who has gone native has also lost the clarity of the original mission. For this reason, even experienced ambassadors for God's reign need the regular teaching of the church in order to keep their focus on the message that they have been sent to convey.

The apostolic tasks of the church are not complete without an intentional process of teaching within the church. To be sent out on behalf of the reign of God is also to gather people into the reign of God and, through the guidance of the Holy Spirit, to help form each other into citizens of the reign of God, who can preach, teach, and heal in the name of Jesus and can share his sufferings and resurrection life.

• 6 •

Missional Community:
Cultivating Communities of the Holy Spirit

Missional communities are called to represent the compassion, justice, and peace of the reign of God. The distinctive characteristic of such communities is that the Holy Spirit creates and sustains them. Their identity (who they are), their character (how they are), their motivation (why they are), and their vocation (what they do) are theological, and thus missional. That is, they are not formed solely by human intentions and efforts, individual or collective, but instead by God's empowering presence: "The Spirit of God is the dynamic, life-giving power of the Church, the unseen Lord, Master, Guide, and Inspirer of the Christian community."[1] Through this power of the Holy Spirit a "people sent" are cultivated through the practices by which they are formed, trained, equipped, and motivated as missional communities.

The Creator Spirit

When you send forth your Spirit, they are created; and you renew the face of the ground. (Ps. 104:30)

The community-forming activity of the Holy Spirit challenges us to move beyond the contemporary assumption that the Spirit's actions center exclu-

---

1. R. P. C. Hanson, "The Divinity of the Holy Spirit," *Church Quarterly* 1, no. 4 (1969): 302.

sively, or even primarily, on the individual soul. Not only does the Creator Spirit renew particular lives, but the Spirit is the source of all life in creation. For example, the Nicene Creed identifies the Holy Spirit as "the Lord, the giver of life." This fundamental understanding of the Spirit is grounded in the biblical witness to the Spirit as the animating principle of all life. The first biblical reference to the Spirit declares that God's Spirit — God's breath or wind — brings life out of chaos: "a wind from God swept over the face of the waters" (Gen. 1:2). As God's life-giving presence to the whole creation, the Spirit is not understood as a pantheistic presence within the natural forces of the world or as the divine rational principle of the universe. Instead, the Spirit's actions are the free acts of the sovereign God. God's Word commands and the Spirit, or breath or wind, carries it out: "By the word of the Lord the heavens were made, and all their host by the breath of his mouth" (Ps. 33:6).

Church tradition has long maintained an understanding of the Spirit as the giver of life. Likewise, it has viewed the Holy Spirit's participation in the primal and ongoing action of creation as the foundation for the saving presence of the Spirit in the life of Christian communities. But modern Western Christianity has more often connected the Spirit with love and grace rather than with creation. Popular images of the Spirit tend to be drawn from subjective human experiences, which tendency has diminished expectations of the Spirit's involvement in historical events and nature. Consequently, a false distinction arises between the spiritual world where the Spirit supposedly resides and the material world of ordinary, everyday life. This distinction limits the Spirit to extraordinary or peak experiences and eliminates the Spirit's immanent and empirical significance. In essence, the Spirit becomes a totally mysterious power used to explain incomprehensible statements of faith, gaps in human knowledge, or extraordinary spiritual experiences.

The biblical testimony offers us the opportunity to broaden and deepen our understanding of the powerful and crucial role of the Holy Spirit. It allows no gnostic dualism of Spirit and matter. That which lives does so because of the Spirit: "The spirit of God has made me, and the breath of the Almighty gives me life" (Job 33:4). As the giver and lover of life, the Holy Spirit is the totally and thoroughly involved presence of the transcendent God — "the beyond in our midst."[2] God's life-giving

---

2. John V. Taylor, *The Go-Between God: The Holy Spirit and the Christian Mission* (London: SCM, 1972), 5.

power is not found in the gaps or on the margins of life but in the very midst of life's natural processes. As the Creator Spirit, God's continuous and energizing presence, the Holy Spirit revitalizes, renews, and transforms life, giving flesh and breath to dry bones (Ezek. 37:1-14) and turning hearts of stone into hearts that beat again (Ezek. 36:25-28).

This biblical conception of the Spirit makes it possible to realize the close connection that existed for the early church between the Spirit and the new life of the resurrection, the new creation, in Jesus Christ. Resurrection life differs from our present earthly reality in that the Spirit, who is the creative origin of all life, permeates it entirely. Because new, everlasting life in the resurrection has already appeared in Jesus Christ, the life-fulfilling power of the Holy Spirit is also present for those who confess Jesus Christ as Lord and Savior.

All who accept the message of the risen Christ and are baptized in his name have already received the Holy Spirit. They are already assured of the new life of the resurrection, for the Holy Spirit is "the pledge of our inheritance" (Eph. 1:14). They are no longer subject to death; by the power of the Holy Spirit they already participate in Christ's triumph over the powers of sin and death. "In this way the Spirit is the first-fruits of future salvation (Rom. 8.23), the foretaste of the new life, a foretaste which lives in hope and believing trust, anticipating the future, even now, in our present existence, in spite of its subjection to death."[3]

Thus the Creator Spirit is an eschatological reality, the dynamic actualization of the *eschaton* — God's final future when "God may be all in all" (1 Cor. 15:28). The *eschaton* represents the fulfillment of God's creative purpose. While this orientation was indicated by Jesus' announcement of the reign of God, the early church spoke of the reality of God's reign in terms of the dynamic presence of the Holy Spirit. Both were declaring that God's future salvation — the reconciliation of all humanity and the healing of all creation — had become a present reality. Although the wholeness or consummation of God's reign awaits Christ's coming in glory, even now in the midst of the brokenness of human life the Spirit enables faith in Jesus Christ and thus brings believers into new life. For this reason, Basil the Great, writing the first treatise on the Holy Spirit in the history of Christianity during the trinitarian controversies of the fourth century, argued that the Holy Spirit is to be worshiped and

---

3. Wolfhart Pannenberg, *The Apostles' Creed in the Light of Today's Questions*, tr. Margaret Kohl (Philadelphia: Westminster, 1972), 139.

glorified with the Father and the Son, not on the basis of ontological or philosophical arguments but because of the marvelous blessings the Spirit bestows on the community of faith:

> Through the Holy Spirit comes our restoration to Paradise, our ascension into the Kingdom of heaven, our adoption as God's sons [and daughters], our freedom to call God our Father, our becoming partakers of the grace of Christ, being called children of light, sharing in eternal glory, and in a word, our inheritance of the fullness of blessing, both in this world and the world to come. Even while we wait for the full enjoyment of the good things in store for us, by the Holy Spirit we are able to rejoice through faith in the promise of the graces to come.[4]

The *Koinonia* of the Holy Spirit

And they devoted themselves to the apostles' teaching and fellowship, to the breaking of bread and the prayers. (Acts 2:42)

Contemporary categories, presuppositions, and experiences have largely blinded us to the radical nature of the biblical sense of community that the Spirit brings. Because in Jesus Christ "everything old has passed away; see, everything has become new" (2 Cor. 5:17), the Holy Spirit is at work "creating and sustaining a community in whom [humanity] can be enlightened by faith and return to [God] in worship and love as the first fruits of a new creation."[5] The church owes its origin, its destiny, its structure, its ongoing life, its ministry — in short, its mission — to the divine Spirit of life, truth, and holiness. At Pentecost, with the outpouring of the Holy Spirit, promise becomes actuality. God's promised reign of love and hope, compassion and reconciliation, harmony and justice, is incarnated in a new humanity, a people commissioned to represent the gospel of peace to the alienated and hostile powers of the world.

This communal reality of holy living, mutual support, and sacrificial service the New Testament calls *koinonia*. Challenging the old competitive order of independence, self-interest, and private privilege

---

4. St. Basil the Great, *On the Holy Spirit* (Crestwood, N.Y.: St. Vladimir's Seminary Press, 1980), 59.
5. Hanson, "Divinity of the Holy Spirit," 302.

(idios), Christian community indicates a new collaborative order of interdependence, shared responsibility, mutual instruction, and commonality *(koinos).* Within this new company of believers studying, sharing, eating, and praying together, the promised fulfillment of creation is visible, tangible, and experienced, even though not yet perfected. While the Spirit is "the unseen Lord," the movement of the Holy Spirit has real and visible effects. The experience of the Spirit brings "the touch of God's presence, the power of God's healing, the liberating experience of forgiveness, the reality of fraternal community, the joy of celebration, the boldness in witness, the blossoming of hope, and the fruitfulness in mission."[6]

The Distinctiveness of Christian Community as the Fruit of the Spirit

The Apostle Paul indicates the distinctiveness of Christian community by contrasting "the works of the flesh" with "the fruit of the Spirit" (Gal. 5:16ff.). Within this context, "flesh" and "Spirit" are not competing forces within the human person; a contrast between natural and supernatural is alien to Paul's thinking. "Flesh" and "Spirit" for Paul are eschatological realities. They indicate the essential characteristics of two ages, before Jesus Christ and after Jesus Christ. Christ and the Spirit mark the turning of the ages. Life "according to the flesh" is lived in conformity with the values and desires of the age that has now been condemned through the cross and is passing away. Life "according to the Spirit" is lived in keeping with the commitments and norms of God's promised reign inaugurated by the resurrection of Christ and empowered by the gift of the Holy Spirit.

Because these two ages overlap, Christian communities are eschatological. They live between the times in the "already" and the "not yet" of eschatological salvation. Having "died with Christ" to the former way of life and by the power of the Holy Spirit participating in God's "new creation" (Gal. 6:14-15), believers do not "gratify the desires of the flesh" (Gal. 5:16). Instead, they "are guided by the Spirit" (Gal. 5:25) and evidence the "fruit of the Spirit" (Gal. 5:22). They manifest an alternative

6. Mortimer Arias, *Announcing the Reign of God: Evangelization and the Subversive Memory of Jesus* (Philadelphia: Fortress, 1984), 61.

social order of "Spirit-empowered Christ-likeness lived out in Christian community as loving servanthood."[7]

Confronting a community in which people "bite and devour one another" (Gal. 5:15), Paul concretely illustrates in his letter to the Galatians alternative — and incompatible — ways of life. The two lists in Galatians 5 are meant to be not exhaustive but representative. The works of the flesh include the attitudes, motivations, and behaviors of those persons who live in accord with their own and the world's basic fallenness — life before and outside Christ. Rather than focusing on the isolated individual or characterizing internal warfare within the human breast, the majority are sins of discord — behavior that disrupts and destroys social relationships. Such a way of life is not in accord with the reign of God (v. 21). Christ has died to deliver us from the grip of such works (v. 24), and the Spirit has come to empower us not to cave in to their desire (v. 17).

A missional people walking in the Spirit, led by the Spirit, and sowing the Spirit manifests the fruit of the Spirit. The very phrase "fruit of the Spirit" emphasizes divine empowerment rather than human works. It is God's life-giving presence, the Holy Spirit, who informs, sustains, and guides communities of "faith working through love" (5:6). Yet believers are not called to passivity by these works. These works require active obedience as believers in community learn to live as God's people together in a fallen world. As both certain evidence that God's redemptive future has dawned and the absolute guarantee of its final consummation, the Spirit empowers this community to manifest love, to work toward peace, to express patience, kindness, and goodness, and to exhibit gentleness and self-control (Gal. 5:22). In this way, the Holy Spirit alone is the antidote to the works of the flesh.

As difficult as it may be for modern persons to grasp because of their sociological and functional understandings of the church, the believing community represents for Paul the sphere of God's eschatological salvation in Christ. When the Holy Spirit transforms the life and practice of Christian communities, they demonstrate that God's promised future has been set in motion. The joy, freedom, and wholeness of life within the reign of God can already be tasted even if not yet fully consummated. While not perfection, life within the Christian community reflects, embodies, and witnesses to a "divine infection."

---

7. Gordon Fee, *God's Empowering Presence: The Holy Spirit in the Letters of Paul* (Peabody, Mass.: Hendrickson, 1994), 370.

The character and purpose of God are revealed in the way God's people worship, care for one another, and live within the world. The role of the Holy Spirit is to form loving community: "to create a people for God's name, who bear God's likeness in their character, as that is seen in their behavior."[8] Far more than simply desirable human virtues, the "fruit of the Spirit" is none other than the Spirit's bearing in and through the believing community's life and witness the righteousness that characterizes God as revealed in Jesus Christ.

Christian Togetherness

Christians are to conduct their common life "in a manner worthy of the gospel of Christ" (Phil. 1:27). The corporate nature of Christianity is illustrated by a recurrent but frequently overlooked word in Pauline teaching, *allelon* ("one another/each other").[9] Christian faith is not an individual matter; everything is to be done with and for one another. Within the community of those who live "in Christ" by the power of the Holy Spirit, persons are to be "members one of another" (Rom. 12:5), "build up each other" (1 Thess. 5:11), "love one another with mutual affection" (Rom. 12:10), "able to instruct one another" (Rom. 15:14), "become slaves to one another" (Gal. 5:13), and "live in harmony with one another" (Rom. 12:16). Those who have put their trust in Christ have died with him to the "old age" characterized by the works of the flesh. They are thus able to behave in keeping with the Spirit, by whom they live and whose fruit they are to evidence. Life in the "new age" — walking in the Spirit — is not spiritual in an otherworldly or interior sense, but relates to concrete behavior within everyday life. The social practice of Christian togetherness is how love, joy, peace, patience, kindness, goodness, faithfulness, gentleness, and self-control are lived out as believers "bear one another's burdens, and in this way . . . fulfill the law of Christ" (Gal. 6:2).

The experience of Christian togetherness is not simply for the benefit of those who choose to participate in Christian community. A

---

8. Ibid., 816.

9. See Fee, *God's Empowering Presence*, 871-72; Gerhard Lohfink, *Jesus and Community: The Social Dimension of Christian Faith*, tr. John P. Galvin (Philadelphia: Fortress, 1984), 99-106.

community of love rooted in the redemptive reign of God can never be an in-house enterprise, for such love is contagious and overflowing. It seeks to embrace all humanity. The church too often accepts the modern dichotomy between private and public life. Therefore it attempts to find ways to enable private religious experience to be relevant within the public sphere of social and political discourse. This search to be responsive to the needs, problems, fears, and anxieties of its culture can unwittingly allow the "old age" — life according to the flesh — to set the agenda. As a result, the church loses its ability to challenge the world's presuppositions and to offer an alternative perspective of reality as well as an alternative social order.

The church is not only to be a distinct and peculiar community but one that nurtures the social relationships that embody the reconciliation and healing of the world in Jesus Christ. While in practice *koinonia* is experienced only by those who by faith participate in Christ's death and resurrection, in principle the manifestation of the "new age," of life according to the Spirit, indicates the future destiny of the whole of God's creation. The church's missionary imperative is to proclaim, to manifest, and to witness to God's will for the world. "The community, in its corporate life, is called to embody an alternative social order that stands as a sign of God's redemptive purposes in the world: this is the concrete social manifestation of the righteousness of God."[10]

The Process of Cultivating

I beg you to lead a life worthy of the calling to which you have been called, with all humility, gentleness, with patience, bearing with one another in love, making every effort to maintain the unity of the Spirit in the bond of peace. (Eph. 4:1-2)

The fullness of Christian life in the Spirit does not spring forth without intentional cultivation. Through social interaction within the community of God's sent people (the sharing of stories, friendships, and projects), we learn what it is to lead a life worthy of our calling. "The church is

---

10. Richard Hays, "Ecclesiology and Ethics in First Corinthians," *Ex Auditu* 10 (1994): 10.

God's people gathered as a unit, as a people, gathered to do business in His name, to find what it means here and now to put into practice this different quality of life which is God's promise to them and to the world and their promise to God and service to the world."[11]

The modern emphasis on the autonomous self too often ignores, or even denies, the formative power of the various communities in which we participate. We assume that our "habits of the heart" — the notions, opinions, commitments, and desires that motivate, order, and guide our lives — are chosen and formed in isolation from other human beings and social realities. Robert Bellah and associates conclude that this view is "based on inadequate social science, improvised philosophy, and vacuous theology." They assert:

> We find ourselves not independently of other people and institutions but through them. We never get to the bottom of our selves on our own. We discover who we are face to face and side by side with others in work, love, and learning. All of our activity goes on in relationships, groups, associations, and communities ordered by institutional structures and interpreted by cultural patterns of meaning.[12]

Our identity and our vision are both taught and caught from our interaction with others in diverse social groupings. The question is not whether we will be socialized, but what kind of society will have its way with us.

In a technological world of mass communication, entertainment, and advertising, we are often unwittingly instructed, in elaborate, skillful and expensive ways, how we should understand ourselves, the good life, and our true worth. Whether we like it or not, and whether we are explicitly aware of it or not, our most intimate and profound habits of the heart are being shaped by societal influences. We are being formed — cultivated — as a people.

11. John Howard Yoder, *The Original Revolution: Essays on Christian Pacifism* (Scottdale, Penn.: Herald, 1977), 30-31.

12. Robert Bellah, et al., *Habits of the Heart: Individualism and Commitment in American Life* (Berkeley: University of California Press, 1983), 84.

The Formation of Culture

A particular people's view and way of life is usually indicated by the term *culture*. Despite its familiarity and extensive use, *culture* is "one of the two or three most complicated words in the English language."[13] Culture names a reality that we all vaguely know something about but cannot really explain. It is usually employed in an all-encompassing, static, and abstract manner, indicating an independent or self-sufficient reality (i.e., "American culture" or "Hispanic culture").[14]

But the modern use of the word *culture* obscures its original dynamic and creative meaning. In all its early uses in English, *culture* was a noun of process referring to the tending of animals or the harvesting of crops. Thus *Webster's New Twentieth Century Dictionary* gives the following as its first definition of culture: "the act or process of tilling and preparing the earth for crops; cultivation of soil." Retaining this active, process sense of cultivating alerts us "to the fact that culture is not some inert abstract reality but is always in process, both in the sense that it is always affecting us but also in the sense that it is always being actively produced."[15]

As the church interacts with all cultures, the issue is not to identify the characteristics (language, tradition, beliefs, values, needs, customs) of a particular culture and then figure out how to relate or apply the beliefs and practices of Christianity to it. The primary issue, instead, is to identify, name, and critique the ways in which various social realities form or make — cultivate — a people. While unmasked through the cross and resurrection of Jesus Christ, idolatrous principalities and powers continue to influence the dynamics and structures of all human cultures (we examined these processes in the last chapter). Consequently, culture is not a monolithic stationary entity that Christians should reject, accommodate, or even transform as a whole; it is, instead, a dynamic process with which Christians should interact in a critical, discriminating, and constructive manner.

13. Raymond Williams, *Key Words: A Vocabulary of Culture and Society* (New York: Oxford University Press, 1976), 76.

14. Contributing to this misleading tendency, H. Richard Niebuhr defined culture as a given "reality sui generis," a social heritage to which all humans, including Christians, are inevitably subject (*Christ and Culture* [New York: Harper & Row, 1951], 32).

15. Michael Warren, *Faith, Culture, and the Worshiping Community* (New York: Paulist, 1989), 172.

Cultivating Missional Communities

The early church theologian Justin Martyr characterized the dynamic culture of the church in the following manner:

> We who have been filled with war and mutual slaughter and every wickedness, have each one — all the world over — changed the instruments of war, the swords into ploughs and the spears into farming instruments, and we cultivate piety, righteousness, love for [humanity], faith and the hope which is from the Father Himself through the Crucified One.[16]

Justin Martyr believed that the old implements that cultivated a people of war had, through the cross of Jesus Christ, been replaced by implements that now cultivate a people of peaceableness. The aim of the church is not simply to make a given culture more just or more caring, but to shape a people into an alternative way of life. Missional communities representing the reign of God will be intentional about providing the space, the time, and the resources for people to unlearn old patterns and learn new ways of living that reveal God's transforming and healing power. As a culture-forming endeavor, Christianity is "a cultivating process that produces people in a particular way."[17]

Tertullian, another early theologian, declared: "Christians are not born, they are made." Just as the various forces and influences of the modern world socialize or enculturate us into the values of freedom, individualism, self-reliance, and self-advancement, so the church is challenged to form a people with distinctive habits of the heart. As an alternative social reality, the church is called to teach people how to talk, how to act, how to fight, how to love, how to see the world in a peculiar way — a Christlike way. As pointedly expressed by Stanley Hauerwas, the role of the church is to cultivate a people who "can risk being peaceful in a violent world, risk being kind in a competitive society, risk being faithful in an age of cynicism, risk being gentle among those who admire the tough, risk love when it may not be returned,

---

16. Cited in C. John Cadoux, *The Early Christian Attitude to War* (1919; repr. New York: Seabury, 1982), 61.

17. D. Stephen Long, *Living The Discipline: United Methodist Theological Reflection on War, Civilization, and Holiness* (Grand Rapids: Eerdmans, 1992), 9.

because we have the confidence that in Christ we have been reborn into a new reality."[18]

The purpose of missional communities is to be a source of radical hope, to witness to the new identity and vision, the new way of life that has become a social reality in Jesus Christ through the power of the Holy Spirit. The persistent problem is not how to keep the church from withdrawing from the world, but how to keep the world from distracting the church from its purpose of cultivating the people of God. As sign, foretaste, agent, and instrument of God's reconciling love and forgiveness, the church makes Jesus Christ visible in the world. The church is a social reality that continually engages in the practices that cultivate a people of truth, peace, wholeness, and holiness. The forming of Christian community is therefore not an option but the very lifestyle and vocation of the church.

Ecclesial Practices

Do not be conformed to this world but be transformed by the renewal of your mind, that you may prove what is the will of God, what is good and acceptable and perfect. (Rom. 12:1-2)

As a people sent to and for God's reign, missional communities are cultivated through participation in particular social or ecclesial practices.[19] Within our discussion, the concept of "practices" has a specific meaning: socially established cooperative human activities carried in traditions that form people in a way of life. The cultivation of a people who follow the way of Jesus Christ is a lifelong process of participation in "a community that embodies the language, rituals, and moral practices from which this particular form of life grows ... [because] the Christian gospel is at once belief that involves behavior and a behavior that involves belief."[20] Active in-

---

18. Stanley Hauerwas, *Against the Nations: War and Survival in a Liberal Society* (Notre Dame: University of Notre Dame Press, 1992), 118.

19. The choice of the term *ecclesial* is intended to provoke an image that moves beyond a static, provincial, and bureaucratic image of church to the New Testament *ekklesia*, which designates a community of people "called forth" (the literal meaning of the Greek) by God to participate in the new creation that has become an historical reality and human possibility in Jesus Christ.

20. Stanley Hauerwas, *Character and the Christian Life: A Study in Theological Ethics*, rev. ed. (Notre Dame: University of Notre Dame Press, 1995), 210-11.

volvement in such practices provides meaning, orientation, and purpose. Therefore it is essential to the formation of intentional missional communities of the Spirit.

North American culture holds a deep-seated belief in the freely choosing, autonomous individual who out of rational self-interest forms his or her own life (the "modern self" we analyzed in chap. 2). Consequently it tends to overlook or even dismiss the role of self-conscious, disciplined processes that regulate and shape both personal and communal life. But even when this culture does attend to such practices, it sees them as ahistorical (isolated actions or events), individualistic (focused on the actions of lone individuals), utilitarian (aimed at producing a specific product or effect), or abstract (culturally and historically neutral).[21] By contrast, those practices that cultivate Christian communities are distinctly historical, communal, experiential, and dynamic. Moreover, these four characteristics of Christian practices are interrelated in that they overlap, mutually influence, and enrich one another.

First, the church's practices are historical. Within the life of the church we do not construct our own ecclesial practices. We do not have to reinvent the wheel. We learn the patterns of faith, the practices of the church, from those who have learned and practiced them before us. We participate in a received tradition.

The contemporary Christian community is enriched by a long heritage of communities discerning and participating in God's creative, redemptive, and transformative activity. This is not a static or dead tradition. We participate in established and received practices, but we are continually called to reinterpret them in light of God's call for our common life and shared ministry in our present situation. Missional communities are challenged to be both faithful and innovative as they contribute to and pass on the historical practices that shape the life and purpose of the Christian community.

For example, prayer does not come naturally. We must learn how, when, and for what to pray. In response to the request: "Lord, teach us to pray," Jesus responded with what is traditionally called the Lord's Prayer (Luke 11:2-4). From the earliest days this prayer has occupied a place of singular honor in the life and liturgy of the church. "It is the

21. Craig Dykstra, "Reconceiving Practice," in Barbara Wheeler and Edward Farley, eds., *Shifting Boundaries: Contextual Approaches to the Structure of Theological Education* (Philadelphia: Westminster/John Knox, 1991), 35-41.

basic prayer of the gathered Christian community, serving as the true test and the instructive model of all Christian prayer."[22] As the prayer of the church, the Lord's Prayer provides the pattern — the content and the focus — for all those who would follow Jesus. This centrality is due not only to its origin in the life and teaching of Jesus but also to the breadth and depth of its content. Thomas Aquinas observed, "The Lord's Prayer contains all that is to be desired and all that we ought to avoid." The essentials of life, the essentials of our redemptive relationship with God, are found in the petitions of the Lord's Prayer.

As we learn to pray this prayer we become the people God has called us to be. Christian prayer is not our own creation — individual and private. It is shaped by our participation in the historical journey of the communion of saints, those who have gone before. As a community praying in his name and for his sake, we join in the prayer of the church, the prayer given to the disciples by Jesus Christ.

Second, the church's practices are communal. A practice is a socially established form of cooperative human activity. Within the life of the church we do not engage in isolated, private, and individualistic activities. Ecclesial practices involve people in actions with one another, even if these people are not engaged in this activity at the same time and in the same place. An ecclesial practice involves a complex tradition of interactions among many people sustained over a long period of time. One person's action becomes an ecclesial practice only insofar as it is participation in the practice of a community and a tradition. We are not born knowing how to live the Christian life. We cannot discover or learn the practices of the church on our own. We need mentors, teachers, and partners who will provide the advice, challenge, and support to enable us to extend and deepen our participation. Ecclesial practices are communally defined, communicated, and transformed.

The ecclesial practice of prayer is again instructive here. Quite often prayer is contrasted with liturgy or corporate worship. Prayer is understood in such cases as individual and private while liturgy is considered to be communal and public. Prayer is certainly personal, but it is never individual in the way that such comparisons would suggest. The language used in the Lord's Prayer is not "mine" and "me," but "our" and "us." In giving advice on prayer, Martin Luther counseled, "Remem-

---

22. Theodore W. Jennings Jr., *Life as Worship: Prayer and Praise in Jesus' Name* (Grand Rapids: Eerdmans, 1982), 19.

ber that you are not kneeling or standing there alone . . . all devout Christians are standing there with you in one unanimous, united prayer which God cannot ignore."[23] Whether we are in the presence of others or physically alone, when we pray we are united with all those who through faith in Jesus Christ have become the adopted children of God. The whole of the Lord's Prayer is public and communal. It is not the prayer of isolated individuals, but of the entire household of God. As we journey in relationship with our beloved Parent, our brothers and sisters serve as guides and supports, mentors and teachers. When we pray "Our Father," we "are naming the way we are saved — as a group, praying together, correcting one another, forgiving one another, stumbling along after Jesus together, memorizing the moves until his way has become our way."[24]

Third, the church's practices are experiential. The benefits of an ecclesial practice can be gained only through participation in that practice. Watching a televised worship service from the comfort of our living room may be inspirational and informative, but it does not engage our minds and hearts in the same way as involvement in the complex and rich pattern of community praise and celebration. The internal goods — for example, the fruit of the Holy Spirit — are not the end results of a particular activity but are realized in the process of being physically, emotionally, and spiritually engaged in the life, worship, and service of the Christian community. In a similar fashion, the indicators of a successful missional community are not determined by quantitative measures: the size of its budget, the number of its members, the quality of its musical efforts, or even the amount of social services. Instead, success is exhibited in the quality of Christian love experienced in the midst of its common life and ministry. The value of a congregation's ecclesial practices is not exhausted by the resulting product or by external goods as defined by society (status, power, influence), but is to be found in the actual process of involvement and participation.

To return to our example of prayer as an ecclesial practice: Christian prayer is grounded in and gives rise to experience. Prayer is experiential in the sense both of our total life experience and of the specific

---

23. Martin Luther, "A Simple Way to Pray," quoted in John S. Doberstein, ed., *A Minister's Prayer Book* (Philadelphia: Fortress, 1986), 443.

24. William H. Willimon and Stanley Hauerwas, *Lord, Teach Us to Pray: The Lord's Prayer and the Christian Life* (Nashville: Abingdon, 1996), 29.

experience of actively engaging in prayer. As we pray "your kingdom come," we affirm that Jesus Christ has triumphed over the powers of sin and death, but we also declare that the joy and freedom of life within the reign of God are not yet a full reality. The promise of a time when God will dwell with us and wipe away every tear, when death will be no more, when mourning, crying, and pain will disappear (Rev. 21), is still to be fulfilled. Thus the rhythm of prayer is that of praise and lament. Praise expresses our gratitude for God's amazing grace already in our midst; lament expresses our yearning for the not-yet fullness of God's kingdom. The Lord's Prayer does not gloss over the harsh realities of life, but announces "forgiveness for the guilt-laden, health for the diseased, hope for the despairing, and restored relations for the alienated."[25] Prayer is an experiential practice that enables us to confront the truth of our lives with eyes wide open yet hearts filled with hope. As Paul reminds us, it is only through the intercession of the Spirit that we are able to experience God's empowering and comforting presence: "For we do not know how to pray as we ought, but that very Spirit intercedes with sighs too deep for words" (Rom. 8:26).

Fourth, the church's practices are dynamic. Christians are called to "press on toward the goal for the prize of the heavenly call of God in Christ Jesus" (Phil. 3:14). As persons who live in Christ we are to grow in Christ. Thus ecclesial practices are dynamic; they grow and change as the community is open to and receives the Spirit's empowering presence. The more deeply we participate in a practice, the more we are empowered to engage in that activity in fresh and creative ways. We are called not simply to repeat various ecclesial practices but to use our insight, intelligence, discernment, imagination, judgment, skill, and commitment in order to be intentional about and to evaluate the faithfulness and the effectiveness of the missional community's various practices. The purpose of all ecclesial practices is to enable the community of faith to see, grasp, and participate ever more deeply in the creative power, redeeming love, and transforming presence of God in the ongoing mission of the reconciliation of all humanity and the healing of all creation.

To pray the Lord's Prayer is a dangerous activity. True prayer is life-creating and life-changing. To pray "your will be done" is to submit ourselves to God, to be open to God's testing and to God's initiatives. Prayer is not about getting what we want — the fulfillment of our will;

---

25. Arias, *Announcing the Reign of God,* 76.

it is about learning what God wants — the bending of our will to God's will. Nor are we left in the dark about what it is that God wants. As Cyprian of Carthage put it, "Now that is the will of God which Christ both did and taught. Humility in conversation; steadfastness in faith; modesty in words; justice in deeds; mercifulness in works; discipline in morals; to be unable to do a wrong, and to be able to bear a wrong when done; to keep peace with the brethren; to love God with all one's heart; to love Him in that He is a Father; to fear Him in that He is God."[26] Open to the movement and the illumination of the Holy Spirit, we grow and change, so that we more closely resemble the One to whom we pray. Not simply a process of human development or progress, nurturing our relationship with God means that we more fully and more profoundly manifest our prayer in our lives and our lives in our prayers.

We live as we pray. Through the transformation of attitudes, expectations, and behavior the witness of missional communities is that of a living prayer. The prayer of the church is the Lord's Prayer because here we discover to whom and for what we are to pray. Prayer is not a tactic for acquiring our hearts' desire, but a cry for God to be God, for the realization of God's kingdom, power, and glory.

The Social Embodiment of the Reign of God

Many people within North America view the Christian life from an individualistic or, at best, an organizational perspective. Yet to be true to its divine mission to embody and proclaim God's reign, the communal body called the church is the central and foundational unit of societal life for Christians. As a people sent to pray "your kingdom come, your will be done, on earth as it is in heaven," the church is to be an imperfect but perfecting social incarnation of God's inbreaking reign of love and reconciliation, joy and freedom, peace and justice.

The quality, character, and witness of Christian missional communities are determined by the social or ecclesial practices that shape, train, equip, guide — cultivate — their identity, vision, and action. As

26. "The Treatises of Cyprian," treatise 4, "On the Lord's Prayer" (tr. Ernest Wallis), in Alexander Roberts and James Donalson, eds., *The Ante-Nicene Fathers*, 5 (repr. Grand Rapids: Eerdmans, 1951), 451, §15.

they share in the standards, purposes, and orientation of these practices, so will their standards, purposes, and orientation as a community be shaped. The church is not simply a gathering of well-meaning individuals who have entered into a social contract to meet their privately defined self-interests. It is, instead, an intentional and disciplined community witnessing to the power and the presence of God's reign. "The church is the place in which the freedom and reconciliation opened in principle by Christ must be lived in social concreteness."[27]

The ecclesial practices of missional communities are many and varied. Among them are baptism, the Lord's Supper, reconciliation, discernment, hospitality, the reading and interpretation of Scripture, the development and exercise of leadership, the loving care and support of one another, the proclamation of God's Word, the active evangelization of all peoples, the exploration and learning of the faith, as well as the responsible and responsive stewardship of all of God's abundant gifts. Many more ecclesial practices currently exist and may be added in the future through the leading of the Holy Spirit. But to stimulate reflection on the formative power of such practices, let us focus on a few in order to see how they cultivate a people sent to represent and proclaim God's reign.

Baptism: Cultivating Communities of God's New Age

In those days Jesus came from Nazareth of Galilee and was baptized by John in the Jordan. (Mark 1:9)

Incorporation into the new humanity of God's reign comes about through the ecclesial practice of baptism. Although there continue to be debates about how, when, where, and whom to baptize, the key issue is not age or form but the faithful and effective cultivation of the community of disciples that the gospel demands and the world desperately needs.

According to the Synoptic Gospels, Jesus himself, and even the disciples in the pre-Easter period, did not baptize. The roots of Christian baptism lie in Jesus' baptism by John. John's water baptism was a prophetic call of repentance and readiness for the long-awaited Messiah

27. Lohfink, *Jesus and Community*, 145.

who would "baptize with the Holy Spirit" (Mark 1:8). When Jesus submits to this baptism in the Jordan River, a dramatic event occurs: the Holy Spirit descends and a voice from heaven proclaims, "You are my Son, the Beloved" (Mark 1:11). With this announcement John's rite of repentance and preparedness is transformed into an event of God's revelation and presence. There is now nothing to get ready for. The long-awaited reign of God is here, present in the life and ministry of Jesus of Nazareth. The meaning of the ecclesial practice of baptism is found in Jesus' fulfillment of John's eschatological anticipation of the promised reign of God.

The Flood That Drowns

Christians are baptized "into Christ Jesus." According to Paul, this act implies a transformation, a conversion of identity and life (cf. Rom. 6:3-11). The cross and resurrection break the universal reign of sin and death and begin a new reign of forgiveness and freedom. In Jesus Christ the depth of divine love, the seriousness of human sin, the power of evil, and the faithfulness of God are revealed. As incorporation into the crucified and risen Lord, baptism is not simply turning over a new leaf, or adopting a few new beliefs, but a matter of life and death: "Baptism is a training in dying — specifically to sin, to the old self — so that people may be brought to newness of life."[28]

More than merely a symbol, instructive analogy, or rite of passage, baptism actualizes the radical reorientation that humanity needs and only God can bring about. Baptism is far more than a bath that washes. We are drowned with Christ in baptism. The old self disintegrates and the new emerges as participation in resurrected life. Because baptism is a drowning with Christ, the powerful significance of this practice may well have diminished as the amount of water used in baptizing has decreased. The sprinkling of a few drops does not communicate the drastic nature of the burial indicated by baptism. Life in Christ involves a rebirth, a new creation. It is not a private event but rather a public declaration of a new identity and a transformed way of life. Thus baptism indicates "a far-reaching reconstruction of one's humanity: a liberation

---

28. L. Gregory Jones, *Transformed Judgment: Toward a Trinitarian Account of the Moral Life* (Notre Dame: University of Notre Dame Press, 1990), 138.

from servile, distorted, destructive patterns in the past, a liberation from anxious dread of God's judgment, a new identity in a community of reciprocal love and complementary service, whose potential horizons are universal."[29]

The Challenge of God's New Humanity

The rebirth of baptism forms a new people sent into and for God's new age: "If anyone is in Christ, there is a new creation: everything old has passed away; see, everything has become new!" (2 Cor. 5:17). The practice of baptism introduces persons into a radically new kind of social relationship; no longer isolated individuals, they have become brothers and sisters adopted into the body of Christ to live a communal life as a sign of God's reign in the midst of human history. Incorporation into Christ involves movement from the alienating independence of competitive and self-interested individualism to the affirming interdependence of a community grounded in the obedience and self-giving of Jesus Christ. "The rebirth of humanity requires that we should die as an individual through baptism and enter into a new life, a mode of existence where life is realized in communion in love and relationship. At baptism the whole of one's life becomes an ecclesial event, a fact of communion and relationship."[30]

Consequently, democratic principles and values are not the basis for Christian equality — baptism is the basis.

> As many of you as were baptized into Christ have clothed yourselves with Christ. There is no longer Jew or Greek [categories of ethnicity and tradition], there is no longer slave or free [economic and social power], there is no longer male and female [gender and role]; for all of you are one in Christ Jesus. (Gal. 3:27)

This well-known text from Scripture is frequently spiritualized, individualized, and idealized. As a result, too many contemporary Christians remain comfortable with, or at least reconciled to, living in neigh-

---

29. Rowan Williams, "Trinity and Revelation," *Modern Theology* 2, no. 3 (1986): 202.

30. Christos Yannaros, *The Freedom of Morality* (Crestwood, N.Y.: St. Vladimir's Seminary Press, 1984), 62.

borhoods and congregations where race, class, ethnic background, gender, and other stratifications separate and isolate individuals and groups of people from one another. Modernity constructed homogeneity for the sake of efficiency. The emerging postmodern perspective celebrates diversity as an end in itself. But Christian baptism confronts and challenges both perspectives. Through the Holy Spirit, missional communities are empowered to participate in God's shattering of all barriers. Such bodies manifest the new humanity of God's kingdom. They provide a model or demonstration of a faithful, open, and inclusive community. They manifest the hope, compassion, love, and unity of those who have died and risen with Christ, and they invite the world to join in the freedom, struggle, and joy of the new way of life in Christ.

Even though the liberating power of the Holy Spirit grasps the eschatological community of the baptized, the church continues to experience the power of evil. The principalities and powers have suffered ultimate defeat through the cross and resurrection of Jesus Christ, but they are still at work in the world. Baptism plunges believers into a situation where the old (the power of all that is hostile to the reign of God) has passed away (2 Cor. 5:17), although the old can still afflict, perplex, persecute, or strike down (2 Cor. 4:7-18). The present reality of alienation, brokenness, and injustice demonstrates the gap and tension between our contemporary world and the fullness of the reign of God. Because baptism links believers with the death as well as the resurrection of Jesus Christ, missional communities participate in his suffering and self-giving ministry (cf. Phil. 3:10). They are called to live into their baptism, to learn daily how to die and thus how to live. They are summoned to offer their lives and their service in the fulfillment of God's ministry of reconciliation. As such, baptism goes far beyond the private salvation of the individual soul or the isolated moment of baptism. It forms a new humanity by incorporating believers into the body of Jesus Christ and beginning their formation as a missionary people.

Breaking Bread Together:
Cultivating Communities of Gratitude and Generosity

This is my body, which is given for you. Do this in remembrance of me.
(Luke 22:19)

Missional communities of the baptized are sustained and nourished in their ongoing life and ministry by breaking bread together as they gather around the Lord's Supper. The Supper has its origin in the history of Jesus Christ, and its pattern and authority stem from the last supper of Jesus and his disciples. This final meal occurs within the context of the Passover, which commemorates God's past deliverance of the Jewish people from Egypt, and it anticipates their future blessedness in the fullness of God's reign. Jesus' words over the bread and wine foresee his suffering and look forward to the great messianic banquet in the kingdom of God (cf. Luke 22:14-20). The Lord's Supper remembers and proclaims the new life to be found in table fellowship with the crucified and risen Lord in whom the coming reign of God becomes experienced reality.

Breaking bread together is an ecclesial practice of remembered hope. Rather than a commemoration of one who is deceased, it is the realization of the risen and living Christ. Thus it is "not a meal looking back in memory of the dead, but a meal which looks forward to the future, full of confidence and hope."[31] As a foretaste of the promised reign of God, it is a meal not of mourning but of joy and thanksgiving.

The Bread of Life

The elements of the church's worship are the things of everyday material life: bread, wine, water, touch, gesture, movement. The actions of eating and drinking at the Lord's Supper are not otherworldly but mundane and natural. The Bible is intensely interested in the human realities of hunger and thirst. Whether as parable or event, as warning or promise, the mention of food and drink can be found within every strand of the biblical tradition.

The style and manner of eating and drinking place the satisfaction of human hunger within a broader context. Human meals are social

31. Hans Küng, *The Church* (Garden City, N.Y.: Image, 1967), 284.

occasions that both express and form the identity and vision of those who participate. Biblical accounts of table fellowship manifest an alternative set of table manners that both reflect and shape a particular way of life: a life sustained and enriched by the abundant promises and gifts of God. "Since food and drink nurture and restore life, they are exemplary gifts of God's care."[32] The Lord's Supper gathers committed believers in communal meal and prayer to offer thanksgiving to God as they support and share with one another in daily life. The Lord's Supper is a protest against and an alternative to the world's use of food and community. Luke ends his account of the Christian community's formation at Pentecost by noting that "there was not a needy person among them" (Acts 4:34). The economy of God is not one of scarcity but of shared abundance, the promise and the experience of full and abundant life for all. The reign of God manifested in Jesus Christ shows forth a redeemed society of reconciliation, justice, and peace where God's will is "done on earth as it is in heaven." The new life in God's reign includes the meeting of all basic and bodily needs: "They will hunger no more, and thirst no more" (Rev. 7:16). In short, the Lord's Supper is an economic act since it is a participation in God's economy of freely given love and grace. To do rightly the practice of breaking bread together is a matter of economic ethics. The community formed by the outpouring of the Holy Spirit participates in the firstfruits of the reconciling work of Jesus Christ, a new way of eating, drinking, and living together as a people. Therefore the church is called to share in and advocate for the physical well-being of all those for whom Jesus gave his life.

An Open Invitation to a Common Table

Shared meals construct and sustain human relationships. Inviting someone to share a meal powerfully symbolizes solidarity. Indeed, the word *companionship* comes from the Latin *cum* + *panis*, meaning "breading together."[33] Meals are social realities of great importance. Because meals express the very texture of human associations, they often exhibit social

---

32. John E. Burkhard, *Worship: A Searching Examination of the Liturgical Experience* (Philadelphia: Westminster, 1982), 79.

33. Ibid., 76.

boundaries that divide human communities. We make decisions about not only what we will eat but with whom we will eat. Patterns of table sharing reveal a great deal about the way of life — the norms and commitments — of a particular community.

Within the Gospels, Jesus' meal patterns receive special attention. Many of his critics observed that "this fellow welcomes sinners and eats with them" (Luke 15:1-2; Mark 2:15-17; Matt. 11:19). They were shocked and appalled that Jesus welcomed everyone to his table. His behavior indicated acceptance and friendship with those who had been judged unfit for table fellowship: the tax collector, the Gentile, the prostitute. His open invitation "manifested the radically inclusive nature of his kingdom, a kingdom that cuts across the barriers we erect between insiders and outsiders, the saved and the damned, the elect and the outcast — barriers often most rigidly enforced at the table."[34]

In the Lord's Supper the followers of Jesus Christ are called to practice eating as he ate, to be a people of gratitude and generosity, of openness and acceptance. They are summoned to be a community where amazingly diverse people allow themselves to be formed by one Lord into one body around a common table. When our table is less than the fullness of Christ's invitation, we eat and drink to our judgment (cf. 1 Cor. 11:29).

Blessed Are the Hungry

The ecclesial practice of the Lord's Supper is not a withdrawal from the world, but provides a pathway into the world through an alternative vision. Participation in the Lord's Supper, by reminding Christians of their fundamental creatureliness, teaches them to recognize and to appreciate the interrelatedness of all of life. The bread, when lifted up and blessed, "thrusts our vision both forward toward all of God's gifts and backward toward the bread we had for breakfast, to the gifted and social nature of our existence, to the interconnectedness of worship and life."[35] Acknowledging their own hunger and their own need for forgiveness and reconciliation, the community which gathers around the Lord's

34. William H. Willimon, *The Service of God: How Worship and Ethics Are Related* (Nashville: Abingdon, 1983), 133.

35. Ibid., 131.

table stands in solidarity with the hunger, the dispossessed, and the marginalized. Nourished and strengthened into a new relationship with Jesus Christ, those who break bread together are drawn into and participate in his ministry of conquering need, overcoming alienation, and accepting the despised.

The church offers the world an invitation to a new communal life, a new social identity, and a new way of receiving and sharing the basic necessities of life. Celebrating the Lord's Supper makes possible the living of the eucharistic life — a life of overwhelming gratitude and overflowing generosity. The community formed around the Lord's Table is a redeemed and transformed society where love, hope, forgiveness, and mutual accountability are palpable and the divisive attitudes and actions of hostility and hate spurned. The church proclaims and embodies a new social ethic in which deeds of mercy and acts of charity are a natural and organic part of its life as it manifests the liberating possibilities of God's reign to the world.

Reconciliation: Cultivating Communities of Mutual Accountability

If your brother or sister sins, go and reprove that person when the two of you are alone. If he or she listens, you have won your brother or sister. . . . Truly I tell you, whatever you bind on earth will be bound in heaven, and whatever you loose on earth will be loosed in heaven. (Matt. 18:15, 18)

As the baptized community that gathers around the Lord's Table, the church is called to deal responsibly with conflict and to utter public statements about morality. But it is called to be much more since its participants are invited to become ambassadors for Christ entrusted with the ministry of reconciliation (cf. 2 Cor. 5:16-21). Reconciliation — confession, judgment, and forgiveness — is not an individual and private matter, but an ecclesial practice that fosters, shapes, and sustains missional communities. Such a practice is an antidote to the competitive, alienating individualism of North American culture. While central to the biblical understanding of the nature of salvation, reconciliation may be the most difficult practice for contemporary Christians even to consider, much less to actualize within their congregations.

The Call to Repentance

In the Gospel of Matthew, the opening word of Jesus' proclamation is "Repent!" (4:17). Jesus' call to repentance moves beyond personal sorrow, guilt, or remorse to a profound and far-reaching *metanoia:* "Turn around! Change your ways! Receive a whole new identity!" Such repentance is possible only because the healing power of God's reign is present in Jesus Christ: "the kingdom of heaven has come near" (4:17). In his challenge and triumph over the principalities and powers, a new order of life and freedom emerges in the midst of the old order of death and bondage. Therefore repentance involves "a new lifestyle of obedient faith and active participation in the community of faith whose common life is characterized by the twin features of forgiveness and liberation in Christ."[36]

Binding and Loosing

To "bind" means to hold someone accountable or to obligate, while to "loose" means to free from obligation or to forgive. This ecclesial practice, as outlined in Matthew 18:15-22, is a communal pastoral process of reconciliation rather than the legalistic method of community discipline with which it is commonly associated. The intent is not to search out and chastise wrongdoers or to purify and thus protect the community's reputation. It is, instead, to be attentive to and, when necessary, reach out to one another in loving forgiveness for the restoration of community. The emphasis rests on the nature and quality of relationships. "Forgiveness is precisely the deep and abiding sense of what relation — with God or with other human beings — can and should be."[37] Forgiveness is less a legal word of acquittal than a transformative mode of relationships that forms a community of forgiven sinners.

"Sin" in this context is not a violation of abstract divine law but a personal offense or estrangement jeopardizing the love, unity, peace, and thus the ministry and witness of the community. Therefore a definite togetherness is assumed, a togetherness of identity and of life. Because the very identity of God's people involves being members one of another,

36. Jim Wallis, *Agenda for Biblical People: A New Focus for Developing a Life-Style of Discipleship* (New York: Harper & Row, 1976), 22.
37. Rowan Williams, *Resurrection* (New York: Pilgrim, 1982), 52.

and because the living of the Christian life depends on bearing one another's burdens, we are important to and bound up with one another. Consequently, under the guidance of the Holy Spirit, we rely on and owe one another counsel and, sometimes, correction and pardon.

Rather than the recognition and forgiveness of sins taking place in a private transaction between the individual and God, forgiveness is placed within the communal context of the body of Christ, of those who confess Jesus as the Christ. This is the basis for the startling claim of Matthew 18:18 that the community's action is God's action. The authority to bind and to loose is given not to just any group but to a people empowered by the Holy Spirit to be an intentional community of shared standards, mutual trust, and redemptive discipline. Such a community is one whose members have committed themselves to its standards and to its practice voluntarily. "We can pursue reconciling confrontation because we trust one another and because we asked to be placed under this kind of loving guidance."[38] The church is given not a static, once-and-for-all legal code but a dynamic procedure of reconciling dialogue. Such a process offers the opportunity for ongoing moral discernment: the clarification, testing, and, if need be, modification of the community's standards.

As a process of concern, involvement, and reconciliation, the practice of binding and loosing involves truth finding and community building. Thus the communal practice of recognizing and dealing constructively with differences and dissension develops skills and offers a model for dealing with conflict in other social relationships and contexts.

A Community of Forgiven-ness

Matthew (in chapter 18) provides practical instruction in the realism of the commandment of love as lived within the daily life of the church. Matthew is a realist who recognizes that until the consummation of God's reign at the end of history *(eschaton)*, the powers of sin and evil will continue to be active, even within the community of those professing faith in Jesus Christ. Since the world is not yet healed, alienation and isolation from God and from each other still determine much of our lives. Because it is a community that recognizes both its sinfulness and

---

38. John Howard Yoder, *Body Politics: Five Practices of Christian Community Before the Watching World* (Nashville: Discipleship Resources, 1993), 5.

its forgiven-ness in Jesus Christ, the church does not need to look at the world through rose-colored glasses. It can deal honestly yet hopefully with the fallen nature of the world. "Forgiven, the community takes courage to look on the world *and itself* as they really are. Its hope is diacritical, opting neither for cynicism or shallow optimism. It recognizes the world and the community as they really are but struggles to see them changed in the grace of God."[39]

The conditions for God's forgiveness have been fulfilled by the death and resurrection of Jesus Christ. Yet it is only as the missional community is empowered by the Holy Spirit to confess and to repent that it is able to receive and appropriate that forgiveness. The way in which God deals with sin is by judgment that always seeks reconciliation, in both an overall and a specific sense. "Christian forgiveness is at once an expression of a commitment to a way of life, the cruciform life of holiness in which we seek to 'unlearn' sin and learn the ways of God, and a means of seeking reconciliation in the midst of particular sins, specific instances of broken-ness."[40] The community of those who would follow Jesus must realistically and honestly recognize the patterns of sin and destruction within its midst. Only those who are willing to stand under and accept God's judgment will also participate in God's forgiving grace.

In and through the practices of Christian community, Christians learn to be sinners: openly and honestly to acknowledge the grievance or affront to their communion with one another. And they learn to be forgiven: to admit their need for forgiveness, to accept the judgment, and to be reconciled with one another. If the conversation fails, if the offender does not acknowledge his or her need for forgiveness and becomes as "a Gentile or a tax collector," the community remembers that it is exactly to these people that Jesus brought the gospel of God's reign. As a community of forgiven sinners accepting God's forgiveness, Christians are able to forgive those who sin against them. "The whole point of this text, Matt. 18:15-22, is that we confront one another not as forgivers, not as those who use forgiveness as power, but first and foremost as people who have learned the truth about ourselves—

---

39. Robert E. Webber and Rodney Clapp, *People of the Truth: A Christian Challenge to Contemporary Culture*, rev. ed. (Harrisburg: Morehouse, 1993), 64.

40. L. Gregory Jones, *Embodying Forgiveness: A Theological Analysis* (Grand Rapids: Eerdmans, 1995), 230.

namely, that we are all people who need to be and have been forgiven."[41]

Watching over One Another in Love

The practice of binding and loosing — mutual admonition and forgiveness — will not fit naturally within the life of most congregations' current practice. For many people within North America the church is a place where individuals go passively to receive religious goods and services. "My only duty as a Christian is to leave the world for an hour or so on a Sunday morning and go to church to be assured that my sins are forgiven."[42] Some might allow that the church has a role in determining and promoting moral principles, but they would leave the acceptance of and accountability for the fulfillment of those principles to the individual and his or her conscience. Within this perspective it is difficult to conceive that ordinary Christians have the authority to obligate and to forgive on God's behalf with the assurance that the action stands "in heaven."

Within North American culture the usual application of moral standards is impersonal, judgmental, and legalistic. When the church adopts this approach, it engenders a fear of others' knowing our shortcomings, evaluating our moral worth, or intervening in our lives. Issues of sin and confession then become divisive, oppressive, and destructive, rather than redemptive practices that nurture and sustain missional communities.

By contrast, the communal practice of Christian reconciliation is experienced through participation in face-to-face groups that covenant together for mutual accountability. Much like the Methodist class meetings of the eighteenth century, it moves beyond individual edification or emotional support to an intentional and disciplined sharing of the challenges of following Christ in an indifferent and hostile world. Coming together in regularly scheduled gatherings, participants share the bumps

41. Stanley Hauerwas, "Peacemaking: The Virtue of the Church," in *Christian Existence Today: Essays on Church, World, and Living in Between* (Durham: Labyrinth, 1988), 93-94.

42. Dietrich Bonhoeffer, *The Cost of Discipleship*, tr. Reginald H. Fuller, rev. ed. (New York: Macmillan, 1959), 54.

and bruises of encounter with the world, as they comfort and strengthen one another. John Wesley believed that intentional and disciplined small groups could be a wellspring for faithful Christian discipleship.

> It can scarce be conceived what advantages have been reaped from this little prudential regulation. Many now happily experienced that Christian fellowship of which they had not so much as an idea before. They began to "bear one another's burdens," and naturally to "care for each other." As they had daily a more intimate acquaintance with, so they had a more endeared affection for, each other. And "speaking the truth in love, they grew up into him in all things, who is the Head, even Christ."[43]

Those within fragmented and transient modern societies have much to learn from this historical experience of accountable fellowship that nurtures Christian discipleship.[44] In the sharing of temptations and weaknesses, and of strengths and accomplishments, participants can begin realistically to confront and acknowledge their bondage to sin as they learn to live as a forgiven and forgiving people. The intent is to create a social space and climate that encourages honest, caring relationships within a community of people who make time for one another, who celebrate and rejoice together, who know and serve each other, and who are accountable one to the other. Skills and habits of listening, praying, studying, thinking, sharing, disagreeing, comforting, planning, working, and thus discovering and building up each other will need to be developed. Within communities of mutual account-ability, the living of the Christian way of life — a life worthy of our calling — is not the responsibility of isolated individuals. It involves the shared insight, the tangible support, and the committed obedience of the entire community.

43. John Emory, ed., *The Works of John Wesley* (1831; repr. New York: Lane and Scott, 1850), 5:180.
44. For more information about Covenant Discipleship Groups, one may contact the Center for Congregational Life, The General Board of Discipleship, The United Methodist Church, P.O. Box 840, Nashville, TN 37202-0840.

Discernment: Cultivating Communities
of Spirit-filled Deliberation

When the Spirit of truth comes, he will guide you into all the truth.
(John 16:13)

Missional communities witness to the nature and quality of God's presence in their midst through worship and their service. But they also witness just as strongly in the way they share power and influence in their decision making. The processes of making decisions within the church are usually viewed as an organizational concern. Modernity has placed great trust in reason's ability to uncover a shared understanding of the truth. In contrast, postmodernity has so stressed the contextual nature of truth and the diversity of human perspectives that all truth claims have become relative. As a result, the processes of making decisions are now largely viewed as a matter of power dynamics in which either competing forces are balanced or one side seeks an advantage through manipulative strategies.

Within the North American context, the democratic process of one person, òne vote is considered the best way to make decisions. Yet the presuppositions behind adversarial win-lose debates, parliamentary maneuvers, special interest group lobbying, and majority rule are seldom examined. These processes are deeply grounded in modernity's commitment to individual autonomy and freedom, maximizing or protecting personal preferences, and a suspicion of power and influence. Instead of offering an alternative, church meetings small and large tend to reflect the conflicts and the inadequacies of these processes, commitments, and suspicions of secular society.

The ecclesial practice of discernment in missional communities indicated a different approach. Discernment is a process of sorting, distinguishing, evaluating, and sifting among competing stimuli, demands, longings, desires, needs, and influences, in order to determine which are of God and which are not. To discern is to prove or test "what is of the will of God — what is good and acceptable and perfect" (Rom. 12:2). Thus the goal of decision making in the church is not simply to discover the will of the community, but instead to discern together the will of God. It is the role of the Spirit to convict, convince, and lead those who profess faith in Jesus Christ into God's truth. Discernment requires this guidance because God acts and speaks in and through the ambiguous circumstances of worldly life. Thus the church is called to "test the spirits to see whether they are from God" (1 John 4:1) through cautious, attentive, and humble discernment. As can be documented through historical review, not only the Holy Spirit but also destructive forces operate and multiply within Christian communities. As the *ekklesia* of God, a people gathered and sent to be about God's business, the church is called to a way of making decisions that articulates and correlates with listening, hearing, testing, planning, and obeying together in the power of the Holy Spirit.

The Pneumocratic Nature of Discernment

The practice of communal decision making assumes a community of giftedness. Through baptism and faith in Jesus Christ all have received gifts of the Holy Spirit for the edification, encouragement, and consolation of the entire body. Therefore it is important that all be involved in discerning what God requires of them. Paul continually insists that every member of the body of Christ has the responsibility to share the particular insights she or he has been given. All are called "to instruct one another" (Rom. 15:14), to speak God's word "so that all may learn and all be encouraged" (1 Cor. 14:31), to "teach and admonish one another in all wisdom" (Col. 3:16), for it is through "speaking the truth in love" that they are to "grow up in every way into him who is the head, into Christ" (Eph. 4:15). Thus the most characteristic setting in which the community receives guidance is when Christians assemble to share and evaluate the gifts given to them. Here in a variety of complementary ways guidance is conveyed through each to all, and through all to each.[45]

Discerning communities are not hierarchical in structure, but neither are they egalitarian. Because all receive gifts to contribute to the common good, everyone enjoys the right and the obligation of participating authoritatively in decisions of faith and practice. Yet because the Spirit distributes different gifts, responsibilities, and functions, there is also an element of differentiation. Spiritual gifts are not distributed in monotonous uniformity but in rich diversity. The focus here is not on the prerogatives of designated leaders or on the equal privileges of

45. Robert Banks, *Paul's Idea of Community: The Early House Churches in Their Historical Setting* (Grand Rapids: Eerdmans, 1980), 141.

members, but on corporate responsibility for discerning the wisdom and prompting of the Holy Spirit. Thus communities of giftedness are neither autocratic (the rule of one) nor democratic (the rule the people) but pneumocratic (the rule of the Holy Spirit). Authority within missional communities is found neither in particular status nor in majority opinion. It is dispersed throughout the whole body through the illumination and empowerment of the Spirit. None is given advantage; all are equipped for service. The image is of a participatory community earnestly expecting and seeking the guidance of the Holy Spirit in its midst, utilizing the diverse gifts of all participants, and willing to be bound by what is mutually decided.

As we shall explore in the next chapter, the role of leadership in such a pneumocratic community must be fundamentally reconceived. The community's leadership serves the process of discernment that results in the witness of communal decision making. It provides the distinctive gifts of biblical and theological insight needed for that discernment. But it is not the exclusive agency of the Spirit within the community. Rather, it is rooted in, emerges from, and is identified by the community's process of discernment. The calling and affirming of leadership is perhaps one of the most important functions of pneumocratic discernment.

Spirit-moved Deliberation

Church meetings often do not deal with the vital challenges of life and faith. Worship, prayer, Bible study, mutual support, sharing of personal and communal issues occur elsewhere. Because of perceived limitations of time and energy, the goal is to get through the agenda. Uncritical compliance (going along with recommendations of the leader), easy compromise (seeking the lowest common denominator), or majority rule (overriding minority voices) are considered the most practical ways to make decisions. Yet if missional communities are called to discern and to participate in God's creative, redemptive, and transformative activity within the concrete circumstances of contemporary life, a much different approach is needed. God's will and God's truth cannot be legislated by prudent and efficient decisions. They require open conversation in which we listen for the Spirit in the midst of communal dialogue. The Holy Spirit works through group processes — the interaction of the two or three gathered together in the name of Jesus Christ.

As with all other ecclesial practices, communal decision making both assumes and creates an intentional community of believers, a community that recognizes the need for the gifts and insights of all members to shape and guide a faithful and effective ministry. Only then will members make the effort to set aside the necessary time to listen, share, study, struggle, pray, and plan together in the continual search for God's truth. Opening themselves to the challenge of seeking God's wisdom in the midst of the community's lived experience, members will eagerly seek out the insights of their brothers and sisters as they bring the issue under deliberation into conversation with Scripture and Christian tradition. The feelings and commitments of all members will be affirmed and considered as they carefully analyze all the available evidence and perspectives on an issue. Diversity of opinion and even conflict will be utilized to enrich the discussion as they talk with one another in frankness and honesty. A discerning community will not rush to judgment since it will know the importance of waiting on the Spirit in silence and prayer.

Having participated in a communal decision-making process of open dialogue, critical reflection, genuine respect, mutual trust, and active collaboration, members will pledge themselves to live out together the conclusions they have reached. Within a discerning community, when a decision "has been prayerfully tested with the authority of Scripture and the presence of the living Christ, seriously taking into account subjective feelings, factual evidence, and the testimony of other Christians and tradition, and the result is a deep sense of peace, love, joy, and humility, we can trust that we have discerned God's will."[46]

Hospitality: Cultivating Communities of Peace

Welcome one another, therefore, as Christ has welcomed you, for the glory of God. (Rom. 15:7)

The optimistic expectation in North America that modernity's individual freedom, reason, democratic rule, market capitalism, and advanced technology would conquer all human ills has been replaced with increasing

46. Arthur G. Gish, *Living in Christian Community* (Scottdale, Penn.: Herald, 1979), 130.

disillusion, anxiety, and cynicism. The headlines of our daily newspapers report increasing crime, violence, and hatred as groups seek to separate and distinguish themselves from those who appear to be a threat. As illustrated by the current debates about affirmative action and immigration, more and more individuals and groups see themselves competing for personal safety, financial security, and general well-being in an age of scarcity. The tribalization of postmodernity that celebrates difference will only increase the division and distance between various groups as they discover their identity by distinguishing themselves from others.

The Peace of the Gospel

It is to such people in such a world that the church is sent courageously and joyfully to proclaim the gospel of the reign of God. As surprising as it might be, the most frequent command in the Bible is not "Be good" or "Be moral" but "Fear not."[47] This good news is not a naïve optimism. It is the affirmation that in Jesus Christ the principalities and powers of a fallen and alienated world have been overcome. It is the promise and assurance that through the power of the Holy Spirit all humanity is invited into God's new world order of compassion, kindness, humility, meekness, patience, love, and harmony (Col. 3:12-14). All things — whether on earth or in heaven — have been reconciled to God; peace has been made through the blood of the cross of Jesus Christ. We have been rescued from the power of darkness; we have been transferred into the kingdom of God's beloved Son; we have received redemption, the forgiveness of sins (Col. 1:13-20).

The church's proclamation of the gospel has validity and relevance only when it confronts head-on the often terrifying circumstances of human life, when it expresses hope in the face of despair, when it honestly and realistically accepts its vocation to convert hostility into hospitality. As the baptized body of Christ that gathers around the Lord's Table, missional communities are called to be peacemakers — reconciled and reconciling communities — making God's peace visible through the quality of their life and ministry as model and invitation.

47. N. T. Wright, *Following Jesus: Biblical Reflections on Discipleship* (Grand Rapids: Eerdmans, 1994), 66.

Henri Nouwen succinctly describes the church's role within our modern context:

> Our society seems to be increasingly full of fearful, defensive, aggressive people anxiously clinging to their property and inclined to look at their surrounding world with suspicion, always expecting an enemy to suddenly appear, intrude, and do harm. But still — that is our vocation: to convert the *hostis* into a *hospes,* the enemy into a guest, and to create the free and fearless space where brotherhood and sisterhood can be formed and fully experienced.[48]

Through the practice of Christian hospitality the church participates in God's peaceable kingdom. Such hospitality indicates the crossing of boundaries (ethnic origin, economic condition, political orientation, gender status, social experience, educational background) by being open to and welcoming of the other. Without such communities of hospitality, the world will have no way of knowing that all God's creation is meant to live in peace.

The Stranger as Spiritual Guide

The stranger represents an unknown and ambiguous figure: friend or foe, resource or thief, giver or taker. Yet three key events in the New Testament — Christmas, Easter, and Pentecost — all recount the coming of a divine stranger. In each case the newcomer brings blessings that both disorient and transform. "The child in the manger, the traveler on the road to Emmaus, and the mighty wind of the Spirit all meet us as mysterious visitors, challenging our belief systems even as they welcome us to new worlds."[49] When the despondent travelers on the Emmaus road extended hospitality to the stranger who had joined them, "their eyes were opened" and they discovered that he was none other than the resurrected Christ (Luke 24:13-35). The stranger plays a central role in biblical stories of faith, and for good reason. "The religious quest, the spiritual pilgrimage, is always taking us into new lands where we are

48. Henri J. M. Nouwen, *Reaching Out: The Three Movements of the Spiritual Life* (Garden City, N.Y.: Doubleday, 1975), 46.

49. John Koenig, *New Testament Hospitality: Partnership with Strangers as Promise and Mission* (Philadelphia: Fortress, 1985), 5.

strange to others and they are strange to us. Faith is a venture into the unknown, into the realms of mystery, away from the safe and comfortable and secure."[50]

Christian hospitality that represents the reign of God includes but is not limited to the offer of aid and comfort to the visitor or outsider. The openness and receptivity of hospitality draws attention to otherness in its many expressions. For example, consider the surprise and the disruption involved in welcoming children into our families: the things we learn about ourselves, the difficulties we face in trying to explain the ordinary customs of our culture, the new perspectives we gain by seeing the world through their eyes, the ways in which our lives become more focused and yet also expanded. Strangers not only challenge and subvert our familiar worlds; they can enhance and even transform our way of life and our most intimate relationships. By honoring others precisely in their otherness, we embrace the new, the mysterious, and the unexpected: "Do not neglect to show hospitality to strangers, for by doing that some have entertained angels without knowing it" (Heb. 13:2).

The Manifestation of God's Hospitality

Jesus came as a stranger, as one who had no place to lay his head (Matt. 8:20), and in his ministry he crossed conventional boundaries and propelled himself into the lives of strangers. As Rodney Clapp has observed,

> Jesus spoke parables honoring such despised ethnic groups as Samaritans, thereby ignoring racial boundaries. He scandalously taught women and conversed with them in public, thereby trespassing sexual borders. He included among his disciples Simon the Zealot and spoke the words of new life to Nicodemus the Pharisee, thereby opening himself to the array of people who were strangers to one another by virtue of their politics. He called the adulteress from the estrangement of the stoning circle back into the circle of community, thereby crossing moral borders. And he invited the ritually "unclean" to his table, thereby breakinq religious taboos.[51]

50. Parker Palmer, *The Company of Strangers: Christians and the Renewal of America's Public Life* (New York: Crossroad, 1986), 56.
51. Rodney Clapp, *Families at the Crossroads: Beyond Traditional and Modern* (Downers Grove, Ill.: InterVarsity Press, 1993), 139.

We too often forget the radical nature of Jesus' life and work. Religious insiders challenged him not because of his doctrine but because of those to whom he extended God's gracious and loving hospitality. As we emphasized above in our exposition of the open invitation to a common table, missional communities are called to cross society's boundaries, to eat as Jesus ate, to be a people of openness and acceptance, of gratitude and generosity.

Missional communities of hospitality do not seek the homogeneous oneness hoped for by modernity, nor do they celebrate the fragmented diversity of postmodernity. They welcome and nurture the incredible richness and particularity of perspectives, backgrounds, and gifts but always within the embrace of God's reconciling unity.

The Creation of Free and Fearless Space

Contemporary images of community or hospitality tend to exhibit what Parker Palmer calls an "ideology of intimacy."[52] They emphasize sameness, closeness, warmth, and comfort. Difference, distance, conflict, and sacrifice are alien to this approach and therefore are to be to be avoided at all costs. Modern communities maintain a facade of unity and harmony by eliminating the strange and cultivating the familiar, by suppressing dissimilarity and emphasizing agreement. The traumatic and tragic events of human life are glossed over, ignored, or explained away. Those who are strange — other than we are — are either excluded or quickly made like us. "People with whom we cannot achieve intimacy, or with whom we do not want to be intimate, are squeezed out."[53] These images portray homogeneous communities of retreat where persons must be protected from one another as well as from outsiders, and where reality is suppressed and denied due to fear and anxiety.

Missional communities, shaped by faith in Jesus Christ and the gifts and fruit of the Holy Spirit, present a different image. Rather than seeing themselves as one more civic institution offering religious goods and services to individuals (or to society at large), such communities take the time to create gracious and caring space where they can reach out and invite their fellow human beings into a new relationship with God

---

52. Palmer, *Company of Strangers,* 108.
53. Ibid., 120.

and with each other. They offer both the protection and the freedom to enable estranged and fearful human beings to bring the actual circumstances of their lives into conversation with the peace of the gospel. They lay aside their occupations and preoccupations, and they attend to one another. Hostility is converted into hospitality, strangers into friends, and enemies into guests. In a world increasingly "full of strangers, estranged from their own past, culture, and country, from their neighbors, friends and family, from their deepest self and their God,"[54] missional communities such as these evidence the good news of Jesus Christ. The welcoming news of the reign of God shapes them into welcoming communities, open to all creation.

The Common Witness of Missional Practice

The cultivation of faithful missional communities is an ongoing process of formation and transformation. Regular and intentional participation in ecclesial practices is God's way of cultivating the missionary people who are sent as the witness to the gospel into the world. Through the empowering presence of the Holy Spirit, these social processes exhibit the incarnation of divine activity within human activity: "They are actions of God, in and with, through and under what men and women do. Where they are happening, the people of God is real in the world."[55]

In the scriptural witness, God's actions reveal the character of God. That God is a loving God is evidenced by the fact that God sent his only begotten Son (John 3:16). Similarly, the missional purpose of the church is made manifest by the practices of the community of believers. In spite of the great cultural diversity that shapes the details of the ecclesial practices, they represent the true unity of God's missionary people. A fundamental commonality in the ecclesial practices testifies to the same God calling forth the church in every culture, the same Lord saving and sending the community, the same Spirit empowering its witness in its public worship, the community draws together and centers its entire life, all its practices, upon the inviting and sending presence of God.

However baptism is celebrated, it is to cultivate communities of inclusion and interdependence where the barriers that separate and

54. Nouwen, *Reaching Out,* 46.
55. Yoder, *Body Politics,* 73.

divide people are dissolved. The practice of breaking bread together is to cultivate communities of gratitude and generosity in solidarity with the hungry, dispossessed, and marginalized.[56] As Christian communities learn to practice reconciliation, their mutual accountability, reciprocal trust, and redemptive discipline become powerful testimonies to the inbreaking reign of God. The practice of communal discernment is to cultivate communities of Spirit-moved deliberation that affirm the unique and important contribution of all believers to building up the community. The practice of hospitality is to cultivate communities of peace that intentionally structure themselves as safe and fearless spaces in the face of the despair and hostility of the world.

Therefore all ecclesial practices that cultivate missional communities, shaped by historical, communal, experiential, and dynamic elements, while varied, share a common pattern.[57] Fundamentally, they are always based on and shaped by the witness of Scripture. While requiring interpretation within varying cultural contexts, they are always apostolically prescribed social processes that witness to the inbreaking of God's reign in Jesus Christ. They derive from, depend on, and participate in his redemptive ministry: Jesus' fulfillment of John the Baptist's eschatological expectations, Jesus' last supper with the disciples, the authority Jesus gave to his disciples to bind and loose, Jesus' promise of the continued guidance of the Holy Spirit, Jesus' controversial practice of befriending the outcast and despised.

The ecclesial practices are never esoteric or supernatural, but involve ordinary human behavior: joining and sharing, eating and drinking, listening and caring, testing and deciding, welcoming and befriending. They relate not to an abstract or private religious realm but to the real challenges of contemporary moral and social issues: social inequality, economic injustice, destructive conflict and alienation, lack of personal dignity and esteem, fear and hostility. The doing of these practices makes a church body what it is: they shape and express the particular way of

---

56. The diversity of sacramental theologies and traditions that are so sadly divisive of the church need urgently to be addressed in the larger missional context of the church. As ecclesial practices that are given to cultivate God's missionary people for obedience and faithfulness, they should not divide Christians but unite them.

57. The expression of the common pattern builds upon Yoder's discussion in *Body Politics*, 43-46, 71-80.

life — the belief, commitment, and action — of a particular community. They have communal and missional meaning from the outset: by their very nature they are social, visible, practical, and public. Because they are the result of the Spirit's empowering guidance, they are not static, given once and for all. They grow and change as communities creatively participate in and responsibly interpret the particular practices within their concrete missional contexts. Yet in this dynamic diversity, they are always the tangible witness to the once-and-for-all gospel of the apostolic witness.

However they take shape, these practices not only form and guide the internal life of the community but also define the church's action within the world. Witnessing to God's creative intent for all humanity, they model and thus proclaim a different way of life to a watching world. They demonstrate how to confront division by practicing a unity that relativizes prior stratifications and classifications. They contend with materialism and consumerism by sharing the basic economic necessities of life. They confront moral relativism and societal conflict through processes of mutual accountability and loving guidance. They challenge competition and power politics by engaging in open conversation and sharing wisdom. They transform hostility and fear by creating safe spaces that welcome and honor the stranger.

Not isolated individuals but a redeemed people who are experiencing reconciliation with God and fellowship with each other is called to witness to God's intent to overcome the rebellion and alienation of humanity through the establishment of a new society of joy, righteousness, faith, and love. Salvation is not a private transaction between the individual and God, but a social reality of transformed relationships. The cultivating of missional communities through ecclesial practices is not simply an instrumental means to a desired end, but manifests in itself the very mission of the church: "The life of the church *is* its witness. The witness of the church *is* its life. The question of authentic witness is the question of authentic community."[58]

58. C. Norman Kraus, *The Authentic Witness: Credibility and Authority* (Grand Rapids: Eerdmans, 1978), 156.

Missional Leadership: Equipping God's People for Mission

Leadership in the Missional Community: Leading from the Front

The key to the formation of missional communities is their leadership. The Spirit empowers the church for mission through the gifts of people. Leadership is a critical gift, provided by the Spirit because, as the Scriptures demonstrate, fundamental change in any body of people requires leaders capable of transforming its life and being transformed themselves. The fundamental pattern is provided in the story of the conversion of Peter in his encounter with Cornelius (Acts 10–11). As the North American church is called to fundamental change, leadership formed by the reign of God needs to be rediscovered. Such leadership will be biblically and theologically astute, skilled in understanding the changes shaping North American society, and gifted with the courage and endurance to lead God's people as missional communities. Ours is a context and a time that require leaders who lead from the front, showing the way toward the recovery of a missional church.

Foundations for Missional Leadership

The purpose of leadership is to form and equip a people who demonstrate and announce the purpose and direction of God through Jesus Christ. Such leadership, through the agency of the Holy Spirit, works to create a people whose life is a witness to Jesus Christ. This point is most vivid in Paul's description of the constitution of the church in Ephesians 4. His directions for leadership emerge from his understanding of the life and ministry of Jesus Christ. It is further rooted in the Spirit's formation of the post-Pentecost community. It reaches forward to the eschatological future of God's kingdom that has already dawned with the outpouring of the Spirit and reaches back into the Old Testament to the very nature of creation. Each of these biblical perspectives illustrates that the formation of a redeemed community of the kingdom is essential to the focus of missional leadership.[1]

Paul is eager for the Christians of Ephesus to understand how essential the oneness of the church is to the life of the body of Christ. This emphasis on the oneness of the body is missiological.[2] It incarnates and demonstrates the reality of Ephesians 1:9-11, where Paul's doxological introduction announces that in Christ has been revealed the secret of God's purposes for all creation. That purpose is to make all things one in and through Jesus Christ. The church, as the body of Christ, is called to live this new reality.

Alongside the theme of oneness, Paul speaks of the church's calling or vocation. These words describe the constitution of the church and "involve the appointment to, and the equipment for, a task to be fulfilled among other peoples or persons."[3] The church comprises those bound together by this vocation as the signal and announcement of what God has accomplished in Jesus Christ. Ephesians 4:11-13 indicates that certain ministries in the form of individuals (apostles, prophets, evangelists, pastor-teachers) are given to the church by Christ, "in order that the church fulfill her present task (vs. 12), and, at the end, reach the goal set

---

1. In this discussion with Paul's account of leadership in Ephesians 4 we are not unaware of the critical questions which surround this epistle. Those issues do not, in our view, diminish the widely shared conviction that this document is essential for the foundation of a missiological leadership. This passage is one of the paradigmatic sections of Scripture in many contemporary renewal movements that seek to reestablish a lay-centered church functioning out of a gift-empowered community. This has been a healthy and appropriate corrective to much of the clericalization of the church, but it often misses the crucial missiological character of these texts for leadership.

2. Marcus Barth, *Ephesians: Translation and Commentary on Chapters 4–6*, Anchor Bible 34A (Garden City, N.Y.: Doubleday, 1974), 457ff.

3. Ibid., 454.

for her (vs. 13)."[4] These ministries of leadership are given to enable the church to carry out its fundamentally missiological purpose in the world: to announce and demonstrate the new creation in Jesus Christ. This purpose necessarily involves leaders in equipping and guiding the body in those ecclesial practices that form the community in a oneness that is a living demonstration of the ethics of God's reign.

Although contemporary discussions of the Ephesians 4 texts on leadership concentrate on the ways they liberate ministry for all God's people, Paul directs his underlying argument primarily at how leaders form and equip missional communities to be demonstrations of the radical new reality of Christ's reign in the midst of the world. Paul's conception of this process of leadership comes directly from his understanding of Jesus Christ as the one who fulfills God's promises and reveals God's purposes for all creation.

Missional leadership is shaped by the revelation of Jesus Christ. In the incarnation, through Jesus' life, death, and resurrection, what was hidden from before creation is now out in the open: God is bringing all things into a healed oneness under the authority of Jesus. Jesus brings a new social reality, a healed creation. By implication, leaders, in the name of Jesus, guide the community of God's pilgrim people as the sign and witness of what has happened to the world in and through the incarnation of Jesus Christ.

In Jesus the reign of God has become present. In his actions and resurrection he demonstrates that God is acting incarnationally to redeem and renew creation. He announces that the future of creation is directed toward this community of God's reign. This reign is grounded in the Old Testament but its meaning and scope are filled out in the revelation of Jesus. In calling and sending out disciples, in his prayer for those who followed him that they would, in their love and unity, be the new people who belong to God (John 17), Jesus indicated that his mission was the formation, fulfillment, and empowerment of a new community, a new people created and sent by God. By implication, leadership finds its most significant definition in the same mission.

Throughout his ministry, and preeminently in his death, Jesus faced the opposition of the principalities and powers. His resistance to these powers indicates that the way toward God's new future is built on the faithful obedience of the Son to the Father. Thus we understand that

4. Ibid., 478.

the reign of God comes into being amid opposition. For the church, this means that it encounters in all times and places the same opposition from the principalities and powers, as we have emphasized in chapter five. Any missional leadership must face the temptation to reduce the life of the church solely to abilities and skills offered by the principalities and powers. Jesus shows that leadership in the reign of God only comes from obedience to the Father. Therefore missional leadership requires a spirituality that lives in close relationship with and reliance on the directions of the Father through the Spirit. The practice of regular spiritual disciplines (the ecclesial practices) is essential for such a life in Christ's footsteps.

Because Jesus was given the messianic task of inaugurating the reign of God by living and announcing its presence, his leadership was fundamentally apostolic. In his calling of the disciples, he brought together a group of followers to demonstrate the character of the reign he came to announce. But the method by which Jesus formed his disciples was as central to his apostolic task as was the invitation to become a disciple and his proclamation of the good news. Jesus led the disciples into the ways of God's reign through a dynamic, reciprocal interaction between demonstrating the nature of that reign himself and teaching about its meaning.

When Jesus spoke about his "sheep," he was referring to those wandering outside God's reign who needed to be reached by the good news. Thus, even in this most pastoral of images, the central meaning is apostolic. Jesus provides us with a clear sense of how leadership is to function in our day. Its central focus is to be that same apostolic mandate of leading out a people as the community of the kingdom. The place of leadership is to be at the front of the community, living out the implications and actions of the missional people of God, so all can see what it looks like to be the people of God. This means that leadership can never be done in solo. Jesus himself spoke of leading apostolically in the context of the Trinity. Leadership that demonstrates this apostolic nature of the kingdom will take place through a plurality of leaders. They will guide the particular community in their cultivation as a missionary people, especially through the responsible use of the ecclesial practices (see chap. 6). Their leadership will be especially evident as they equip and inform the community to discern God's will for its missionary action.

Leadership in the missional church will therefore necessarily be more than preaching and teaching. These critical aspects function in the dynamic interaction of kingdom demonstration. This is what makes leadership in the missional church inherently apostolic. It must be directly involved in the works of the divine reign for an effective communication of the words of God's reign. Jesus made clear that his apostolic mandate was itself operative out of the relationality and plurality of the Trinity. He did nothing without the Father's direction; he did all the works of the kingdom through the power and anointing of the Spirit.

Missional leadership is shaped by the Spirit's formation of the post-Pentecost community. At Pentecost the Spirit inspired the new community of God's reign and sent that community of the resurrected Christ into the world. The apostles' speech in many tongues at Pentecost signified the Spirit's intent to make of this community a people sent as a sign, foretaste, and agent and instrument of the Father's redeeming actions for the whole creation throughout its diverse cultural contexts. The nature of missional leadership is understood against this background. It is shaped by the determinative action of the Spirit in the formation of the church for the sake of the world.

As Paul indicates in Ephesians 4, the Spirit calls leaders for the church. The book of Acts further indicates that these leaders function in a variety of ways. Not all are apostles, although they are all, in some sense, interpreters of the Word. Their foundational identity is inextricably tied to the forming of a people whose life witnesses to the reality of Jesus Christ and the presence of God's reign for a world deeply in need of both. No matter what specific forms leadership must take at any one point in time, the Spirit guides leadership in order to bring into reality a future-present messianic community of the reign of God, and the Spirit equips that leadership to lead the community into missional engagement with the context in which they live. Missional formation as a community, missional identity through practices of the divine reign, and missional engagement in the actions and announcements of God's reign are the ways leadership functions under the Spirit.

Missional leadership is shaped by the recovery of eschatology. The Spirit of God, which is the Spirit of Jesus, leads the people of God's reign and their leadership into an eschatological future that is present among them now, even if only imperfectly. Eschatology is not only about the end of the world. It is about the future breaking in today with an alternative order known as the reign of God. The announcement of Jesus that in his coming the kingdom of God had drawn near (Mark 1:14-15) was a declaration that God's future — the *eschaton* — was present in the world.

Jesus' acts of healing were signs that God's reign had broken into the world. His language of entering the house of the strong man to bind him demonstrated Jesus' own self-understanding of his role in relation to the kingdom. The church is the future-present messianic community promised throughout the history of God's dealings with his people.

Missional leadership is formed within the context of this eschatological understanding of the church. William Abraham described how, for the early Christians, eschatology had to do with events that had recently transpired in their midst. It was not just a matter of future hope beyond the horizon of history. Their experience was that God's reign had already dawned, bringing new direction and power to their lives. In Jesus, the events of the new age were already under way.[5] The closing images of Revelation are a vision of what God is doing in the present and will bring to completion in the future: a redeemed creation characterized by a new people in a new city where God dwells in their midst. Missional leaders are to form a people shaped by this vision. "They guide and serve the process of ecclesial formation . . . and ecclesial mission — that is, to enable the church to *realize* its ecclesial essence, to be a community of faith, hope, and love, a sign and sacrament of the kingdom of God."[6]

Missional leadership shapes a people who demonstrate and announce God's intention for creation. The church's eschatological vision of the future-present reign of God is universal. But it is always and everywhere lived out in the particular locales of created existence. The created order locates people in specific cultures, and God invites the missional community to cooperate with the ongoing work of God's creating in their particular location.

The creation is a missional act of the triune God. The God who creates is the three-in-one of the Trinity. Out of the dynamic relationship within the Trinity the creation is called forth. As an expression of God's own nature, creation itself is to reflect the dynamic interrelationship of God. This means that creation is fundamentally and inherently relational in nature and intention. Thus the stewardship and dominion given to created humanity is to cooperate with the Creator in calling

5. William J. Abraham, *The Logic of Evangelism* (Grand Rapids: Eerdmans, 1989), 19-38.
6. Peter Hodgson, *Revisioning the Church: Ecclesial Freedom in the New Paradigm* (Philadelphia: Fortress, 1988), 98.

forth a relationally shaped creation. Humanity's awesome dignity is found in its call to be the ambassador of God in the ongoing creation of community. In this sense, humanity is given a deeply and profoundly priestly role between God and the rest of creation. God has begun the great work of creation, and the *imago Dei* invites us to take up the task of completing the work of creation. As priests to the God of creation, we are offered the opportunity to unfold the relational mystery of the created order and present it complete to our Lord and God. As priests to the creation, we have the missional responsibility to show forth both the sovereignty and the healing power of the Creator in relation to the creation.

Leadership in the redeemed community will be shaped by these understandings of humanity's original purpose and God's missional intention for creation. Although the unity of creation has been broken, God's purpose is to make it one and whole again. This divine missional intention is carried forward through God's Son, the outpouring of the Spirit, and the creation of the redeemed community.

Like the community it serves, leadership is shaped by this holistic framework, but it participates in the healing of the whole creation by addressing the relational dysfunctions in the creation in that part of the whole where particular missional communities reside. We have emphasized that creation locates people in culture. The first humans were placed in a specific location and so too have been all humans since. We cannot escape the reality of place nor should we, and the fact that creation locates us contextually has important implications for leadership.

Located always in particular places, the church inevitably sits between the gospel and a specific cultural context. Therefore the church's leadership seeks to express the gospel in ways that speak to the realities of their sociocultural setting. Missional leaders must understand their context and interpret that context to the church so that a faithful and relevant witness emerges. As God's wise stewards, they will love that part of creation in which they have been placed, but also aid God's sent people in calling their part of creation into the relational fullness that God originally embedded throughout creation and that the gospel seeks to restore.

Contextuality, however, implies limitations. While we are called to embrace our location, we neither see nor understand all that is going on either in our portion of creation or in the whole. Therefore leaders will never have the whole answer nor will they be able to see clearly through the glass of their context. These limitations mean that leadership must be self-critical of its very relative vision, and leaders should not operate in the certainty of their own knowledge and skills but rather under the sovereignty of God, who leads in ways far beyond our understanding.

While wanting to be shaped by biblical models, our current forms of leadership often do not fit the description of scriptural missional leadership just presented. In order to understand the ways in which this apostolic leadership should be formed in the context of North America, it is necessary to examine briefly how elements of our heritage have altered our images of leadership away from this apostolic identity. This overview will provide a bridge to a proposal for how missional leadership might be recovered in the North American churches.

The Context of Leadership: Priest, Pedagogue, and Professional

The shape of leadership in any particular location is a matter of historical antecedents and deep cultural values. History and culture affect our present understanding of church leadership, and in North America two movements in particular have dramatically informed our present understanding of such leadership rules. They are Christendom and modernity.

Leadership in Christendom: From Apostles to Priests

By the time that Constantine began the process of establishing Christianity as the official religion of the Roman Empire, a priestly model of church leadership had already emerged in response to the pressures of heresies and the need to disciple the converted. By the third century, Clement of Alexandria (d. 215) could describe an early hierarchy in which priests controlled the saving knowledge of the gospel. This represented an emerging shift from a functional notion of leadership in which individuals' gifted abilities were dynamically employed among the people of God to a distinct and separate clergy office entrusted with the knowledge required for the proper life of the church.

The term *priest* was not applied to Christian clergy until around the year 200. But thereafter a theology and practice were forged that created a priesthood of sacramental, holy orders in which the power of Christ's presence resided. The emerging priestly order removed church leadership from ordinary existence, as priestly leaders were expected to practice a specialized order of life different from everyone else. Amid this transposition in leadership, then, rank and role increasingly displaced the New Testament experience of gift and charisma. Concomitant with this development were related changes in the church's condition and self-perception. The church moved into a more settled, established, and organized form. No longer a mission band of God's people, it became a religious organization in which the means of grace were sacramentally communicated through an ordained priesthood and the reign of God identified with the church structures and its sacraments.

Constantine's sanction of Christianity in the first half of the fourth century accelerated these changes as the church forged a radically new relationship with the state. Many viewed the state's embrace of the church as the hand of God working in church and empire to bring God's reign to earth. The practices and training of the church's leadership were significantly formed by the assumptions of the empire even as the empire was itself transformed by the Christian presence at its center.

Becoming the empire's official cultus transformed a struggling church into the conquering, victorious people of God. Images of the body of Christ as a minority band following in the footsteps of an alternate Lord from the margins of society disappeared. Priest and cleric now served as spiritual guides to a huge empire. From the perspective of the fourth century, Christianity appeared to be the culmination of human history. The fight and struggle were over. Kingdoms of this world had become the kingdom of the church's Lord and Christ. Such a new location signified divine favor, and leadership in the now ascendant church was reshaped to fit its new status. Following the protocols of Roman organization and codification, an administrative hierarchy received greater distinction. As state regulators, bishops accredited those coming into the priesthood. The emergence of celibacy among the clergy further accentuated the division between leader and people. No longer based on gift and function, ordination was state sanctioned and an institutionalized office gained through rank and study. Clerical embodiment of the means of grace and office defined the church. The governing principle became "No clergy, no church." From a community of God's people, the church became a "place where" one received grace through a state-sanctioned priesthood.

As the church took over pagan basilicas or built worship centers with similar design, liturgy and order took shape to fit both the basilica and the social appropriation of power implicit in the building's forms. Priests became the manufacturers and operators of liturgies and orders shaped by empire and basilica. Although one may fault these changes because of their long-term consequences, they were nevertheless quite understandable given the circumstances. After a long period of struggle and periodic brutal persecution, it would have been difficult not to believe that the purposes of God had been achieved through the Constantinian settlement. There was certainly an alternative history of protest from the edges of the official church theology, but the pattern was nevertheless set and Christendom born. From the fourth century on, the ideologies and normative structures of power at the heart of the state slowly, silently, but potently came to define the nature of leadership within the church. Transposition became co-option.

Christendom represented a settled, static, Christian world in which clergy functioned as a separate order of society. The priesthood symbolized the unity of faith and life. Membership in the church through baptism was concomitant with citizenship in the state. Thus mission was politicized and the *missio Dei* completed. The church was a community focused on worship, sacrament, and spiritual care. The priest was shepherd to a static people and the provider of the focused and limited mission of caring for the church's members by ordering and dispensing the means of grace in a geographic locale. Leadership had a settled, pastoral identity now. The apostolic, as in missional, nature of leadership evaporated under these conditions.[7] While early creeds affirmed the church as one, holy, catholic, and apostolic, now these marks defined priestly orders as expressions of its essence. These marks were held as attributes defining the priestly orders. Apostolicity no longer described the action of the people of God in missional engagement. Instead, it meant the succession of priestly authority.

7. Wilbert Shenk, *Write the Vision: The Church Renewed* (Valley Forge, Penn.: Trinity Press International, 1995), 35.

Leadership in the Reformation: From Priests to Pedagogues

The Reformation did not substantively alter the role or understanding of clergy developed in earlier centuries. Christendom's assumptions about the nature of ecclesial leadership continued. The magisterial Reformers addressed ecclesiological questions to the institutional church that had been and would continue. New definitions of the "true church" based on the marks of pure doctrine, pure sacramental administration, and pure discipline shaped the Protestant-Christendom conception of church and clergy. The church as static server of religious grace and power within a Christian society was neither challenged nor transformed by the Lutheran, Reformed, and Anglican reformers.

The Reformation challenged and reformed the inherited priestly categories of leadership only to create a more pedagogical identity for the clergy in which such leaders became the keepers and guarantors of the Word. Teaching and preaching, oversight of right doctrine, and proper administration of the sacraments became the normative forms of Protestant leadership. The clerical paradigm remained embedded in the practices of these churches. Leadership continued as a separate clergy class, and gradually the qualifications for leadership came to be closely identified with schooling and academic qualifications. Even the priestly vestments were exchanged by some Reformation traditions for the gown of the pedagogue.

The Radical Reformers, or Free Church movement, created alternative, if minority, ecclesiologies. Rejecting Christendom, they sought to recover a more apostolic and functional leadership based on neither a priestly-sacerdotal nor pastoral-pedagogue model of leadership. Although this recovery of an organic, lay-led church seeking to restore pre-Constantinian images of church and leadership remained a minority movement, it is currently being reassessed as churches come to terms with their post-Christendom context.

Leadership Following the Enlightenment: From Pedagogue to Professional

From the mid-seventeenth century to the mid-eighteenth century, Christendom began to unravel as modernity took shape.[8] In the words of John Donne:

> 'Tis all in peeces, all cohaerance gone;
> All just supply, and all Relation:
> Prince, Subject, Father, Sonne, are things forgot,
> For everyman alone thinkes he hath got
> To be a Phoenix, and that there can bee
> None of that kinde, of which he is, but hee.[9]

The Enlightenment particularly challenged the church and its place in the social context. The church and its theologians sought to respond to the new demand for a foundation rooted in reason. The place of theology and the training of clergy were significantly altered by these efforts. Training clergy for parish leadership had a long-established history at the center of European educational institutions. In the nineteenth century, theologians like Friedrich Schleiermacher attempted to sustain theology's place in the academy by proposing a new model based on the scientific study of religion's role in culture. This model would create a paradigm for the religious leader as a professional among other professionals and the theological faculty as equals to their counterparts in the empirical sciences.

Arguments for this shift in understanding were founded on science and rationalism as applied to the study of culture. It was argued that scientific study showed religion to be an irreducible dimension of human activity and one essential for the proper functioning of a culture. Since faith and religion were critical to society and both were the focus of the church, the church required an educated leadership as did other dimensions of society like law and medicine. A university education provided the cognitive foundations for law and medicine, and so it should provide the same for church leadership. Just as the faculties of law and medicine, based on scientific rationalism, trained practitioners with high levels of skill fitting their particular profession, the faculty of theology, with the

---

8. See Stephen Toulmin, *Cosmopolis* (Chicago: University of Chicago Press, 1990).

9. Ibid., 66.

same scientific rational foundations, should train clergy practitioners as professionals in the skills of ministry.

This shift essentially placed the training and functioning of church leadership in a new setting organized or controlled by Enlightenment categories of competency. Religion represented a positive science, and this positivist knowledge formed the basis for educating a professional clergy for tasks and responsibilities within the religious culture of a fading Christendom. This educational paradigm has continued into the twentieth century; seminary training remains firmly committed to the model of preparing a professional clergy for a set of tasks considered to be "ministry."[10] Edward Farley emphasizes that in the twentieth century the clerical paradigm of Christendom has shaped and determined the curricula and ethos of seminaries in North America. Indeed, its most potent expression was and is the seminary. This paradigm and, therefore, seminaries make the "discrete, public, and congregational tasks of the ministry the rationale and unity of theological studies. . . . This means that the areas and disciplines of theological study either directly deal with those tasks or find their justification in those tasks."[11]

Moreover, across the varieties of today's models of ministry, there remains this underlying notion of church leadership functioning as specialized professionals. Whether the leadership is that of the social activist, the megachurch entrepreneur, or the therapist-pastor, all are seen to require some aspect of professionalized training.

This view effectively eclipses the gifts for leadership in the non-ordained contingent of God's sent people, those known in Christendom as the laity. Ministry remains identified with the static roles of clergy as priest, pedagogue, or professional, all dispensers of spiritual resources. Even where the priesthood of all believers stands as a theological conviction of an ecclesiastical community, it is rarely practiced in the church. In most denominational structures, leadership in the church involves a series of clearly marked requirements that mean few can give leadership without some form of seminary education that prepares them for ordination to the professional ministry. Therefore the priesthood of all believers is continually undermined by the practices of ordination.

---

10. Edward Farley, *Theologia: The Fragmentation and Unity of Theological Education* (Philadelphia: Fortress, 1983), 114.

11. Ibid., 115.

Recent Shifts in the Professional Paradigm

The image of the ministerial professional has proved to be as unsatisfying and subject to change as its two predecessors, the priest and pedagogue. Urbanization, capitalism, the nation-state, and rising demographic diversity from immigration particularly in North America have restructured society and the location of the church within it. The North American perception of living in a churched culture has collapsed under the weight of such change. The identity of religious leaders at the center of society was lost as clergy found themselves in a social context that did not recognize, honor, or require their function except in the passages of life. In like manner, the church was decentered as its role shifted from public cultus to private vendor of inner spiritual resources.

This decentering resulted in an anxious search for identities and roles to replace those that were being displaced. A rediscovery of the laity returned to the agenda for future church leadership, but the symbols that continued to dominate leadership indicated that the North American churches still sought to restore themselves to the center of the public square. Clergy leadership paradigms, rooted in the professionalism of the schools, were reformed but not replaced as the revised symbols focused on the provisioning of personal, individual needs and the technical management of growth, market, and success so admired in modern culture. The three revisionist images of counselor, manager, and technician (which we will examine next) illustrate that the churches appropriated without question modern images of the leader as their primary means of equipping their leadership for a return to the cultural center. In doing so, they missed the opportunity to receive their marginalization, or disestablishment, as an opportunity to recover a missional identity. The problem with this move was not that it was adaptive to its cultural context but instead that its prime motivation was to regain the center rather than engage the culture with the gospel.

The Leader as Counselor

The modern notion of the individual engendered a revised form of pastoral leader. Privatized Christianity shifted from a theocentric to an anthropocentric focus with ecclesiologies shaped by human need. Pastoral identity was recast into psychological categories, with a reductionistic gospel centered on meeting the human potential of the private individual.[12] Clinical and therapeutic models of leadership began to dominate pastoral education. The pastor as counselor was an identity indicative of this shift. Questions like "What does the gospel do for me?" and "How does it further my personal development?" became paramount. This reduction of the gospel and its shaping of leaders have created a church that does not act as a sign or foretaste of the reign of God or the *missio Dei*. The assumption has seemed to be that by training leaders professionally to meet the personal, spiritual needs of the individual, the church could reacquire relevance at the cultural center. This assumption has proved not to be the case.

The Leader as Manager

Technique and rationality form an interpenetrating complex characterizing modernity. They have also become dominant paradigms for congregational leadership. Modernity required leaders shaped by management and organizational skills. But the leadership skills of management are neither morally nor ethically neutral. They are rooted in presuppositions about how the world is constructed and about human control of that world. One of the most important of those presuppositions is effectiveness. Effectiveness assumes that the goal of management is to control the processes of intricate social reality for specific ends. In late modern societies, those ends are defined in terms of market, consumption, and privatized personal need. The manager maximizes organizational effectiveness in resource capacity and market growth. These management skills have become central images of church leadership. Unless the assumptions of this paradigm are understood within the framework of a more foundational ecclesiology, leadership falls into the reductionism of effectiveness and the market.

Operational ecclesiologies have come to be based on managerial paradigms. The church renewal movement emphasizes inner organizational design. The church growth movement focuses on effectively reaching specific target groups of people. The church effectiveness movement

12. David Lowes Watson, "Christ All in All: The Recovery of the Gospel for North American Evangelism," in George Hunsberger and Craig Van Gelder, eds., *The Church Between Gospel and Culture: The Emerging Mission in North America* (Grand Rapids: Eerdmans, 1996), 180ff.

stresses leadership paradigms with ecclesial assumptions rooted in modernity. At denominational, local, and seminary levels, the management paradigm dominates models of leadership development as if it were a neutral set of techniques and skills. The nature of leadership is thus transformed into the management of an organization shaped to meet the spiritual needs of consumers and maximize market penetration for numerical growth. Schools of management now replace medical and law schools as the professional model shaping seminary leadership training.

The Leader as Technician

The technical application of scientific rationalism assumed that it is possible to control life by manipulating our environment to achieve the ends we desire through specific techniques. With the right tools and skills it is always possible to get the job done. Technique makes the inscrutable, scrutable. The reign of God, an opaque reality wrapped in the mystery of God's purposes, becomes achievable with human wit and ingenuity. As a result, the perception is created that there is always a right technique to fulfill the church's mission statement or meet strategic goals. Technology is the handmaiden of an anthropocentric church. It is not value neutral. When training institutions equip leaders with a variety of techniques, the value system inherent in those techniques easily becomes the operational ecclesiology, defining the church's nature.

Numerous seminars offer church leaders methods on "how to _____" (fill in the blank). They provide a technique and skill ethos no different from any found in a non-Christian environment. This factor does not invalidate the insights but indicates how our ecclesiologies are shaped by factors other than a biblical understanding of the church and its leadership. What we have lost in the ascendancy of technique is the openness to mystery and the understanding of God's own inscrutable work in our midst.

As the older legitimizing roles of priest and pedagogue lost their power, that of professional came to the forefront. In this new identity, the three images of leadership as counselor, manager, and technician became the legitimating criteria that promised the church an effective means of reclaiming its place in the culture. But these professional forms of leadership, once adopted without critical assessment of their presuppositions and functionality, drive the agendas of church leadership and become operational ecclesiologies in and of themselves.

Missional Leadership in the North American Church

Missional Leadership and the Formation of Covenant Communities of the Kingdom

The marginal reality of the church is an opportunity to recover the character of the gospel as God's reign in Christ through the power of the Spirit. But leaders have had little preparation for a marginal identity. There can even be an air of unreality about this concern. Resurgent interest in religion suggests anything but marginality.[13] But the church's pacification to the private sphere of North American life indicates how much it functions on the margins of people's lives. Leadership in this context is a terra incognita. Images of exile and diaspora seem appropriate since they hold the promise of a recovery of Christian identity at the margins.[14] Such a location calls for leaders to form a covenant people who will learn again that minorities "do not prosper when majorities write their agendas."[15]

For such communities to emerge, leaders will need to become like novices, learning to recover practices that have become alien to current church experience. Becoming a novice is a difficult transition. It requires waiting and listening to the Spirit's directions, listening to the Lord's song in a strange land (Ps. 137:4).

Paul's account of leadership in Ephesians 4 is a voice novices might well attend to as [they] listen for the Spirit. Paul's definition of the function of leadership as "to equip the saints for the work of ministry" emphasizes the formation of God's people so that they can "lead a life worthy of the calling to which [they] have been called" (Eph. 4:12, 1).[16]

13. Phyllis A. Tickle, *Re-Discovering the Sacred: Spirituality in America* (New York: Crossroad, 1995).

14. This is the useful language by which Douglas John Hall describes the actual setting of the church in North America; see *Thinking the Faith: Christian Theology in the North American Context* (Minneapolis: Augsburg, 1989), 204.

15. Glenn T. Miller, "Dreaming," *Theology Today* 52, no. 2 (1995): 253.

16. The formation of such a community is what Elton Trueblood was urging upon the church immediately after World War II. See Elton Trueblood, *The Company of the Committed* (New York: Harper & Brothers, 1961). See also the description of the Church of the Saviour in Washington, D.C., in Elizabeth O'Connor, *Call to Commitment* (New York: Harper & Row, 1963); and *Journey Inward, Journey Outward* (New York: Harper & Row, 1968).

This definition calls for a leadership whose attention is directed to making concrete and practical those practices that form covenant missional communities. Such communities find their life in the tension of the already and not yet. They are on their way, moving toward the reign they experience and anticipate. Between-the-times leaders are neither triumphalistic nor quiescent. They are re-forming a collection of consumer, needs-centered individuals to live by an alternative narrative. Making a transition from the optimism of modernity to the humility of a people in exile evokes the experience of brokenness. Voicing this brokenness enables churches to feel the gulf between their present forms and the covenant community of Jesus. Evoking this voice is a deeply pastoral task. Leadership evokes, opens, and brings forth the experience of confusion and brokenness waiting to be given expression in the church today. A people who have grasped their brokenness understand that the reign of God is received as a gift. It is at this point that one can appropriate the covenant nature of the missional community.

For covenant community to emerge, church life must be repatterned. In an individualist, voluntaristic culture, people need to be led into forms of covenant identity. Few pastoral models exist that show this way forward. The exilic experience of Israel called forth such an alternate leadership. Psalm 137 describes a weeping, angry people eager to return home, unable to imagine worshiping God in a strange land. Yet there emerged people like Daniel who chose an alternative story. As a result, a people were forged into an identity for exile living. For this to occur in our situation, we must overcome current notions of *solus pastor* leadership. The corporate, Spirit-empowered leadership described in Ephesians transcends clergy-laity difference. In the missional community all are ordained to ministry in their baptism; all receive the same vocation to mission; and all are gifted in various ways for that mission as they participate in the twofold journey of the reign of God that is both inward and outward. Overcoming the professional, clergy-shaped leadership models is an essential shift toward a missional leadership.

Because it forms at the margins, missional leadership requires courage and perseverance. Missional communities will be minority churches, and minorities question the veracity of their identity over against the ascendant culture. The temptation is to lose hope, to allow the dominant culture to write one's agenda. How may leadership function in this setting?

The Shape of Missional Communities

Two issues currently pressuring the shape of pastoral leadership are the loss of ecclesial identity among those who attend churches and the priority given to reaching the unchurched and activating the inactive (affiliates). Denominations are ceasing to be important markers for religious life. Until the onset of their decline in the 1960s, they provided a framework for people's belief systems. The erosion of this religious identity, linked with the religious pluralization of society, results in more and more churches filled with people who have little sense of a cohesive belief system. People enter churches with undifferentiated assortments of beliefs — some often quite vague — garnered from a mixture of sources. They enter also as individual consumers looking for churches that meet personal needs.

Such factors place leaders in complex situations. They must deal with diverse groups and a wide spectrum of needs, beliefs, and expectations. Added to this spectrum are all the fragmenting tensions of generational needs. Leaders are pulled in multiple directions by congregations of expressive individuals whose belief systems are amorphous and changing. Further, a whole series of other pressures compels leaders to structure churches around strategies for reaching the increasing number of unchurched people. Church growth and evangelism models direct the attention of churches to reaching the unchurched and connecting with disaffected affiliates.[17] A majority of these approaches are technique and method driven. Generational studies and demographics are increasingly used as tools to develop effective strategies for reaching various groups in North America. Such tools are important resources, but they can become false substitutes for forming a missional identity. Often missing from their application is reflection on the nature of the church.

As leaders seek to address this complex situation, the tools and resources offered to them generally assume but rarely reflect on the nature of the church. Thus evangelism often is a function of recruitment. What is absent from the conversation is the crucial discussion of a missional ecclesiology. Consequently, the church is viewed as the religious, or

---

17. See, e.g., Reginald Bibby, *There's Got to Be More! Connecting Churches and Canadians* (Winfield, B.C.: Wood Lake Books, 1995); George Barna, *Church Marketing: Breaking Ground for the Harvest* (Ventura, Calif.: Regal, 1992); and *Evangelism That Works* (Ventura, Calif.: Regal, 1995); George H. Hunter III, *How to Reach Secular People* (Nashville: Abingdon, 1992).

spiritual, side of social life. It is conceived in terms of a particular expression of a universal, human religious need that must be given specific shape in North America. This shape is generally assumed to be determined by the needs of contemporary individuals. Figure 1 illustrates the relationship between the larger culture and the understanding of the church as the vendor of religious goods and services to the wider social context.

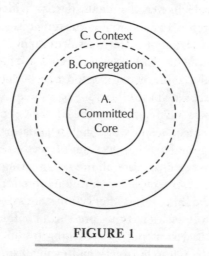

FIGURE 1

In this series of concentric circles, the inner circle A represents the committed core of a church community. These are the people active beyond attending worship services. This core is generally composed of people serving as officers, on committees, in choirs, or in other groups. They seek to live out faithful lives but give most of their church time to providing services to those who only attend. They are being consumed by the needs and demands of these people. Circle A represents people with a genuine commitment to function as bearers of the gospel. But the gospel itself is reduced to the categories of our culture. It has an anthropocentric shape since it addresses privatized individuals' needs. The church thus becomes a voluntaristic association, providing individuals with personal, spiritual influences. David Lowes Watson comments that "we find narcissism . . . and individualism . . . masquerading as personal salvation and religious experience, . . . as a privatized soteriology and spiritualized discipleship, . . . leaving the powers and principalities of the present world unchallenged."[18] This

18. Watson, "Christ All in All," 180.

results in the core of the church spending an enormous amount of its time servicing those who attend and consume what the church offers. The core is focused on how to meet the needs of attenders in the name of the gospel. This is where leadership currently expends a great deal of its energies and skills. Seminaries train leaders for this role.

The next circle (B), the congregation, includes the core (A). Circle B is composed largely of affiliates who expect services but have minimal ownership. It is a voluntary association of expressive individuals. Again, leadership spends a large part of its time responding to the expectations and needs of these people. Leaders have been equipped to look after the mixture of personal spiritual needs that function in this circle of affiliates. This task becomes increasingly complex as more and more people lose any essential sense of Christian identity. Leaders respond to this circle by spending an increasing amount of time developing strategies to move these affiliates into the core that they perceive as being the real church. Circle B is represented by a dotted rather than a solid line to indicate that there is no longer a clear line of distinction between those who belong to a congregation and those who are outside.

The final circle (C) represents the context. The unchurched and the seekers reside here. Much of the activity in A and B is spent convincing unchurched people to connect with a particular brand of church. The energies of leaders are dissipated, first, in meeting the needs of individuals within the core and affiliates segments of the congregation (A and B), and second, shaping the congregation's ethos to meet the needs of those in the context who are not yet in the congregation. The focal energy of leadership is directed toward getting people into the center, A, but the location where the leader expends most of his or time and energy is in circles B and C. All of this assumes a reductionistic gospel of meeting personal, individualistic needs. This assumption is what generates vendor-type ecclesiologies. Because the gospel is envisioned in terms of private, individual, subjective experience, leaders struggle to form religious identity out of an assortment of individuals, each with one's own sense of how one's spiritual needs are to be met. Direction is determined by the needs of both those in the church and the unchurched. The professional pastor needs, obviously, the skills of counselor, manager, and technician to begin to meet all these demands. Energy moves outward toward the periphery and adjusts the inner life of the congregation and the activity of the pastor to individualized needs.

A way of leading is required that takes seriously the creation of a covenant community as sign and foretaste, agent and instrument of the reign of God. In this community, direction is determined by God's intention to create a pilgrim people "who are always on the move, hastening to the ends of the earth to beseech all to be reconciled to God. . . . Therefore the nature of the Church is never to be finally defined in static terms, but only in terms of that to which it is going. It cannot be understood rightly except in a perspective which is at once missionary and eschatological."[19] Such an understanding redirects the church away from a needs-determined perspective. Context is placed under the larger call to be the pilgrim people of God.

When leaders are shaped primarily by contextual needs, they fail to connect the gospel in a specific setting with its eschatological nature. The gospel's eschatological horizon makes leaders aware that the church is always more than context. The needs of the churched and unchurched are not the primary agenda of leadership. The reign of God in Christ, the social reality of the redeemed community, determines the church's direction. The pointer in figure 2 indicates this eschatological direction that must shape all that the church is and does in a context. The image of the pilgrim people, moving in and toward the reign of God, is the center of the church's life and identity.

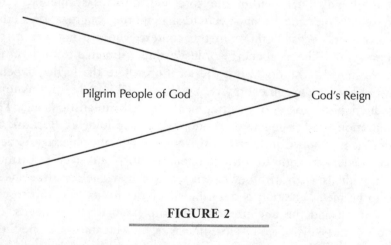

Pilgrim People of God   God's Reign

FIGURE 2

19. Lesslie Newbigin, *The Household of God: Lectures on the Nature of the Church* (London: SCM, 1953), 18.

From this directional basis it is possible to reshape the ways in which leaders function. The understanding of missional leadership that we are developing is based on a way of interpreting the nature and structure of the particular community or local congregation. To develop this interpretation, we propose to use concepts taken from sociological analysis: bounded and centered sets. The difference between these two dimensions of the life of the missional community will be crucial for the formation of missional leadership.

Bounded Sets and Churches. Bounded and centered sets are two ways that organizations establish identity. Biological cells are examples of bounded-set structures. Their membranes provide structure and shape to the cell. The membrane controls and defines what enters or leaves the cell. Organizations like clubs and societies have initiation rites through which prospective members must move before they can join. People accept the rules of an organization before being allowed into membership. Bounded sets give mechanisms of structure and control to institutions. Generally, such bounded sets are clearly articulated and understood by those within and outside the organization. They act as walls of demarcation establishing boundaries for the group and defining its identity.

Congregations and denominations have functioned by providing just such spiritual, social, and cultural boundaries. They have established at the outset the rules, expectations, and folkways of the particular denomination. People used to be clear about what belonging demanded and involved. If not committed to them, they understood that these bounded sets existed. Those within a congregation (A and B in fig. 1) are more or less committed to these boundary expectations that form their identity. In this sense, the understanding of church schematized in the diagram above represents a bounded-set model. The operative function of leaders and those at the core is to move people across the boundaries. As the church continues to lose its identity in North America, we witness the erosion of these boundaries. Continuing the bounded-set model now creates significant obstacles for people entering the church, and the erosion of bounded-set identity creates confusion around the nature of belonging.[20]

---

20. This situation is illustrated by the widespread tendency to make the process of becoming a church member as simple and unchallenging as possible; this is called the "low threshold approach," and it assumes that disciplined nurture of new members will follow — which rarely happens.

Denominations once provided bounded-set identity. People could travel from one church in the denomination to another, and the worlds within those churches would have had a clearly identified commonality. Congregations had clearly set understandings of what it meant to belong. Written into constitutions were detailed descriptions of the processes for getting in and the rules of belonging. Membership was all spelled out up front. This has broken down in recent times as this kind of bounded-set identity becomes increasingly difficult to sustain in a pluralized setting.

Centered Sets in the Church. Centered-set organizations do not define membership and identity at the entrance points or boundaries. The centered-set organization invites people to enter on a journey toward a set of values and commitments. For example, in the model that we have been developing in this book, the direction toward which people would be invited to move is the gospel's announcement of God's reign that is forming a people as God's new society. Therefore the center to which we would be moving has two components. First, it is the biblical understanding of the reign of God that is present and yet ahead of us, awaiting its completion in Christ. It is always before us, always a direction toward which we are moving. That is why the language of "pilgrim people" is so appropriate. Second, it takes concrete form and expression in the formation of a covenant people living in faithfulness to the reign of God. The center has an identity and location among a people. Here the language of the "city on a hill" is appropriate. In our pluralistic context, where people search in multiple directions and struggle to understand the nature of Christian life, a centered-set model represents the church as a people on the way toward the fullness of God's reign in Jesus Christ. People are constantly being invited to move toward and into a covenant, disciple community. This kind of centered-set church is open to all who may want to be on this journey. It has a permeability that is open to others since it seeks to draw others alongside and minister to people at every level on the way.

In this model, what we have traditionally defined as the congregation (indicated by circle B in fig. 1) becomes a centered-set structure.

The dotted line in figure 3 indicates that entrance on the journey is not a bounded-set commitment. This reflects, contextually, the missionary situation of the churches in North America. Many of those in congregations are confused about what it means to be a Christian. As religious hunger increases, people attending churches bring with them a wide variety of spiritual beliefs. They are testing meanings received

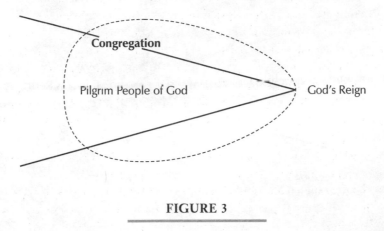

FIGURE 3

in the church through their own filtering systems. Christian teaching is grafted onto personal belief systems. These people make up an increasing percentage of congregational populations. A centered set invites such people to go on a journey. It addresses our situation missionally, enabling leaders to understand the actual situation in congregations. This is not a sufficient understanding of the church; it is hardly the church as the sign, foretaste, agent, and instrument of the reign of God. But congregation as centered set begins to lay out a framework for forming congregations into missional communities.

Missional communities are more than centered-set congregations. A pilgrim, covenant people require an alternative way of life. This calls for bounded-set identity. Within the centered set will form a covenant community, illustrated by a second ellipse in figure 4.

The solid line symbolizes a bounded set. The missional community must be both centered and bounded. But where does each operate? The centered-set congregation invites people onto a journey with Jesus in order to understand its contours, to hear its stories, to sort out the issues and questions of commitment and discipleship. While the direction of the journey is the reign of God, the community is where people can discover and encounter the meaning of this larger journey. This journey, as a pilgrim people, calls for commitments to practices of the reign of God that can be made only in covenant. Such practices need to be encountered and demonstrated so that people might see the implications of the journey. The covenant community is a bounded set composed of

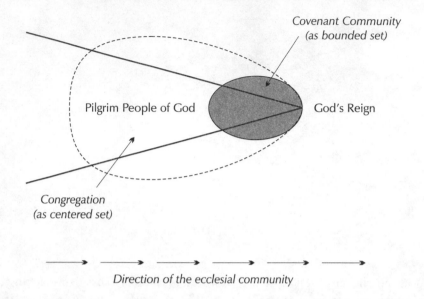

Covenant Community
(as bounded set)

Pilgrim People of God

God's Reign

Congregation
(as centered set)

Direction of the ecclesial community

FIGURE 4

those who have chosen to take on the commitment, practices, and disciplines that make them a distinct, missionary community.

Leading the Missional Church as a Covenant Community. Those choosing to enter this kind of covenant community would become part of an order bound together through specific practices and disciplines. Missional leaders would focus their time, energy, and thinking on the formation of this covenant people. They would be shaped by clearly identified disciplines of Christian life and accountability.[21] In such a community, disciplines of three types would form a secular order. They would be spiritual disciplines of a common life, disciplines of learning, and disciplines of mission.[22] "Secular order" means that people commit them-

---

21. This covenant community aspect of the church has affinities to Wesley's band of disciples. The missions groups that shape the Church of the Saviour in Washington, D.C., are an example of such a covenant community. See O'Connor, *Journey Inward;* Gordon Cosby, *Handbook for Mission Groups* (Waco: Word, 1975).

22. One contemporary example of this approach would be the Servant Leadership School developed out of the Church of the Saviour and now being appropriated by a variety of groups in North America.

selves to an ordered, covenant life within the reality of their everyday callings as spouses, children, siblings, workers who live in neighborhoods, and those who work in the larger community. We need to shape and direct the formation and equipping of leadership toward the generation of these new orders within existing churches. Leaders will need skills in spiritual formation and missional encounter as well as organizational development and management of complex systems.

The mission community is a bounded set within a centered-set organization. This language reflects the biblical imagery of a pilgrim people and gives concrete form to what it might mean for a church to reappropriate the language of being a city on the hill. The bounded-set nature of the disciple community reflects how Jesus chose a group of disciples (a bounded set) while at the same time inviting many to come and see where he was going. Thus the bounded-set style of the covenant community is not closed to the outside but constantly inviting others to come and see that they too may participate. The covenant community has a missional ministry to those who are journeying within the centered-set congregation. People can enter the covenant process at many points along the journey as they see the way of Jesus and choose to follow him.

A centered-set community invites all to enter the journey at any point they choose. There is no demand to have arrived at a specific point along the way. The way in which the community functions, that is, its worship, its fellowship, its opportunities for biblical and spiritual exploration, all announce and point toward the center. It is by definition inclusive of any and all who sense that they are attracted to the gospel and to the service of Jesus Christ but have not determined what that will mean concretely in their lives. As we describe the church in its particular community form, it functions on a continuum as illustrated in figure 5.

The Mission Community as a Continuum from Centered to Bounded Set. Figure 5 places the centered and bounded set in a relationship of continuous movement from the one to the other.

On the journey of the congregation there are places where one cannot go further without choosing to take on practices unique to the Christian life. These are points where the journey can continue with integrity only when people are intentionally bound by a common language and story, a common set of practices particular to the Christian way. When people in the congregation (the centered set) observe and participate in the ecclesial practices, they find themselves exploring the meaning of Jesus' invitation to follow him and become fishers of people. They begin

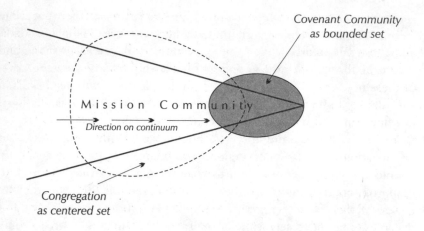

Covenant Community
as bounded set

Mission   Community
Direction on continuum

Congregation
as centered set

FIGURE 5

to grasp something of what it means to take up his cross and follow him. In the life of the missional community, there are points of movement and disciplines of transition where one may enter into the covenant community. Those in the congregation are invited to become novices in the new orders of God's missional people. For those who have never been baptized, this could be the beginning of a process of catechesis leading up to baptism as an incorporation into the covenant community.[23] For those who have been baptized but have been unclear about their Christian vocation (e.g., many who experienced infant baptism), this could become a radically revised understanding of confirmation that guides the individual into an affirmation of one's personal calling to be a disciple of Jesus Christ and an accountable member of his missionary people. In some way this envisioned process will enable the individual to make his or her confession of submission to Christ together with some clarification of what this confession will now mean missionally. The priesthood of all believers and the understanding of baptism as ordination to Christ's ministry will merge in a disciplined exploration of one's gifts, calling, and opportunities to minister as part of a missional community. In this approach, one of the primary responsibilities of the covenant community would be to guide, support, explore, and

---

23. See Patrick Keifert, *Welcoming the Stranger: A Public Theology of Worship and Evangelism* (Minneapolis: Fortress, 1992), for a provocative exposition of "liturgical evangelism" that could serve as this transition into the covenant community.

affirm these commitments as people move through a novitiate into membership. As this kind of community emerges, churches will be shaped in ways that will then engage their context missionally with the gospel; they will send their members as they understand themselves to be a sent community.

In such a missional community, leaders function on the continuum from centered to bounded set. In the centered set, the leaders need the skills that will enable them to welcome those who are outside moving in and to present those gathered in the congregation with the gifts and grace of the gospel that invite them to discipleship. These leaders need skills for reaching those who are nominal, the seekers, and the unchurched people. Their work will equip and support the congregation on its journey, however tentative and exploratory that may be. But what determines these skills and strategies for leadership is the larger image of the pilgrim people of God as a covenant community. The leaders' primary skills are directed toward intentionally forming such orders within the community.

This can only happen as leaders themselves participate in such orders. Leaders must exert the greatest attention and energy at this point for a number of reasons. First, it is the covenant community that witnesses to the gospel as an alternative logic and narrative within the social context, including in particular the larger unbounded congregation. Second, this area is precisely where leaders have been given almost no preparation; there are few models from which they can learn. The leaders themselves must therefore become a novitiate, embark on a missional apprenticeship, in order to give the kind of direction needed by the emerging missional community. This is a demanding task that cannot be given a secondary role in the church.

The two ellipses may be put together within the directional pointer. Surrounding the entire image is a larger ellipse that represents the context of the missional community. The directional pointer moves through all the ellipses. It signifies that the missional community is first and always a journeying people. The final, surrounding ellipse emphasizes that the context is critically important. The way the new community shapes its life is essentially related to the outer ellipse. But now a twofold direction takes place. First, the pointer indicates the focus of the missional community in everything it does: its life is a continuum as a people moving toward covenant commitment, toward disciplined witness. The pilgrimage of this pilgrim people moves from centered, open-ended, exploratory engagement with the gospel toward bounded, covenanted, accountable, missional commitment to the community's witness to God's reign in Christ. But this movement is not inward, turned in on itself, focused on the spirituality of the committed. The outer ellipse defines the constant goal of the missional community: to be God's witness in the larger context. The dynamic of God's reign shaping the community orients it toward engagement with its context, as a sent people. The inbreaking reign of God shapes the covenant community, invites and draws the congregation, and sends the entire missional community into its immediate context as "a royal priesthood, a holy nation, God's own people" (1 Pet. 2:9).

In this model, the orientation of leadership is transformed. In the professional model that currently prevails in our churches, leadership orientation goes two ways: inwardly toward servicing multiform congregations of expressive individuals, and outwardly toward developing strategies for reaching the religious market. The model offered here also has a twofold direction required of the leadership. First, the leaders call into being a covenant community; second, they direct its attention out toward their context. But the location of the leadership in this process is at the front of the pointer. In other words, the leadership plays primarily an apostolic role. Pastoral gifts remain critical but are relativized by the nature, purpose, and directional movement of the missional community. In this context, leadership is a calling that both engages the context with the gospel and leads in the formation of the disciplined community.[24] Being at the front means that the leadership lives into and incarnates the missional, covenantal future of God's people. The model may now be completed (fig. 6).

Forming Missional Leaders in the North American Context. How will missional leaders for such a church be formed? It will require a combination of factors. First, formation must relate to a deep sense of vocation. In many religious orders, the initiate spends time within the community listening, praying, and discerning the call of God for this particular vocation. This kind of initial formation is essential. It might mean that potential candi-

---

24. A helpful book for our approach is Eugene Peterson, *The Contemplative Pastor: Returning to the Art of Spiritual Direction* (Grand Rapids: Eerdmans, 1989). The title may suggest a return to some form of interiority that is a removal from missional engagement, but Peterson is outlining a way of leadership that is deeply missional in character.

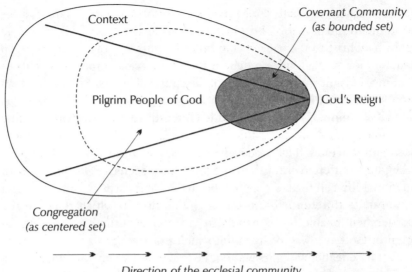

Context

Covenant Community
(as bounded set)

Pilgrim People of God

God's Reign

Congregation
(as centered set)

Direction of the ecclesial community

FIGURE 6

dates spend a year as initiates, during which time they enter theological and biblical studies and live in the context of a covenant community as preparation for discerning their calling to this vocation. Second, such leadership will be defined personally by its distinctively Christian character. This is clearly the understanding of congregational leadership that the Pastoral Epistles emphasize with their lists of the qualifications of church leaders. The integrity and spiritual maturity of those who bear responsibility for missional leadership are essential to the health of the missional church. This means that the process of selection will require a missional orientation lacking in most polities up to now. Third, academic and intellectual competency will be crucial. Missional leadership must be biblically informed and theologically grounded leadership. If the gospel of God's inbreaking reign in Jesus Christ is to shape the missional church, then that gospel must be faithfully articulated, studied, explored, and heard over and over again. The formation of missional communities is not a matter of simple methodologies but of biblically centered, continuing evangelization of the church, for which skilled evangelists are needed. Finally, skill development in spiritual and communal formation will be essential. If those who are today's "apostles, prophets, evangelists, and pastor-teachers" are truly "to equip the saints for the work of ministry, for building up the body of Christ" (Eph. 4:11-12), then they will be people given by Christ to the church with both the gifts and the ability to learn and appropriate the skills needed for this ministry of formation. Creating, forming, and cultivating new forms of the church will require far more than merely managing its present forms.

To summarize, missional leadership will require skills in evoking a language about the church that reshapes its understanding of its purpose and practices. The practices of a disciple community will require a language different from that of a voluntary society. The practices of missional life call forth a people who live by standards of judgment and action quite different from those of the culture in which they are set. Leaders will enable God's people to give voice to this language of the reign of God as a way of living into such practices.

These leadership gifts will not be found in a single individual. God never intended the church to function that way. The roles of pastor-teacher and apostle function in a plural leadership. Pastoral gifts are important, but in the current setting of the North American church, the apostolic gifts need to be called forth and equipped. While Ephesians 4 outlines a series of leadership gifts, the contemporary church focuses most of its energy on identifying, training, and credentialing that limited section of those gifts related to the pastor-teacher. This indicates the levels at which the model of the settled parish culture continues to prevail. In the marginalized, missional setting that lies ahead for the church in North America, this pastor-teacher model is insufficient.

Apostolic, missional leadership will be learned through apprenticeship within communities. Such leaders will learn firsthand how to live out the practices of community formation that require a profound involvement of the self and deep roots in Bible and theology. Becoming a people who are a sign, foretaste, agent, and instrument of the reign of God, who embody the life of Jesus through the Spirit, and who function as the city on a hill, calls for leaders schooled in such communities.

Missional leadership moves away from current models of *solus pastor*. Ephesians 4 suggests leadership teams expressing varieties of gifts and functions. The order in which Paul presents the gifts of the various leaders may not have been significant in his mind, but in terms of our discussion, that order is noteworthy. The purpose and direction of the church as a missionary people shape apostolic leadership. As we emphasize in chapter 9 the primary mark of the church is its apostolicity, its sent-ness as the witness to the good news of God's saving rule. Today apostolic leadership's function is to reestablish the reality and vitality of missional congregations. The prophetic gifts of leadership are rarely recognized or given place in our day. Yet here is a leadership calling that is truly prophetic, for its purpose is to direct the saving Word of God to the specific context into which a Christian community is sent. This is a profoundly missional expression of leadership.

We have come to see evangelists as manifesting a particular kind of leadership gift for nonlocal settings. Our current models of evangelist generally include images of itinerant ministry and mass rally events. But what if we began to think of the evangelist as having a particular leadership gifting in the local congregation? The pastor-teacher is essential to grounding and caring for the missional people of God within the community. But in dynamic combination with the evangelist he or she would best lead a missional congregation. This kind of plural leadership raises obvious questions for denominations' identification of leaders and ordination procedures as well as for schools' understanding of equipping disciples for leadership.

One potentially fruitful way of understanding this plurality is to pursue leadership as a team function in any particular geographic area. Hence the particular community would not be seen as a relatively independent unit with its own, *solus pastor* leadership. Instead, a team of leaders, each bringing unique gifts, would function within a number of connected congregations, equipping and empowering them as a missional people for a particular area. A leader among the leaders with overall apostolic gifts could provide oversight within the team of leaders as they create and lead a series of missional communities related through some structure of connectedness. Current ecclesiastical systems and judicatories could take the first steps to such an approach by examining how those in positions of bishop or area minister could make the apostolic function the heart of their callings. At present, these kinds of leaders are primarily administrators, advisors, or consultants. Certainly in congregational and free church models, area ministers function largely as consultants with vague pastoral identities. A missional church in North America needs apostolic gifting at these critical points. This would have significant implications for the way in which denominations identify bishops, area ministers, general presbyters, or conference ministers.

The gift of apostolic leaders is one that creates leaders, like Paul, who are driven by a passion to see the reality of the church as a missional people of God. Such apostolicity challenges the conserving tendencies of institutions by confronting and naming areas where change must take place. Denominations have rarely known what to do with these kinds of people. When Paul came to the church in Jerusalem after his conversion, he was cautiously received and sent off to Tarsus, a long distance from the perceived center in Jerusalem, where he waited for them to initiate contact. It was the church at Antioch that risked Paul's apostolic leadership through the support of Barnabas. It was also at Antioch that we first meet a church that had a deeply missional identity.[25] In our day, denominational systems tend to be suspicious of these more apostolic leaders and look for those with conserving, pastoral, and administrative skills to fill the roles of bishops and executive ministers. More apostolically gifted leaders tend to be placed at the edges of church bodies. They are distant from the key areas of leadership where their gifting is critical in our day. As denominations examine the ways in which they might recover a missional identity, they will need to address this key area of apostolic identity.

Denominational judicatories and educational institutions should recognize that the current processes of leadership identification and training were designed for a settled, churched culture in which the congregations are led by a pastor whose gifts are largely those of the pastor-teacher. Fundamental changes need to occur in these institutions. Just as congregations face radical transformation, denominations and seminaries must go through a similar process. Like many organizations formed in modernity, these institutions and their paradigms of leadership preparation need to be altered fundamentally in order to participate in the creation of missional congregations for North America.

Seminaries are seeking to reorient their training philosophies to equip more adequately leaders today. Such changes need to be shaped by the kind of missional ecclesiology outlined in this book. This shaping would mean the redesign of theological education. The learning process would be shaped by covenants and an intentional missional thrust. The first year of such an education might be a year for initiates who are discerning whether God is calling them to the vocation of missional leadership. Classrooms would become communities, and the initiates would live in these communities shaped by ecclesial practices and dis-

---

25. David Bosch, *Transforming Mission: Paradigm Shift in Theology of Mission* (Maryknoll, N.Y.: Orbis, 1991), 43-44.

ciplines of accountability. The remaining years of preparation would involve the initiate in a close covenant relationship between the theological training school and an actual missional community. Together they would initiate leaders-in-formation into the ways of God's sent people. The actual learning of spiritual disciplines and spiritual direction would need to shape all the work of the gathered community that made up the school.

This model of leadership formation may well require theological schools to move deliberately away from graduate school models of education with their paradigm of theory separate from practice and academic learning as an abstract enterprise based on observation rather than personal involvement. Issues of theological pluralism within the seminary would need to be addressed openly. It is often this kind of pluralism, based on the abstract, graduate school model, that makes it impossible for covenant communities of the reign of God to be formed in the schools. This may imply that the schools themselves must be shaped as bounded sets.

Structured intentional formation needs to be rediscovered within this changed paradigm of leadership formation. In this regard, the training of leaders might move in several related directions at once. In one direction, theology, history, and biblical studies — the classic or core curriculum — need to bring the great traditions of the church to bear on the diaspora situation in North America. These crucial areas of learning must be related to the actual situation of the church in North America rather than taught in the abstractionist modes of modernity. The meaning, contextuality, and theology of our exile need to inform the way leaders are prepared in these foundational areas.

Further, leaders are needed who are more than practitioners trained in methodologies. The language of "practitioner" is extremely misleading when used by those in pastoral leadership as a code word for lack of skills in theological evaluation and integrative action. They have learned the mechanical skills of managing a system when what are required are the skills of system transformation and formation. The latter require far more than learning methodologies. When the people of Israel entered their exile (Ps. 137), those well trained in the theology and practices of Jerusalem suddenly found themselves in a situation where what they were trained to provide no longer sustained or gave meaning to the people. The tradition had to be reentered to shape the new practices and theologies that would speak from the profundity of the tradition but also form and sustain a people shifted to the margins, disoriented and sorely tempted by the gods of Babylon. That is our context. Training leaders for the continuation of life in our churched-type Jerusalem will not enable those leaders to embrace our current reality. Alternative forms of training will certainly emerge outside these established centers if they do not embrace the need for missional leaders. Exile requires more than the priest, pedagogue, or professional. Leaders are needed who can think deeply about the faith in a contextual and significantly theological manner. The reorientation of the seminary as a place where theological and biblical thinking at high levels is nurtured is much needed in the missional church.

In the other direction, the practice and orientation of practical theology must undergo a fundamental transformation. Training leaders in the formation of a covenant people demands learning contexts in which classrooms have become covenant communities where spiritual formation and discipleship are practiced. One thinks of Dietrich Bonhoeffer's small pastoral training seminary in pre–World War II Germany where students lived together in covenant community, the Catholic monastic orders bound together in far more than an academic learning experience, or John Wesley's weekly class meetings around a common set of disciplines and commitments. These are examples of the direction that this kind of training needs to take. They are far closer to the type of preparation needed today. Some voices within the theological schools are calling for a return to this kind of leadership formation.[26]

Current seminary offerings in counseling, preaching, church administration, and methodologies of growth will not develop the missional leaders identified in this book. These offerings are inadequate for the formation of leaders for covenant communities. The schools will need to develop systems of training in which students become like novices who, on entering an order, assume a set of disciplines and are thereby shaped by a process of accountability far beyond these external forms of identification. The seminaries may need to become the pivotal places where these transformations occur. But they will have to become very different structures from those presently preparing leaders for the church. They themselves may need to discern how to become covenant communities in order

---

26. David Lowes Watson is currently developing this kind of program for leadership formation at Wesley Theological Seminary in Washington, D.C.

to equip leaders for the church. This is more than a schedule and management issue. It involves introducing students into a way of life.

The process of credentialing leaders in many denominations demands a similar rethinking. Credentialing depends on congregations' affirming the call and gifts of the potential ministerial candidate. The only model those congregations and candidates have by which to measure call is the *solus pastor* professional-pedagogue minister vendoring to private spiritual needs. This situation cannot be simply legislated out of existence.

Denominational judicatories need to make fundamental commitments to the development of missional leaders. They need forms of credentialing that work with the processes of formation outlined above. At the moment, those who sense God's call to a form of church other than the normative church-culture, vendoring models find few places for vocation. We are constantly losing the best and most creative leaders to more visionary and challenging areas of life because the systems of leadership identification that we have created are for a form of church life that no longer has the veracity or the power to engage these kinds of people. The maintenance and servicing of these institutions does not challenge those wanting to give their lives to something more. This is why our churches and seminaries tend to attract and educate individuals whose leadership skills enable them to do little more than manage the current institutions of North American church life. The credentialing process should be opened up so that alternative forms of leadership for missional communities emerge and attract gifted candidates for such leadership.

In the closing section of *The Gospel in a Pluralist Society*, Lesslie Newbigin summarizes the direction of his argument by stating that in such a culture as ours "the only hermeneutic of the gospel is the life of the congregation which believes it."[27] He goes on to ask what kind of leadership will nourish the church in this kind of faithful witness to the gospel in our pluralist society. The task of leadership is "to lead the congregation as a whole in a mission to the community as a whole, to claim its whole public life, as well as the lives of all its people, for God's rule."[28]

---

27. Lesslie Newbigin, *The Gospel in a Pluralist Society* (Grand Rapids: Eerdmans, 1989), 234.

28. Ibid., 238.

Then he concludes with the image of such a leader based on Pasolini's film *The Gospel According to St. Matthew*:

It shows Jesus going ahead of his disciples, like a commander leading troops into battle. The words he speaks are thrown back over his shoulders to the fearful and faltering followers. He is not like a general who sits at headquarters and send his troops into battle. He enables and encourages them by leading them, not just by telling them. In this picture, the words of Jesus have a different force. They all find their meaning in the central keyword, "Follow me."[29]

This is the character of missional leadership that the church in North America sorely needs.

29. Ibid., 240.

· 8 ·

Missional Structures:
The Particular Community

In the final three chapters of this book, we are initiating a discussion of the concrete implications of a missional ecclesiology for North America. In the previous chapter we defined the leadership needed for a church in North America that is truly missionary in nature. There we proposed a structure of the missional community as the pilgrim people of God, which always exists as the centered but unbounded congregation and the bounded covenantal community, living out its witness in its particular context. In these final two chapters, we consider some of the major structural implications of this proposal. As we assume the missional definition of the church as the sign, foretaste, instrument, and agent of God's rule in Christ, we shall ask now, How should the church organize itself for its vocation?

Principles for Shaping the Missional Church

Our basic assumption has been that God's mission is carried out through the calling and setting apart of a particular people for God's purposes. The *missio Dei* is historical and concrete. God's Holy Spirit has begun the implementation of the *missio Dei* in the calling and formation of a particular people: Israel, and from Pentecost onward, the ever-widening church that Jesus Christ engrafted upon the root of Israel. The people of God, the church, is a concrete reality, present and able to be experienced within human history. The New Testament description of the

221

church as the "body of Christ" emphasizes primarily the interdependence of all the members of the church. But at the same time, the "body" metaphor stresses the concrete, tangible, visible presence of the church in the world as the evidence of the gospel. The church is an organization that has structures, continuity, and identifiable functions. "A missional ecclesiology will always include organizational forms, but one should not see these as the essence of the church. Organization needs to serve, not determine the nature of the church with its duality of being both divine and human."[1]

When we consider the structures of the missional church, our task is to apply the theological understandings rooted in the *missio Dei* to the church's structures. The gospel shapes a people who believe, witness, practice, hope, and decide in concrete forms, specific to the culture in which that people are God's sent community. The process of missional organization is always to be carried out in a realistic interaction with the distinct cultural context within which the people of God respond to God's sending. Organizational formation is as much a form of translated witness as is the translation of the Bible into vernacular languages or the continuing exposition of the apostolic tradition in new cultural contexts. We cannot approach the task of being and becoming a missionary church in North America as though our cultural context were a clean slate. As chapters two and three have shown, we stand in the midst and are heirs of a broad and complex tradition. Thus we ask, How do we move on from here?

Three principles for the structuring of the missional church in North America emerge out of the theological approach we have developed:

1. The Scriptures function authoritatively in the formation of the churches' structures.
2. The church's catholicity demands a necessary cultural diversity for its structures.
3. The local particular community is the basic missional structure of the church.

As we examine these principles, we shall draw together the major emphases of our discussion thus far and suggest the trajectories for the formation of missional ecclesial structures in the years ahead.

1. See above, pp. 71-72.

Biblical Formation of the Church

Our approach to a missional ecclesiology for North America has attempted, at every step, to be faithful to the authoritative scriptural witness. The same Holy Spirit who formed the church at Pentecost empowers that community to encounter and respond to God's Word in Scripture from generation to generation.

When we turn to the question of mission and organization, the normative authority of the scriptural witness functions in a distinctive way. We read the Bible using a missional hermeneutic that enables us to recognize in the scriptural testimony not only the content of our message but the way in which that message is to be made known. The Bible gives us both the what and the how of missional obedience. The New Testament writings were addressed to communities already in mission; the purpose of the canonical Scriptures was (and is) to enable them to continue that mission. The Scriptures are thus the warrant for the church's mission, instructing and guiding these mission communities by engaging their situations, their challenges, and their struggles.[2]

Since in North America we are not starting with a clean organizational slate but are heirs of a long organizational tradition, this dimension of the scriptural witness is especially important for us. Our challenge is to become a truly missional church — a vocation we have severely reduced in the course of Christendom. This is not an entrepreneurial enterprise. It cannot happen in divisive ways if it is faithful to the gospel and the scriptural witness. Rather, Scripture is the Holy Spirit's powerful tool to guide our formation in the mission community that God has called us to be. "The approach needed, however, is one that starts with the biblical intent God has for the church and then reflects on how organizations might be designed to carry out that intent."[3] This ongoing effort will be shaped by the marvelous diversity of biblical images for the church that speak constantly in new ways to the organizational

2. George Hunsberger, "Is There Biblical Warrant for Evangelism?" *Interpretation* 48, no. 2 (1994): 131-44; James V. Brownson, "Speaking the Truth in Love: Elements of a Missional Hermeneutic," in George R. Hunsberger and Craig Van Gelder, eds., *The Church Between Gospel and Culture: The Emerging Mission in North America* (Grand Rapids: Eerdmans, 1996), 228-59 (originally in *International Review of Mission* 83, no. 330 [1994]: 479-504).

3. See above, p. 69.

passage of the church within history.[4] This means for the church, at every time and in every culture, a continuing process of correction, admonition, repentance, conversion, encouragement, growth, and change.

"A missiological reading of the New Testament makes clear that no one church form existed in that context. The early church was developmental in character and found expression in a number of different organizational arrangements."[5] Nevertheless, the scriptural record makes abundantly clear that the church must have structures, and that the way these structures are formed is integral to the church's witness. Some patterns of organization are found everywhere in the New Testament church, much like the way that the ecclesial practices are found everywhere that Christians are called and formed into mission communities. We see the formation of particular communities in Jerusalem, Samaria, Antioch, across Asia Minor and Greece, and in Rome. These communities formed as house churches, as assemblies in rented halls or on riversides, or as alternative synagogues. The ecclesial practices began to be practiced immediately, and the structures for continuing Christian witness emerged, borrowing from the cultural context. Regular meetings for worship, instruction, and mutual encouragement took place. Patterns of celebration developed, including liturgical hymnody, as we see in the many hymns quoted in the New Testament.

These communities adopted behaviors that expressed their witness. These were distinctive forms of witness that often challenged the norms of their social context. The communities brought Jew and Gentile, male and female, slave and slave owner into a new kind of relationship. They crossed cultural and ethnic boundaries. They evoked radical changes in the practice of land ownership and personal wealth, established common treasuries, and mandated the sharing of all worldly resources. They did not take each other to secular courts but managed their disagreements internally. They disciplined each other when circumstances required, for the sake of their witness.

Each community appears to have arranged its structures of leadership for its particular mission: elders or overseers were chosen, apostolic emissaries were sent, qualifications of leaders for the communities were

4. See Paul Minear, *Images of the Church in the New Testament* (Philadelphia: Fortress, 1977).

5. See above, p. 68.

defined. The communities recognized and evoked the spiritual gifts needed for the church's ongoing witness: hospitality, administration, generosity, as well as the various ministries of the Word. The apostolic leadership shaped communities as their teaching was drawn together into the canon, the rule for the life and practice of the church.

Special needs were addressed, such as the practical problems of the daily provision for the Hellenistic widows described in Acts 6. This serves as an example of the continuing organizational creativity of the church. To meet the needs of this group, which the Jerusalem church was not treating fairly, a board of welfare commissioners was formed. This organizational division of duties prevented the distraction of the apostles from their responsibilities, while still addressing the legitimate concerns of these women. Another example of organizational structures meeting special needs is found in the apostolic collection throughout Asia Minor to support the impoverished church in Jerusalem.

One of the most telling examples of organization for mission was the Council of Jerusalem described in Acts 15. The question of Gentile Christians presented a theological issue with profound organizational implications. It had to do with membership, rites of initiation, status and mutual recognition, and the formation of new communities as a result of mission. The theological issue at stake here was the fundamental translatability of the gospel. The apostolic community was to carry the gospel across cultural boundaries and form mission communities in new cultural contexts. This witness was to extend to the "ends of the earth" (Acts 1:8). In every process of translation, beginning with the movement from the Palestinian church to the diverse churches of the Hellenistic world, the church forms itself within a receiving culture for its continuing witness.[6] This process parallels the translation of the Scriptures into the vernacular; it is the translation of the missional community into relevant organizational forms in a given context.

The story of the council in Acts 15 illumines the character of this process. The council's decisions led to a next organizational step, the sending of a delegation with Paul and Silas to explain the council's decisions to the church at Antioch. Thus the council established the understanding that the church's decision making, however organized,

6. See David Bosch, *Transforming Mission: Paradigm Shifts in Theology of Mission* (Maryknoll, N.Y.: Orbis, 1991), 190-214; Lamin Sanneh, *Translating the Message: The Missionary Impact on Culture* (Maryknoll, N.Y.: Orbis, 1989), 9-85.

must always serve and enable its missional witness. The Holy Spirit must inform it: "it has seemed good to the Holy Spirit and to us" (Acts 15:28). The agreements of that council were considered binding guidance for all the churches of the apostolic period, even if the controversy continued. The council's missional focus is normative for the church's decision making today in every cultural context. That focus defines the church's structure.[7]

This example, with many others, indicates that the structures of the church from the outset dealt with the local particular community and the connected family of communities that was the emerging church catholic. Although diverse organizational forms existed, there was no doubt that, everywhere, each distinctive community embodied an expression of the one people of God formed by the Holy Spirit to be the witness to Jesus Christ. The structures of connectedness were likewise diverse, but they were certainly there, especially in the apostolic ministry reflected in the New Testament Epistles. When Paul wrote to Rome, a community he had as yet never seen, he addressed the way they functioned as a community, dealing with their behavior and structures authoritatively. He assumed that their confession of the same gospel (Rom. 1–11) meant that there were necessary practices and disciplines with their structural implications (chs. 12–16) that he could address from across the seas. Their common vocation and what it meant for their distinctive life as a mission community connected them. The structures of connectedness linking all the churches of the first century were necessarily and primarily missional. Thus, while no particular organizational tradition can legitimately claim that its visible shape conforms to the New Testament church, the scriptural witness makes clear that all structures that enable the community to carry out its mission and to engage in the ecclesial practices common to all followers of Jesus can claim to be in succession from the first churches.

Although form follows missional function in the New Testament church, the scriptural witness does show us how missional communities are planted and nurtured in particular contexts. The structures of par-

---

7. "The New Testament's pronouncements on Church order are to be read as a *gospel* — that is, Church order is to be regarded as a part of the proclamation in which the Church's witness is expressed, as it is in its preaching" (Eduard Schweizer, *Church Order in the New Testament*, tr. Frank Clarke, Studies in Biblical Theology 1/32 [Naperville: Allenson, 1962], 14).

ticular churches will always emerge out of the interaction of the gospel with the cultural context. The challenge that ecclesial structures must meet is to enable the missional community to function faithfully in its specific cultural context. To put it another way, the structures of the church are to incarnate its message in its setting. In its visible form, the church is to demonstrate the dominical instruction, "By this everyone will know that you are my disciples, if you have love for one another" (John 13:35).[8]

In every particular cultural setting, the structural decisions of the church are a basic form of witness to the gospel. The church, like the incarnation, is never a nebulous abstraction. It is instead a concrete reality formed in specific cultures for its mission. The missionary story that unfolds in Acts can be read as the first Christians' discovery of the concrete, organized shape of their mission as the church in the Mediterranean cultures of the first century. As summarized above, everything they did had to be done organizationally in a way that demonstrated the transforming power of the gospel in a particular situation.

It was not always immediately obvious how this was to be done in the cultural context of Jerusalem or Antioch, Asia Minor or Greece. Working out the shape of faithful witness entailed struggle, even conflict. How such conflicts were resolved provided a particularly important form of witness, a demonstration of the church's response to the lordship of Christ. The Holy Spirit was given to enable the church to become Christ's witnesses, but that process often meant the continuing conversion of the church, which we see happening in Peter's encounter with Cornelius in Acts 10. The result was the organization of functional missional communities across the then-known world. Their spread is indicated by the list of regions represented at Pentecost (Acts 2), the places to which epistles were sent or mentioned in them, and the seven letters at the beginning of the book of Revelation.

The structuring of the church for mission in North America must similarly be a profoundly scriptural process. Our disciplined use of a missional hermeneutic should shape and guide the continuing formation of the church in our changing society. In this social context, the sciences of organizational development and management are important aspects

---

8. The missiological theme we are speaking of is contextualization; see Louis J. Luzbetak, *The Church and Cultures: New Perspectives in Missiological Anthropology* (Maryknoll, N.Y.: Orbis, 1995), esp. 69ff.

of the culture with which the biblical formation of the church interacts. This interaction is subject to the scrutiny of the scriptural witness. The structural patterns of the missional church in the New Testament must guide the continuing organizational formation of today's church. Yet at the same time we must reject every form of organizational fundamentalism that claims absolute biblical authority for a particular polity.

We urgently need biblical scholarship that will probe the scriptural record, using a missiological hermeneutic, to enable the church in North America to structure itself in radical obedience to God's mandate to be Christ's witness. If we read the biblical witness missionally, we will not fall prey to the naïve and unfaithful notion that the goal lies simply in replicating some particular New Testament church.

Two central themes of the biblical message are especially important for the structuring of the missional church. They have emerged in the biblical-theological discussion of the twentieth century as major and much debated issues. We speak now of the biblical emphasis on the kingdom or reign of God, and the role of eschatology for the ministry and witness of the New Testament community. We have already addressed these themes in chapter four, but we should consider them here in terms of their structural implications. Both of these themes have always been, in some way, part of the church's ecclesiological conversation, but they have often been reduced, adapted, or diluted in ways that the results of much recent biblical scholarship now challenge. Those results have a significant impact on our understanding of the normative role of Scripture for the formation of the church.

The Reign of God and the Administration of Power

What are the implications of the reign of God, as expounded above in chapter four, for the missional structuring and organizational witness of the church? If Christ is the Lord of the church, then the church's submission to Christ's rule will guide its structural formation. If the church is the sign, foretaste, instrument, and agent of God's inbreaking kingdom, then the organizational structure of the community will incarnate that vocation.

As heirs of Christendom, we face a particular struggle in regard to the rule of Christ made manifest in the structures of the church. Our history is marked by compromises with other masters (e.g., the state, property and possessions, ethnicity, class, economic marketplace environment) that profoundly jeopardize our missional integrity. These compromises can be seen with special clarity when we examine the history and impact of the establishment, and the development of ecclesiastical hierarchies based on secular models of monarchy.

In every cultural formation of the church there is the danger of idolatry. Organization entails the administration of power, which constantly reveals itself to be a seductive force trying to distort the gospel.[9] The story of Jesus' temptation in the desert equips every particular church for the constant struggle with power paradigms that are contrary to its mission. Within every culture, the Christian community must examine how it is allowing other gods to replace the triune God as its Lord. When the particular community sees that it is preoccupied with power and factions that focus on winning or losing, then it must hear the injunctions to receive and enter the kingdom as a summons to conversion.

The reign of Christ is jeopardized when any organizational structure becomes an end in itself. This happens whenever the institution places all its energy in its own maintenance. When the visible church is primarily concerned with its image, its growth, its success, and its security, then it is ripe for conversion to the reign of Christ, who lays bare and sets aside all these idols. Just as flirtation with false gods remained a continual problem for Israel, the Christian community must contend constantly with temptations that would set up idols to replace Christ the King. The formation of a missional ecclesiology for the church in North America will be, in this regard, a process of contrition, repentance, and conversion, a continual entering and receiving the gift of God's divine reign. The goal of this formative process is to organize the church in ways that will enable it to "represent God's reign as its community, its servant, and its messenger."[10]

The commitment to do this will lead the emerging missional church to the New Testament record with renewed energy. With the assistance of biblical exegetes, the church must hear Jesus' exposition of the character of the kingdom (e.g., the parables of the kingdom) as highly relevant

9. See Gerhard Lohfink, *Jesus and Community: The Social Dimension of Christian Faith*, tr. J. P. Galvin (Philadelphia: Fortress, 1984), esp. 44ff., 115ff., 157ff.; John Milbank, *Theology and Social Theory: Beyond Secular Reason* (Cambridge, Mass.: Blackwell, 1991).

10. See above, p. 102 and thereafter.

equipping for the realities of North America. We need to understand not only what the New Testament means by "community," "servant," and "messenger," but we must also study how the apostolic communities structured themselves for this task. This encounter with the biblical word will not only shape the missional church but also open our eyes to the many ways in which we continue to distort the message of the kingdom.[11]

Eschatology and Organization for Mission

The eschatological character of the reign of God has strong missional implications for the organization of the church. It is essential to the continuing conversion of the church today that the radical meaning of New Testament eschatology be heard anew.[12] The kingdom has come and is coming. Thus the church finds itself on the way, living out its obedience in the tension between what God has already done and what God has promised yet to do. The particular community grapples with this tension as it goes about its missional witness within a specific culture.

The community in a place makes decisions: it forms itself for its mission and evolves as an organization. But in a variety of ways this process can then foreclose on the eschatological open-endedness of the church's mission. A church can decide that it has organizationally reached a point of institutional perfection and therefore view itself as permanent, sacrosanct, even salvific in its structures. This happens when any form of the church declares itself to be "the true church," over against others who are considered to be not the true church. Even more fateful is the claim that a particular church *is* the kingdom of God. But it can also happen when a particular church tradition allows itself to become the religious servant of its society, fulfilling the assigned roles of religious master of ceremonies, vendor, or chaplain to the world. When the church

11. See Mortimer Arias, *Announcing the Reign of God: Evangelization and the Subversive Memory Of Jesus* (Philadelphia: Fortress, 1984), for an incisive analysis of the fateful dichotomy the church makes between the gospel of salvation and the message of the reign of God. See also Stanley Hauerwas, *A Community of Character: Toward a Constructive Christian Social Ethic* (Notre Dame: University of Notre Dame Press, 1981), esp. his discussion of "The Moral Authority of Scripture: The Politics and Ethics of Remembering," 36-52.

12. Bosch, "Eschatology," in *Transforming Mission,* 196-99; and his discussion, "Where the Early Church Failed," 50-52.

succumbs to such reductions of its vocation, it denies the future orientation of the gospel. It denies its continuing need for confession, renewal, and change; and it stagnates in its false sense of completeness or security within its societal position.

God's faithful movement toward the eschatological consummation of salvation requires the continuing conversion of the church. This is an essential dimension of its identity as the pilgrim people of God. One of the most important tangible forms of that conversion is the church's willingness to change its visible structures in order to become more faithful to its mission. Openness to reform is a crucial expression of the church's petition, "Your kingdom come." Concretely, this openness will mean that the constitutional definition of every ecclesial organization must contain procedures that call for the biblical and theological assessment of its structures and provide for ways to alter them. To be missional, church organizations do not need sunset laws, but they do need regular evaluation and orderly change toward more faithfulness.

Every organizational expression of the missional church must understand itself as witness to the reign of Christ and the firstfruits of that kingdom. The church lives in the eschatological confidence that God will complete what he has begun in it. Thus the church, in all its diversity, wears its organizational structures lightly, since it knows that in some way it is always conforming to this world and needs to be transformed by the renewal of its mind (Rom. 12:2).

The Cultural Diversity of the Church's Structures and Its Catholicity

From the outset, the church of Christ was mandated to be multicultural: to witness in the distinctive contexts of Jerusalem, Judea, Samaria, and to the ends of the earth. The Spirit was given to empower the apostolic community to translate the gospel into particular cultures as it expanded across the world. The formation of mission communities in Jerusalem, Samaria, Antioch, Philippi, Ephesus, and ultimately Rome represents a continuing witness to the translatability of the gospel.[13] Those gathered

---

13. Sanneh, *Translating the Message,* esp. 1-8; Andrew F. Walls, "The Translation Principle in Christian History," in *The Missionary Movement in Christian History: Studies in the Transmission of Faith* (Maryknoll, N.Y.: Orbis, 1996), 26-42.

in Jerusalem on Pentecost heard the apostolic preaching in all their languages. Presumably many of those converts took the gospel back into their own cultures and continued the process of translation that God's Spirit intends. Every cultural context, as Lamin Sanneh has emphasized, may receive the story of Jesus and tell this good news in its particular way. God's love in Christ may be praised in every human language, and the people of God may be formed in every human culture. The ecclesial practices can be carried out in every language and in every cultural setting.

Just as the New Testament does not ordain a particular organizational structure for the visible church, so too no particular culture is ordained to be the normative pattern for all Christian communities. Instead, according to the apostolic instruction, one should "lead a life worthy of the calling to which you have been called" (Eph. 4:1), wherever that calling is heard and responded to. The church's task in every culture is to find the visible organizational form that is worthy of its calling to be the witness to Christ in that particular place. This is a process that demonstrates faithful response to the gospel, appropriation of the Spirit's empowering gifts for continuing ministry, and dynamic translation of the gospel into the structure and functions of the community. Wherever that empowered translation takes place, communities will confess our Lord and Savior Jesus Christ, practice his presence and rule in ways common to all Christians (the ecclesial practices discussed in chap. 6), and function as God's city on a hill, as salt, as leaven, and as light.

There are risks in the cultural shaping of the visible church. Organizational modes profoundly express the basic assumptions and values of a culture. This becomes clear when any organizing church begins to deal with issues like power, decision making, conflict resolution, leadership roles, administration of money and property, or the education of its young. The Christian church of the second century developed in a social and political world shaped by monarchy and centralized hierarchical power. It is no wonder that the monarchical bishop emerged as the most authoritative figure within the church. The papal office followed in the cultural track laid out by the Roman emperor, assuming even his title "Pontifex." In like manner, the established Christianity of the fourth and fifth centuries took over the former temples (basilicas) of various ancient religions and made them into meeting places for Christian churches. We can find similar examples today in African and Asian churches that have adapted cultural patterns of decision making and office to the life of the church. This is always a necessary, a risky, and a dynamic process of translation, conversion, and (often) gospel reduction.

The gospel's transforming impact on a culture is constantly in tension with the culture's reductionistic influence on the gospel. In the area of visible organizational witness, the church often appears to submit readily to the forces of its culture. We have shown in our discussion up to now how profoundly this submission has been true of North American churched culture. The formation of a missional ecclesiology for the church in North America entails rigorous examination of the cultural shaping of the church in the piercing light of the gospel. It will have to deal with the multicultural character of North American society clearly reflected in the cultural diversity of North American church traditions. In particular, such an ecclesiology must address responsibly all attempts to define a North American culture in normative terms and then assign to the church the task of defending that culture. The continuing reformation of the church includes the recognition of the ways in which its conformity to this world impedes its faithful witness as well as its willingness to be transformed by the renewing of its mind (Rom. 12:2).

To summarize, the biblical definition of the church's mission makes plain that the church is essentially multicultural, because God's people are formed in distinctive ways in each context, interacting with every culture in order to form itself visibly as a community of witness. This concrete process of translation and formation among all the nations is God's intent. The resulting organizational diversity demonstrates that the gospel is being witnessed to the ends of the earth. This diversity raises questions, obviously, about where the unity and catholicity of the church reside. We will address those questions later, but first let us consider the structures of congregations, or what we prefer to call "particular communities of the church."

The Particular Community as the Basic Missional Structure

The basic form of Christian witness is a company of followers of Jesus called by God's Spirit and joined together as God's people in a particular place. The New Testament concept of *koinonia* defines the Christian church as all those who have Jesus Christ and his mission in common. This community, shaped by God's word, is sent to be the concrete witness to the gospel of Jesus in its particular place. As we have emphasized above, the goal of the New Testament Scriptures is to equip such communities for their faithful witness. The New Testament describes particular mission communities, encountering God's Word as it prepares us to be Christ's witnesses.

The primary organizational challenge for the church is to find ways to structure the life of the particular communities so that they can carry out faithful witness in their places, always in responsible connection to the entire church around the world and cultivated by the ecclesial practices that God's Spirit provides. The particular community happens concretely in the coming together of Christians to worship, to grapple with the Scriptures, to be instructed in the faith, to love each other, and to practice the rule of Christ corporately and individually. All of this focuses on the community being sent into its mission field as Christ's witness. The concrete life of the particular community is the essential expression of "our rootedness in the particularity of Judaism and Jesus."[14]

North Americans almost automatically assume that the particular community will be organized as the local congregation. The local congregation is now receiving increasing emphasis in North America, while denominational structures continue to diminish. The cultural changes we are experiencing, however, force us to ask what we mean by "local congregation." What constitutes the local nature of any congregation in North America? The model we have inherited is the geographical parish. This model originated with Charlemagne's division of all of "Christian Europe" into a system that guaranteed every resident lived in a parish with a church and a priest. Parish membership was defined by where one lived. Where one lived was where one worked. Most lived and worked all their lives in the parish where they were born. Thus everyone was on a church roll somewhere, usually from baptism on. Everyone knew where to go to get the religious services one wanted or needed, and everyone was familiar with the cemetery next to the church that would be their final resting place. In this way, the geographical parish provided a workable organizational pattern in the churched culture of Christendom, even if it was problematic missiologically.

In North America the geographical parish continued to serve as a dominant model, although our history of emigration and voluntaristic

14. John Howard Yoder, "Why Ecclesiology Is Social Ethics," in *The Royal Priesthood: Essays Ecclesiological and Ecumenical* (Grand Rapids: Eerdmans, 1994), 113; see the entire discussion of "particularity," 113-16.

system of church affiliation have produced a layered pattern, in which congregations of differing traditions are close to each other and overlap each other's parishes. Local churches have been in competition with one another from early on, modifying the geographical parish model brought across the Atlantic from Europe. But profound recent social and economic changes in our society have rendered the geographical parish even more unrealistic. As long as we were an agricultural and small-town society with a relatively low level of mobility, our modified parish system served us relatively well, even though there was the constant issue of church competition.

Now, however, everything is changing, and these changes threaten traditional structures. Few people can be cradle-to-grave members of a local congregation. We move for our jobs, our schooling, our families, and our retirement. Christians are constantly shopping for a new congregation. They no longer necessarily end up in the church geographically nearest to their homes. In the American voluntaristic system, in which every dimension of the church's life is shaped by the individual decisions of its members, one's choice of membership is likely to be based on many factors. These factors include denominational affiliation, quality of parish program, services provided, esthetics of worship, opportunities for social relationships, parking and accessibility, economic class, personality and preaching skills of the minister, even prestige or reputation, and perhaps the missional commitments of a particular congregation. One chooses one's congregation as one does one's clubs, social activities, and professional services.

In large urban areas, traditional congregations face particular difficulties. They cannot afford the land and buildings that we traditionally have associated with the local congregation. People do not necessarily structure their lives around the area where they live. Neighborhoods are often nonexistent. The mobility made possible by rapid transit and the car makes social networks across large urban areas possible. People form their communities around interests and activities that have nothing to do with geography. Similarly, the electronic church allows large numbers of people to experience religious servicing without forming any face-to-face relationships with members of a particular community. Some electronic church ministries have even developed a system whereby television viewers become members of a church that they experience only on their TV set!

North American churches are in much ferment with regard to the structure and activity of the local congregation. Experiments abound, ranging from the Church of the Savior in Washington, D.C., with its rigorous commitments and disciplines, to user-friendly megachurches offering a myriad of services to the religious consumer. Mainline denominations are responding to numerical decline by focusing on the priority of the local congregation. A growing and diverse theological consensus supports that focus.[15] In the formation of a missional ecclesiology for North America, the local congregation will continue to be the center of emphasis. But its structures may well look different from the inherited forms of parish in the Christendom paradigm. Shaped by Scripture, creatively translating its witness into the multicultural diversity of North America, the traditional parish must emerge as a missional community. The task is to structure it as an authentic community of the reign of God.

The Challenge: From Parish to Mission Community

A particular community might express what we have proposed as the understanding of the missional church by confessing together:

> We believe that we are the church, that is, we are a community of God's people called and set apart for witness to the good news of Jesus Christ. We are blessed to be a blessing. As the Father has sent Christ, so Christ sends us. Jesus Christ has defined us as his witnesses where we are. We believe therefore that the Holy Spirit not only calls us but also enables and gifts us for that mission. Our task is to determine the particular focus and direction of our mission. We are to identify the charisms given us by the Spirit for mission. We have the responsibility and the capacity, through the Holy Spirit, to shape ourselves for faithful witness. Our purpose defines our organizational structures — which means that our mission challenges us to re-form our structures so that we can be faithful in our witness.

15. See, e.g., C. Ellis Nelson, ed., *Congregations: Their Power to Form and Transform* (Atlanta: John Knox, 1988); Patrick R. Keifert, *Welcoming the Stranger: A Public Theology of Worship and Evangelism* (Minneapolis: Fortress, 1992); Charles Van Engen, *God's Missionary People: Rethinking the Purpose of the Local Church* (Grand Rapids: Baker, 1991); Robert E. Webber and Rodney Clapp, *People of the Truth: A Christian Challenge to Contemporary Culture*, rev. ed. (Harrisburg: Morehouse, 1993).

A particular community's purpose is to hear and translate the gospel in its specific setting so that the witness to Jesus Christ takes place. To use an image developed by Lesslie Newbigin, the particular mission community is always involved in the discipline of becoming culturally bilingual, learning the language of faith and how to translate its story into the language of its context, so that others may be drawn to become followers of Jesus.[16]

We now propose that the structural formation of the church in North America for its mission must be a disciplined, intentional process. This should become the focus of the teaching and preaching ministry in each particular church as well as in the connecting structures that link particular communities to each other. Particular churches should place their organizational processes under the scrutiny of Scripture to see where they need to repent and be transformed. Theological scholarship and teaching should prepare leaders who can guide communities in this disciplined process.

This process of continual reform and conversion can happen only as congregations become aware of their traditions. We need to be students of our history both to receive its legacy thankfully and to discover how we became what we are. Communities will certainly discover much for which they can be thankful and which they can celebrate in their public worship. They will discover models in their histories to emulate and experiences from which to learn. They will also learn a great deal about the many ways their traditions have been shaped to dilute their commitment to Christ and his mission. They will be enabled to recognize their reductions of the gospel and the compromises of the institutional church in their past.

This is an essential process, constantly calling for sensitive guidance on the part of the community's leadership. Leaders need to know and to use research into the social and cultural history of North American Christianity in order to help the local particular community see itself accurately in its context. But most of all, they and their communities must be infused with a profound sense of the particular community's vocation as a mission community. Many communities are working in this direction, as is evidenced by the emphasis on mission statements and the formulation of goals and objectives for a particular community. But we would argue that this discipline requires a more radical critique

16. Lesslie Newbigin, *The Gospel in a Pluralist Society* (Grand Rapids: Eerdmans, 1989), 65, 97-102, 141-54.

of the cultural captivity of North American churches than most contemporary congregations have contemplated.

The disciplined process we envision here must be rigorously biblical and theological. It must be wary of the cultural temptation to locate the entire structural conversation at the level of efficiency, productivity, and success. Such a critique may well be painful, but it need not be destructive if the community desires to incarnate faithfully God's love in Christ in all that it does. This grappling with tradition in its ambiguity should happen as the community is learning to translate the gospel into its own community life, and through that, into its surrounding context.

The testing of any community's structural integrity is its continuing articulation of the evangelistic invitation. How it lives as a community and what it proclaims and confesses should center on Jesus' words, "Follow me and I will make you fish for people" (Matt. 4:19). The Spirit empowers that witness, others see and hear and respond, and the local congregation grows. Such growth is not its goal or preoccupation, but rather the effect of its faithfulness to its calling.[17] That faithfulness is expressed concretely when the corporate ecclesial practices (chap. 6) and the practices for missional leadership (chap. 7) are centered on the mission of God in Jesus Christ.

For this to happen, we need to be willing to work through some hard questions for this moment in the church's pilgrimage in North America.

Is there one normative structural pattern for a mission community? Typically today, a particular community is formed in a place, and formal leadership is appointed. Sometimes an appointed pastor then works in an area to recruit and form a particular community, a new church development. The community develops its membership and resources, invests in property, constructs a building, and designs its ministry with a range of programs. If any missional thinking is attempted, the entire process is accompanied by a discipline of mission study and formulation. The goal in all this activity is the formation of a viable congregation, and viability is usually measured in term of numbers of members, financial stability, and the capacity to function as an organization. All this carries unquestioned assumptions about "what a real church does" as a "place where" religious services are provided.

17. For a compelling exploration of how this might happen, see Raymond Fung, *The Isaiah Vision: An Ecumenical Strategy for Congregational Evangelism* (Geneva: WCC Publications, 1992).

In our changing context, Christian communities may do none of these traditional things. Mission communities will look very different in unchurched North America. The criteria for the structuring of the church that we have outlined previously — namely, the normative influence of the Scriptures, cultural diversity, and the priority of the particular community — will still hold. But these criteria will be translated into a range of ecclesial structures for mission communities. We have not exhausted the resources of the Holy Spirit to guide us toward structural innovation! In this diversity of structures, the gospel will be witnessed to, the rule of Christ will be announced and practiced, and the ecclesial practices will take place.

Christians may form themselves as an intentional mission community living in the same neighborhood, making lifestyle decisions that enable them to organize their daily lives and family interactions as a primary form of witness. But they may worship in their homes rather than own a church building. Christians may form themselves as a non-geographical community centered on a particular form of witness. Their calling may be to demonstrate the gospel in ministry to the homeless, to young people, to the elderly, to prisoners, to the terminally ill, or to an immigrant population. Such a vocation might mean that their congregation meets in a borrowed facility, a rented hall, or a storefront that welcomes their particular constituency. Christians may join together to share church buildings erected for a time when the church was dominant in our society. Their particular vocation may be to conduct public worship in innovative ways that build communication bridges to their society and present the gospel to unevangelized people in ways they can understand. To do this they may find themselves using a local theater on Sunday mornings or taking over an abandoned inner-city church and using its space for untraditional forms of worship and ministry. A particular group of Christians may respond to the loneliness and isolation of the modern city and form themselves as a vowed intentional community, sharing several apartments in order to carry out a ministry of hospitality and friendship in the midst of the highly secularized world of professionals. Other Christians may form themselves around the charism of hospitality, or ministry with the handicapped, or the contemplative life.

However Christians structure themselves, they will have missional leadership and their common life will have a focus on the ecclesial practices that cultivate them as missional communities. They will find themselves forming a bounded covenant community within a centered congregation (described in chap. 7). Depending on their particular vocation, this relationship may vary. Some forms of evangelistic mission may emphasize the centered, unbounded congregation, while other forms of highly focused missional community may emphasize the covenantal and bounded congregation. However they are configured, they will constantly struggle with how to be in and not of the world, how to relate to their culture as a sent but still alternative community, and how to incarnate Jesus Christ where they are.

We should anticipate a growing diversity of structures for mission in the North American situation. This means that denominations must begin to examine critically their present strategies for new church development and encourage both innovation and experimentation. Communities of the reign of God are not defined in terms of demographic feasibility or organizational viability. The criteria currently used for defining the successful organization of a local congregation as a voluntary society are missionally problematic. When Jesus said, "As my Father sent me, so I send you," he did not mean that there was only one way in which God would send his people! But he did mean that God's purposes must define the formation of every particular mission community.

Is the task of a mission community to maintain itself? Organizational constraints quickly eclipse the theological assumption that particular communities exist for their mission. The community owns property, has staff, makes commitments, and must therefore ensure that the budget is raised and the program continued. Maintenance replaces mission as the guiding principle of the community's life. The challenge confronting the church in North America is a radical one. It is that neither maintenance nor survival is an adequate purpose for any particular community or ecclesial structure. The organizational structures that guarantee maintenance and survival are often missiologically questionable. These structures may be transformable, but they are not justifiable as they are.

To state that the local congregation or particular community must have priority in a missional ecclesiology for North America has sweeping implications for the parish structures that we have inherited. The well-known emphasis on the continuing reformation of the church becomes an urgent if not radical imperative. Business as usual will not work if our local congregations are to become missional. We must be willing to question our value systems, particularly with regard to property, wealth, and endowments.

We must scrutinize the criteria of success that we transfer to the church from our society. This is a task that North Americans often resist. It calls for strong and sensitive community leadership, disciplined Bible study, and a willingness to deal with conflict within the community. We cannot, however, develop our understanding of the local congregation as the mission community as though all we needed were the further evolution of our traditional structures, along with some fine-tuning. In view of the reductionism of the gospel and thus of the church's concept of its mission, our communities and their structures need to be profoundly evangelized and to be converted. Mission communities do not automatically emerge from the religious vending agencies of our churched culture.

A missional ecclesiology for North America will address the situations of already existing congregations prophetically and critically. It will lead Christian communities to ask: What is our particular expression of the mission to be Christ's witnesses? What are our charisms for that ministry? What is our sense of vocation as a sent community? Then it will provide the biblical and theological resources for communities to find their answers to such questions. Such an ecclesiology must provide ways to assess the organizational priorities in order to see if they are rooted in a missional commitment or in some other nonmissional motives. Discussion of money and budgets will reveal which motives are truly at work. This missional ecclesiology will significantly shape the leadership of the missional pastor, whose identity we may best describe as missionary to the congregation, so that the particular community may become a mission community.

Not all forms of the church that we inherit must continue. None of the seven churches to which the Revelation of John was addressed exists today. The structures of the mission community should embody in some way the transitional and pilgrim character of the church. Such communities, if they are founded for mission, will be prepared to change and perhaps even to cease existing in a specific form.

Exploring the tension between mission and maintenance will help to determine the viability of many already existing local congregations. These issues can also help to sort out the motives for founding a new congregation or ministry in a particular place.

What is the relationship between corporate worship and a community's mission? The center of any mission community's organized life is its corporate worship. Virtually every theological and confessional tradition represented in North America agrees with this proposition. It is the pervasive assumption of this book. Moreover, in spite of our confessional diversity, there is a strong consensus among the Christian traditions as to the purpose of worship. That consensus includes at least four basic affirmations: Worship is the public celebration of the presence and reality of God; it is the community's gathering to acknowledge, praise, and thank God; it focuses on the proclamation of the gospel in Word and Sacrament and our response to it; and it provides Christians assurance, comfort, and encouragement.

At the same time, the ways in which we gather to worship are enormously diverse. At one end of the spectrum are disciplined commitments to the maintenance of a particular worship tradition, as enshrined in venerable liturgical expressions. At the other end, worship resembles religious entertainment, combining a variety of motifs like praising God, satisfying emotional needs, attracting outsiders, and inspiring believers.

A missional ecclesiology for North America will need to address the centrality of worship for the life and witness of the mission community, both as centered congregation and as covenant community. We need to learn how worship concretely calls and sends us into Christ's service, and how it is a facet of our mission itself. For this to happen, worship must primarily be the people's encounter with the God who sends. We meet the missionary God who is shaping God's people for their vocation, namely, to be a blessing to the nations. For that to happen, the people constantly receive the blessing that makes them a blessing. The people hear the word of forgiveness, experience their own continuing healing, and find the comfort that they need in order to function as Christ's witnesses.

Those in the covenant community hear that same gospel as the empowering word that sends them out. The Holy Spirit empowers the community not only to hear but also to do the Word. In worship we learn how to celebrate our ordination to God's service with every baptism, and we learn how to claim the real presence of Christ nourishing us to live as his witnesses at every communion service.

Most importantly, our ecclesiological discipline will develop in new ways our understanding of worship as public witness. The presence of the unbounded centered community, if taken seriously, will profoundly affect the public character of worship. We need relevant communication, language that can be understood, and music that relates to the experience of the worshiper, who as a seeker is genuinely open to God's call. But the spiritual needs of the centered community are not the ultimate, defining factor for the gospel. Our postmodern society has come to regard worship as the private, internal, and often arcane activity of religionists who retreat from the world to practice their mystical rites. By definition, however, the *ekklesia* is a public assembly, and its worship is its first form of mission. This is the emphasis that the covenant community brings to worship. The reality of God that is proclaimed in worship is to be announced to and for the entire world. The walls and windows of churches need to become transparent.

In its worship, as in its common life, the mission community needs to develop space for people who find themselves in different places as they respond to God's call, from the edges of the centered congregation to the heart of the covenant community. Two basic dynamics are always at work in worship as public witness. It is the worship of God carried out by God's called and sent people. But it also welcomes and makes room for the curious, the skeptical, the critical, the needy, the exploring, and the committed. It practices the hospitality that is rooted in God's presence and invitation, made known and experienced in Jesus Christ. It is that inclusive and open-ended hospitality that recognizes in everyone, whether mature Christian or first-time visitor, a person for whom Christ died. That is the alien dignity that the gospel grants all humans and which Christian hospitality demonstrates.[18]

Above all, the public worship of the mission community always leads to the pivotal act of sending. The community that is called together is the community that is sent. Every occasion of public worship is a sending event. Our worship traditions have vast resources to draw on to implement this vision of missional worship. But much work needs to be done in order to equip those who lead worship to do so with such a vision. Communities need to learn to worship missionally. This worship cannot happen merely as the result of liturgical innovation, nor will it be accomplished by converting the meeting into an evangelistic crusade meeting. Rather, the conversion of worship to its missional centeredness will come about as communities are gripped by their vocation to be Christ's witness and begin to practice that calling.

What does "membership" mean for a mission community? As currently practiced in much of the North American church, the definitions and

18. See Keifert, *Welcoming the Stranger,* esp. 1-13.

disciplines of church membership reveal the poverty of our missional self-understanding. Here the legacy of Christendom and establishment is particularly problematic. The original sense of "member" was linked to the concept of the body of Christ as expounded by Paul in 1 Corinthians. The emphasis rests there on our interdependence and our intimate relatedness to the Head of the church, Jesus Christ. "Membership" in this sense had to do with our calling to be the presence of and witness to Christ. It stressed the importance of each person for that witness as well as the organic nature of the community's witness. Over the centuries, this concept has been diluted by a complex process. Membership has long been associated with an individual's supposed salvation status. To be a member of the church was to be a baptized communicant, a participant in the blessings of the faith in preparation for eternal bliss. Not to be a member was to be outside the pale of the saved. Thus the focus of membership shifted from the mission of Christ's body, the church, to the issue of one's salvation. Becoming a member was less a process of enlistment in Christ's service than an enrollment in the book of life. In the reductionism of the concept of membership, we see a primary example of the dichotomy between the benefits of salvation and the mission for which we are saved, a dichotomy that is the continuing crisis of Western Christianity.[19]

In the voluntaristic church structures of North America, church membership has been even further diluted. Although the formal theologies of the various Christian traditions seek to define membership with integrity, the practice has degenerated into little more than a matter of organizational affiliation. Members are recruited. Thresholds for entering into membership are often purposely low in order to make the process as easy and painless as possible, or they are raised inordinately in order to foster greater organizational commitment. Membership numbers are monitored as a primary indicator of the success and health of a congregation. Membership is easily changed, and in many denominations members have low levels of biblical literacy plus even weaker understandings

---

19. See Karl Barth's discussion of Christian identity in "The Christian as Witness: The Vocation of Man," §71.4 in *Church Dogmatics*, vol. 4: *The Doctrine of Reconciliation*, part 3, second half, tr. G. W. Bromiley, ed. Bromiley and T. F. Torrance (Edinburgh: T. & T. Clark, 1962), 554ff.; see also Darrell Guder, *Be My Witnesses: The Church's Mission, Message, and Messengers* (Grand Rapids: Eerdmans, 1985), especially the emphasis upon "the missions-benefits dichotomy" throughout.

of the distinctive tenets of their traditions. The frequently used term *nominal membership* is symptomatic of this sad situation. In North American denominations shaped by the business and corporate ethos of modern society, membership decline is obviously an indicator of organizational failure linked with loss of income, since members are givers.

One of the immediate implications a missional ecclesiology for North America is a critical rethinking of the meaning and practice of church membership. For the open, unbounded, centered congregation, membership may be an irrelevant concept. Those who are in various stages of engagement and response to the gospel are more like inquirers or candidates than members. Venerable terms like *novices* or *catechumens* may even become useful again.[20] The term *member* may also be unusable for the covenant community as well. Such a covenant commitment is closer to ordination, or to the commissioning of Christians for their particular ministries within the corporate witness of the entire community. There can be none of the passivity we see today in the practice of church membership. Covenant identity implies decision, vows, and accountability.

We do not expect that the structures of membership must be uniform. But we do look for structures and practices that will express the missional calling of the church and foster that sense of calling in the individual Christian. Some are proposing to revive and reinterpret the ancient disciplines of catechesis for the North American church in a post-Christian setting.[21] The ecumenical consensus that views baptism as general ordination to Christian service supports such rethinking of membership's meaning.[22] In effect, the disciplines of membership will have become missional when they are understood and experienced as ecclesial practices.

The challenge for a missional structure of membership can seem daunting. On the one hand, the missional community needs to practice an evangelical hospitality that welcomes into the centered community people who are at all stages of response to the gospel. The movement

---

20. See Keifert, *Welcoming the Stranger*, 95ff.

21. Ibid.; also William J. Abraham, *The Logic of Evangelism* (Grand Rapids: Eerdmans, 1989), 92ff.

22. E.g., the *Baptism, Eucharist, Ministry* statement of the Faith and Order Movement (Geneva: WCC Publications, 1982), and the theological consensus of the Church of Christ Uniting (C.O.C.U.) process in the United States.

from centered to covenant congregation over time could create a wall of division by establishing levels of spiritual status. The missional sense of the covenant community is not that it is a spiritual elite. However, the history of the religious orders should be a constant warning to us that such perceptions can arise, both among those who have made such a covenant commitment and among those who are considering it. How does the mission community deal with this danger?

This needs to be a continuing theme of the church's conversion. The scriptural formation of the community should root deeply the sense of the community as strangers and aliens, people on the road toward the consummation of the kingdom. The overarching sense of the church's life should be that of a pilgrim people, a movement with Christ toward God's promised fulfillment. All Christians are on that pilgrimage, and the community itself is continually being converted as it follows Christ. Membership cannot therefore be defined in terms of achievement, or completion, or having arrived. Nonetheless, there is growth from milk to meat, from spiritual infancy to adulthood, and key points along this process should be marked in the covenanting process. Perhaps we should explore ways to combine elements of the Believers' Church tradition's insistence on rigor and discipline in membership with elements of the openness and inclusivity of the public and people's church of Christendom.

Beginning the Conversation

The foregoing conversation indicates that the way to the formation of missional communities begins and ends in our confrontation with and by the Scriptures. Intensive study of the New Testament will become missionally incisive if one approaches the task asking, How did this text prepare the early church for its mission, and how does it prepare us for ours? What does this text tell us about the gospel? What makes it good news? What does this text tell us about ourselves? about our world? What does this text show us about the way in which the gospel is to be made known? How does this text challenge our organizational forms and functions? How should our organizational practices change in light of this text? How does this text challenge us to be converted?

These questions focus on the visibility of the congregation, on its tangible organization as an essential expression of its missional faithfulness. The organizational task that all particular communities face, whatever their charism and missional focus, whether old or new, is to find ways to shape themselves so that their missional nature and identity are expressed and translated into concrete witness. The biblical conversation will guide that discovery process. As we have emphasized, a congregation needs to learn from the long and varied history of the church as an organization. It can discover models that bear imitation. It may learn as well from the missional and organizational failures of the communion of saints. It will find in the experience of other communities both in North America and in the global church much that will inspire and direct it as it seeks to form itself organizationally.

However the missional community shapes itself, its vocation will be Christ's definition: "You shall be my witnesses." Such witness to faith centers on the evangelistic invitation to others, to one's neighbors, to become Christ's disciples and to join the community in its continuing apostolate. The particular community, empowered by God's Spirit, not only lives out the gospel internally but opens up the gospel externally by the way it lives, so that others may see and respond. This witness may result in growth, as we have noted, but that is not its goal. Rather, it is one possible form of witness that God empowers. For North American churches, shaped as they are by society's preoccupation with success, the issue of growth is a key missional test. Plans and strategies for growth can become idolatrous and result in questionable reductions and distortions of the gospel. They may reveal the degree to which a church is captive to values that are truly alien to the gospel. Such captivity may produce impressive church organizations, but they are not necessarily faithful witnesses of the vocation to be, do, and speak witness to Christ.

The process of movement toward the missional church, then, will be rooted and shaped by intense engagement with Scripture. It will subject all the church's structures to biblical scrutiny. It will confront the particular forms of cultural captivity that mark our conformity to this world in North America.

Missional Connectedness:
The Community of Communities in Mission

We have established that the particular mission community is the central focus of God's mission, as it carries out its witness in a specific cultural setting. It is not biblical, however, for particular communities of the visible, organized church to exist in isolation from one another. Particularity is not exclusivity. The calling of the Holy Spirit at Pentecost began to produce what 1 Peter calls a "race, priesthood, nation, and people" (2:9-10), a worldwide multicultural fellowship of witness.[1] The people of God, in all their cultural diversity, may be understood as a universal community of communities. The particular community is, in an essential sense, an expression of the church catholic. There is a common bond, a relationship among all particular congregations that is part and parcel of their vocation and their faithfulness. That relationship is the result of God's action in calling forth the church as Christ's witness: "There is one body and one Spirit, just as you were called to the one hope of your calling, one Lord, one faith, one baptism, one God and Father of all, who is above all and through all and in all" (Eph. 4:4-6). Just as the members of every mission community have Christ in common,

---

1. See Gerhard Lohfink, *Jesus and Community: The Social Dimension of Christian Faith*, tr. John P. Galvin (Philadelphia: Fortress, 1984), esp. 26ff. and 75ff. Cf. Eduard Schweizer, *Church Order in the New Testament*, tr. Frank Clarke, Studies in Biblical Theology 1/32 (Naperville: Allenson, 1962), 8: "I try uniformly to translate the New Testament term *ekklesia* by 'church,' in order to emphasize that linguistically the New Testament cannot distinguish, as we do, between the local and the universal Church."

its common calling to witness and its submission to its Lord define the community of communities. That calling and all the relationships it implies result in structures, institutional realities, which are an essential part of what we mean when we talk about the church.

Our purpose in emphasizing the particular mission community has been to make it the theological priority for the development of a missional ecclesiology. To be sure, we experience the church today in a great diversity of forms beyond and distinct from the local congregation. But in our theological analysis of these larger structures, we proceed missiologically from the assumptions and principles that define our understanding of the particular mission community. What we say about the community of communities is rooted in the central missiological understanding of God's people called and sent in particular places and structures. We move missiologically from Jerusalem to the larger church with its diversity of communities in Judea, Samaria, and to the ends of the earth (Acts 1:8).

The theological formation of the missional connectedness of the church should be centrifugal in nature. In terms of its biblical and theological approach, it should move outward from the particular communities to the wholeness of the church in all its diversity. This is an important dimension of the priority of the particular mission community in both our theology and our practice. This should, then, be the theological sequence in developing a missional ecclesiology.[2]

How does a missional ecclesiology deal with the essential relatedness of particular communities? How do we form these structures so that they provide a missional connectedness for the universal church in all its diversity? From a missional perspective, the connecting structures are crucial to the nature of the church as the people of God for God's mission. At the level of the community of communities, gospel witness takes place in ways that are inherent in the church's calling. It supplements, complements, and even completes the witness of the particular

2. This approach continues to be true even where we observe that particular mission communities are the result of actions on the part of the larger structures of the church. The obvious example is the way in which congregations are "planted" by many denominations in North America; they are the result of decisions made at the regional or district level of a church. But their purpose is to form a particular community, so that the priority of their work, as a connectional structure, is still the particular mission community, and what they do is defined theologically by the priority of such particular communities.

mission communities. We shall explore some of these dimensions of witness below. As we do, we need to remember that the fundamental sent-ness of the particular mission communities defines the purpose of the connecting structures. They exist too for the mission of the church, and their particular function must in some way relate to the primary form of mission, the particular community.

The Necessity of Structures of Connectedness

In his high priestly prayer, Jesus set out the purpose of the church as the community of communities:

> I ask not only on behalf of these, but also on behalf of those who will believe in me through their word, that they may all be one. As you, Father, are in me and I am in you, may they also be in us, so that the world may believe that you have sent me. The glory that you have given me I have given them, so that they may be one, as we are one. I in them and you in me, that they may become completely one, so that the world may know that you have sent me and have loved them even as you have loved me. (John 17:20-23)

This prayer is a central New Testament passage defining the purpose of the relatedness of the church. It teaches us that the missional connectedness of the church is not merely a matter of institutional unity, and even less of efficiency, stewardship, good public relations, or effective growth strategies. The oneness spoken of here is a matter of obedience to the Lord of the church, obedience that centers on his mission, "so that the world may know that you have sent me." The basic missional task of connecting structures, then, is to witness to the one gospel that relates all Christians to one another under their one Lord and sends the church into the world, "to the ends of the earth."

Some dimensions of the church's calling emerge from the formation of particular mission communities but can only be concretely expressed when these communities are linked as a community of communities. The structures of missional connectedness witness in distinctive ways to the gospel of God in Jesus Christ. These structures make the people of God visible and tangible. They enable the cultivation of the ecclesial practices as the missional witness, which crosses boundaries and breaks down human walls.

One of the most important and earliest ways in which the church's universal connectedness witnessed to the gospel was the process of canonization of Scripture itself.[3] It was not a process carried out by local congregations independent of one other. Rather, the connected church that linked the local communities in regional structures of various kinds accomplished the catholic acknowledgment of these Scriptures. The normative witness of Scripture authenticated that process.[4] The connected church of the second and third centuries affirmed what was already recognized and practiced in the local communities: that these writers were the authoritative witness for the mission of the church in every place. The canonization process was a missional confession of the multicultural church of the first centuries. The church in this process witnessed to God's work in bringing about and preserving these accounts to continue to equip the church for its mission.

These writings continue to be the authority for all that the church says and does. Just as the character of the local church's structure is to be defined by a missiological hermeneutic of the Bible, the development of connecting structures stands under the judgment and correction of Scripture. For this reason, the complex modern debate about biblical authority represents one of the most important challenges we face. If the church in North America is to be able to define with missional faithfulness its shape and practices, this critical debate must reach some consensus. The challenge of biblical authority is not an academic issue — it is essentially a missional one.

Another distinctive missional task of connecting structures has been the formation of doctrine and confessions. There is a widespread, but not total, consensus regarding the doctrinal centrality of the ancient

---

3. "The fixing of the Canon is the basic act of Church confession and therefore the basic establishment of Church authority" (Karl Barth, *Church Dogmatics,* I/2, tr. G. T. Thomson and Harold Knight, ed. G. W. Bromiley and T. F. Torrance [Edinburgh: T. & T. Clark, 1956], 597).

4. "The word 'canon' itself points to the fact that in establishing a canon, the Church acknowledged the existence of a factor which confronts it, its activity, and its speech with unconditional authority.... The Church is not the body which makes the decision about recognition directly, as with the canons of ecclesiastical law or liturgy. Here its decision is simultaneously its acknowledgment of something which it is receiving from an authority over it"; Otto Weber, *Foundations of Dogmatics,* tr. D. L. Guder, 2 vols. (Grand Rapids: Eerdmans, 1981-83), 1:251; see the entire discussion of "The Canon," 248-68.

ecumenical creeds. For our purposes, it is important to recognize that they were evidence of the missional faithfulness of the connected church, or at least demonstrations of the larger church's struggle to be faithful. Similarly, in their confessional documents the Lutheran and Reformed traditions attest to a consensus on the centrality of not only *sola scriptura* (Scripture alone) but also *sola gratia* (grace alone) and *sola fide* (faith alone). These documents are the outcome of processes carried out by the structures of ecclesial connectedness. For several strands of the Reformation movement, the confessions form a common ground that connects the churches in their diversity. Virtually every strand of Reformation Christianity has formulated statements of faith and conviction that help to define their continuing mission. In the latter half of the twentieth century, the Roman Catholic Church has impressively demonstrated the power of such ecclesial connectedness in the missional theology that has emerged from the Second Vatican Council and in many subsequent papal encyclica. In short, church history is full of examples of the distinctive kind of witness that can happen only through the structures of missional connectedness.[5]

The church's structures of connectedness are elements of the church as institution. Together with many critics of institutional Christianity, David Bosch regards it as a "failure of the early church" that it "ceased to be a movement and turned into an institution." But he goes on then to say that "either the movement disintegrates or it becomes an institution — this is simply a sociological law."[6] As Bosch's remarks suggest, the institutionalized church presents the more obvious and problematic dimensions of missional connectedness. Institutional forms of connectedness can express the church's unity and catholicity, or they can dilute these features. The connecting forms of the church have shown remarkable versatility and faithfulness. As we have just seen, they have produced the creeds and confessions. They have defined the church's mission over against the state. They have mandated creative innovations in ministry such as the missionary orders of the Middle Ages, and they

---

5. Among many other examples of the crucial role of structures of connectedness, we could also point to the development of communal structures of peaceableness, service, and diaconic mission. These are further evidence of the distinct missional responsibility of the church's structures of connectedness.

6. David J. Bosch, *Transforming Mission: Paradigm Shifts in Theology of Mission* (Maryknoll, N.Y.: Orbis, 1991), 50, 52.

have preserved venerable legacies of learning, liturgy, spirituality, and art. But institutional "connectionalism" has also proven susceptible to cultural compromise and often resisted missional reform. Here the issues of power, money, political linkages, and influence assert themselves and seriously challenge the missional integrity of the churches.

The radical witness of the Anabaptist movement has resulted in tremendous persecutions of these churches as they have pointed to the compromises of the major ecclesiastical traditions, especially with regard to power, violence, and wealth. Not until recently has this alternative expression of missional connectedness begun to receive a wider hearing. To make it even harder to hear this prophetic witness, the twentieth century in North America has seen the churches' adoption of the corporate ethos and the values of American big business. As our church organizations have centralized, they have become oriented to productivity, efficiency, success, statistics, and public relations, and this orientation has often proved detrimental to the church's missional identity and calling. Power and wealth are especially important and difficult missional challenges in the institutional structures of connectedness.

The formation of a missional ecclesiology will most radically address the concrete realities of ecclesial institutions. The inherited structures of denominations and ecumenical organizations are profoundly marked by cultural captivity. In these structures, the ancient European legacy of compromises with power, property, influence brokering, competition, and empire building is obvious.

The widespread distrust of large, centralizing structures in our society is reflected in increasingly tense relationships between local congregations and their denominational structures. Although the reasons for this crisis are complex, one component is the impression that connectional structures are functioning as ends in themselves. These larger, or perhaps wider, structures of the church in North America are experienced as distant from the realities of the particular local community. While lip service is given to the idea that the connecting structures of the churches exist to serve the local congregations, these overarching structures can become strongly invested in their own agenda and maintenance. It is becoming progressively difficult to define their structural purposes missionally. Their missional renewal will come about as they redefine themselves in terms of the *missio Dei.* They need to submit themselves to the same authoritative formation by the Scriptures that is at work in the particular mission communities. They need to grapple with the implications of the church's cultural diversity. They need to become missional structures of connectedness.

Given such mistrust and the suspicion of the institution generally present in our society, the tendency of local congregations to retreat from connectional commitments is understandable. But for important missional reasons, this tendency must be checked. The denomination may need to be reinvented, and the shape of such emerging structures may be as yet unclear. One can have no doubt, however, that particular communities must be tangibly and structurally connected to the larger church, for the sake of the integrity of their mission.

Missional Connectedness, Structural Diversity, and Faithfulness

We have affirmed that the particularity and translatability of the *missio Dei* will always result in a diversity of organized structures of the church. This we see happening in the New Testament communities. The formative power of the cultural context has obviously contributed a great deal to these diverse structures. In light of this complex variety, how will we then determine if structures for missional connectedness in North America are truly faithful? How do we discern if the diversity of missional structures is biblically legitimate? In light of that diversity, what is common to the Christian church in all places and times? What is the organizational shape of the church's unity in all of its cultural diversity? How shall our church structures be shaped toward greater missional faithfulness? Much of what we have already discussed can apply here to the concrete character of the church's visible witness.

The Marks of the Church

The process of naming and defining the "marks of the church" at Nicea in the fourth century was another important example of missional connectedness at work. The ancient doctrinal development of the marks of the church grew out of the struggle with heresy. The church that is faithful to the gospel tradition, the Nicene Creed proclaimed, will always be experienced as "one, holy, catholic, and apostolic." The Reformation responded to the crisis of the sixteenth century by supplementing these classic marks with its definition of the "true church" in terms of its basic functions: wherever the Word is properly preached, the sacraments rightly administered, and (the Reformed addition) Christian discipline practiced. These traditions are important for the continuing formation of our theology of the church in and for North America. For a missional ecclesiology, the classic marks of the church help us to test and guide the mission faithfulness of both the particular mission community and the connecting structures of the church. Like the ecclesial practices, these marks will always characterize the particular community and the community of communities. In one way or another, the church must express the oneness, the holiness, the catholicity, and the apostolicity of the body of Christ in order to be a church. In one way or another, the church must preach the Word, administer the sacraments, and practice Christian disciplines.

Charles van Engen has suggested that the Nicene marks be read as adverbs rather than adjectives in order to capture the dynamic character of mission faithfulness.[7] Rather than static concepts defining the nature of the church, he proposes that the church's missional ministry is unifying, sanctifying, reconciling, and proclaiming. This constructive suggestion moves us much closer to a way of doing a missional ecclesiology because it focuses on the dynamic work of God's Spirit in and through the church, rather than dwelling on abstract concepts defining the church. But we suggest going one step further. In order to capture the fundamental character of the church's missional vocation, the Nicene marks should be also read and understood in reverse order. The church is called and sent to be apostolic, catholic, holy, and one — or, with van Engen, to be proclaiming, reconciling, sanctifying, and unifying.

The Apostolicity of the Church:
The Church as the Proclaiming Community

It has been customary to understand apostolicity in terms of faithfulness to the apostolic tradition. The church is apostolic in that it is based on the teaching and preaching of the apostles, carries forward their legacy, and, at least according to hierarchical traditions, actually embodies their

---

7. Charles van Engen, *God's Missionary People: Rethinking the Purpose of the Local Church* (Grand Rapids: Baker, 1991), 66ff.

succession. There is important truth in all of these emphases. But the missional nature of the church is more emphatically affirmed when the apostolic activity itself defines the church.[8] What the apostles did, that is, their life and work as witnesses to God's good news in Jesus Christ the Lord, defines and shapes the very nature of the church. The apostolicity of the church is expressed by its witness to the gospel, its obedience to the mandate to go out as Christ's ambassadors. "Based on [the commissioned apostles'] testimony which is preserved in the New Testament and in the life of the church, the church has as one constitutive mark its being apostolic, its being sent into the world."[9]

Such a sent church cannot let the need to maintain itself organizationally eclipse the mission for which it is called and equipped. Faithfulness to the apostolic authority of the church is not, then, merely a matter of subscription to doctrinal tenets. It is a matter of commitment to and practice of the apostles' mission, which comprises both the apostolic message as well as the apostolic incarnation of the gospel in community. The New Testament Scriptures are God's instrument to shape this apostolic community, as they witness to the apostolic message and mission. As the church continues to submit to the work of God's Spirit through the authoritative and normative biblical Word, it is empowered to continue the apostolic ministry.

The fundamental criterion of apostolicity defines and shapes both the particular mission community and the structures of connectedness. They are all apostolic in that they continue the apostolic ministry. They do so as an organic body, in complementary interdependence. But no aspect of their life and work can be called apostolic unless, in reconciling, sanctifying, and unifying ways it demonstrates the love of God through the rule of Christ. Further, the catholicity, holiness, and unity of the church are rooted in and formed by its apostolicity. These marks express the sent-ness of the church; they describe what this sent community does and how it does it.

8. Robert Scudieri argues that for the early church to be apostolic was to be missionary, and that this understanding was important in the development of the episcopal office; see *The Apostolic Church: One, Holy, Catholic and Missionary* (Fort Wayne: Lutheran Society for Missiology, 1995).

9. *Mission and Evangelism: An Ecumenical Affirmation* (Geneva: WCC Publications, 1983), §3.

The Catholicity of the Church:
The Church as the Reconciling and Reconciled Community

The catholicity of the church is demonstrated in all the ways that the church at every level witnesses to the one gospel that draws all people unto Christ. "Catholicity" should be understood in its original Greek sense: *kata holon,* "according to the whole, or appropriate to the whole." The World Council's Fourth Assembly at Uppsala (1968) defined this catholicity as "the quality by which the church expresses the fullness, the integrity, and the totality of life in Christ."

A particular mission community is catholic when its way of serving Christ is appropriate to the gospel while modestly recognizing that it is not the only way to be a Christian community. Its way of being Christian contributes to the reconciling of the entire church by focusing on the center of the gospel: the person and work of Christ, the hope of the gospel, the promised inbreaking of God's rule already begun in the apostolic mission.

Every particular community points consciously beyond itself to the global church as the full expression of the Spirit's work in calling and shaping God's people. This has many ramifications for the life of the particular community. Its work may focus on outreach to its own context, but as it carries out this outreach, it always expresses the catholic character of its faith. It works locally with a global attitude. It constantly learns from the experience of the multicultural church worldwide and seeks to link itself consciously to that community of communities. It communicates with the church catholic; it writes and receives letters, following the New Testament pattern. It rejects all attempts to define its own cultural tradition or its theology as normative for the global church. The particular community will thus reject words or actions that divide the church or set one cultural expression of it against another, knowing that such actions are a betrayal of its mission obedience.

The structures of connectedness have a distinctive set of responsibilities with regard to catholicity. Even as they represent their traditions and constituencies in many forms of interaction with each other, they must demonstrate in the way that they cooperate, listen, decide, and even disagree that the one gospel is authoritative over them all. They must keep their focus on the underlying apostolicity that forms the authentic church everywhere. And they must find ways to relate to each other that are appropriate to the wholeness of the gospel.

It will be especially difficult to practice such catholicity as marginalized churches in North America. We are accustomed to functioning at the center of society, supported and protected by our legal and cultural establishment. In such a system, catholicity appeared self-evident since all Christians were in the same or similar institutional structures. But as churches moved from the center to the margins, we now must discover what catholicity means in terms of our relationships with all Christians of all cultures. Our catholicity must now become much more intentional. It has to be a theme of our continuing repentance, conversion, and obedience.

Catholicity will demand special attention to the relationship, or lack of it, between the traditional denominational structures and the great spectrum of paralocal or specialized ministry organizations. For the sake of missional integrity, these diverse agents of mission need to move toward each other in dialogue. They need to address the much lamented church-parachurch conflicts and find ways to cooperate as one example of truly catholic or reconciling witness. Denominational structures might find it helpful to assess the proliferation of paralocal ministries as an indicator of possible deficiencies in denominations' understanding of their calling. In turn, paralocal ministries need to face the theological question of community. Specifically, in what ways are they valid expressions of mission community as defined above, or are they in accountable relationship with mission communities?

On all fronts, these structures of connectedness must examine their own sense of mission, or lack of it, and consider their conformities to the values of North American culture. We are not suggesting that some type of organizational union must at all costs be achieved, although that kind of union may, in many instances, be the most concrete way to incarnate the witness to unity. But the diversity of ministry agencies does not need to violate either the unity or catholicity of the church, if they practice their diversity in ways that are unifying and reconciling — that is, ways that are appropriate to the wholeness of the gospel.

The Holiness of the Church:
The Church as the Sanctifying Community

The holiness of the church is expressed by the way a particular community understands itself and functions as a community set apart for

God's mission. Since that mission is apostolic and entails the demonstration of the inbreaking gracious rule of God, the impact of the community's witness is sanctifying. That means that God's Spirit (the Sanctifier) works through the community's witness to heal the broken creation, to extend the salvation that Jesus accomplished on the cross. Thus the mission community carries out its mission by making holy through its witness. This holiness is demonstrated in the ways that it practices forgiveness, fosters healing and reconciliation, makes peace, loves righteousness, and walks in Jesus' footsteps in all that it does with all who are "the least of these who are members of my family" (cf. Matt. 25:40). The community sanctifies, by God's empowering Spirit, when it serves God and God's children as the continuing incarnation of Christ's love and invites others to join in this calling. In particular, its holiness must be translated into concrete service to those who are poor, discriminated against, and subject to injustice. The sanctifying community's confident anticipation of the *eschaton* makes its piety into a joyful foretaste and harbinger of the reign for whose coming it prays daily.

In short, the holiness of the church happens in and through the ecclesial practices. The community makes holy as it lives out the gospel in all its organizational processes, both internally and externally. With such an emphasis, the particular mission community is liberated to focus less on its holiness as a concern for its own inward spiritual state and more on its impact as a sanctifying presence where it is sent.

The same emphases need to characterize the structures of missional connectedness. At these levels, the holiness of the church should be demonstrated by the way the church structures go about their business. Their decision-making processes, administrative policies, financial practices, and personnel structures are all opportunities to incarnate the gospel. What our world needs to experience is institutions whose decisions and actions are shaped by God's love revealed in Christ. For the sake of its mission, the church must risk being genuinely alternative in our culture. This alternativeness does not mean a withdrawal of the church from society, but rather an intentional demonstration in the actions of our connecting structures of this basic fact: Christ is our Lord, and we are his witnesses and the firstfruits of his inbreaking rule. One place to begin would be to examine carefully the implications of the Beatitudes for the ways in which our structures of connectedness function.

The Unity of the Church:
The Church as the Unifying Community

The apostolicity of the church, expressed in its catholicity and holiness, must result in its unity. The emergence of the contemporary ecumenical movement out of the worldwide missionary expansion of the seventeenth to early twentieth centuries is an intriguing demonstration of that fact. Where the missional vocation of the church is taken seriously, where the gospel mandate to be reconciled and reconciling, to be "holy even as I am holy" (Lev. 19:2; 20:26; 1 Pet. 1:16), shapes the church, then its visible and tangible unity must follow. This unifying witness is to be understood in the light of the New Testament's radical message of God's healing work that overcomes all human boundaries of discrimination and injustice, especially with regard to the poor. Divisions may arise because Christians disagree among themselves, as they have done since the first century. They may arise because of the cultural setting in which the church is functioning. The tension between Jewish and Gentile Christians in the early church is a first example of this cause. However disunity comes about, the gospel addresses it and the rule of Christ overcomes it.

The catholicity and the unity of the church are two sides of the same apostolic truth, because Christ reconciles us and we therefore are made one in Christ. In the particular community, this truth will mean that we need openly to confront everything that divides us, finding the ways we are "conformed to this world" (Rom. 12:2). The ministries of preaching and teaching are to equip the community to recognize and affirm as Christians those brothers and sisters with whom we disagree, because Christ has taken down the walls of division (Eph. 2:11ff.). We practice unifying mission when we lay bare and seek forgiveness for all the ways we do discriminate within the community. Our ecclesial life is unifying when we follow Paul's detailed instructions in Romans 14 and cease judging one another and causing each other to stumble, and instead seek to "please our neighbor for the good purpose of building up the neighbor" (Rom. 15:2). Unifying missional practice confesses our racism, our sexism, our classism, and it experiences the healing work of the Lord who comes to those who know that they need a doctor. Unifying missional practice deals with our dissension by learning how to disagree Christianly. This is an important part of the apostolic instruction preserved in the New Testament.

In the model of the pilgrim people of God that we are considering, an important expression of this unifying witness is in the relationship between the centered congregation and the covenant community. The missional thrust of the covenant means that these people primarily understand themselves as the servants of their companions in the centered congregation. Their ministry is, first of all, with those who are part of their own particular mission community. Their mission begins within this fellowship. Not hierarchy or spiritual superiority, but Jesus washing the feet of his disciples is the model of ministry for the covenant community. To accept the disciplines of the covenant will mean to redefine oneself within the community as a "servant of the servants of Christ" *(servus servorum Christi).* [10] The New Testament teaching about our neighbor will also guide us in this practice. The neighbor is the one who is next to us, the one whom we encounter in our daily routines, whom to avoid requires effort on our part, and especially the ones next to us within the mission community.

The connecting structures of the church, for their part, should express and implement the mutual interdependence of all the parts of Christ's body. They should do this both in relationship to the particular communities that make up their constituencies (e.g., the congregations of a denomination) and in relationship to other structures. They should foster dialogue, enable contacts, provide resources to their communities, and encourage the public witness to the Lord who is the Prince of Peace and who breaks down walls of separation. This witness will move from the oneness of the community in Christ to the unifying power of the gospel as God's claim on the world. The practice of unity and unifying ministry are ethical expressions of the radical newness of the life made possible by birth from above (John 3:3-8).

The ecumenical movement represented by the World Council of Churches has tended to advocate organizational unity as one, if not the most, important form of Christian witness to the gospel. There have been significant organizational expressions of that commitment during this century, for example, the Church of South India, the Church of North India, the United Church of Canada, as well as various union processes within Lutheran, Congregational, and Presbyterian traditions in North America and elsewhere. The Consultation on Church Union in the United States evolved into the project of forming nine denomi-

---

10. This classic title of the pope applies to all Christians in the missional church.

nations into the Church of Christ Uniting.[11] One can have no doubt that the unity of the Christian community is fundamental to its obedient witness, as defined by the New Testament.

By contrast, we have stressed the multicultural character of the church. We have stated that structure is an aspect of cultural translation, one way in which the gospel is incarnated concretely within human experience. In our organizational structures, we express the translatability of the gospel into our specific cultural contexts in ways similar to the translation of the Bible into vernacular languages. There appears to be a tension between the biblical mandate "to be one" and "to disciple the nations" in their cultural particularity. That tension is present in North America, which is itself multicultural.

When the church in its diverse structures presents to the world a witness of competitiveness, contention, wastefulness, and mutual judgmentalism, then it is not bearing witness to the Christ who makes peace and breaks down the walls of division. The visible church is called by Christ and empowered by the Holy Spirit to be one church. Paul instructs the church to make "every effort to maintain the unity of the Spirit in the bond of peace" (Eph. 4:3). But how does one understand this unity? We suggest that the churches in North America need to analyze what the New Testament means by "oneness" and what we usually mean by "ecumenical unity." To put it briefly, does the New Testament understand the church's oneness as centralized, hierarchically organized church structure? Is it some kind of corporate or bureaucratic institution that provides services and defines denominational identity? Or is it disciplines of community, fellowship, shared ministry, and mutual support that translate the ecclesial practices into every level of the organized church?

The quest for organizational unity is complicated by our Christendom history. Powerful assumptions inform this legacy that in turn shape our understanding of unity.[12] Structural unity has to do with power,

---

11. At this writing, the Church of Christ Uniting (C.O.C.U.) project is faltering. One might ask if part of the reason is its missional weakness. Perhaps the process would have gone differently if the participants had started with their common apostolicity, that is, their common calling to be and become a missional church, and then moved toward the unifying of the church from that foundation.

12. For a thorough analysis of these powerful traditions, see John Milbank, *Theology and Social Theory: Beyond Secular Reason* (Cambridge, Mass.: Blackwell, 1991).

hierarchy, and uniformity of organizational forms and functions. This is even implied in liturgical practice. We often assume that the unity of the church should be defined as national, that is, by the political boundaries of the nation within which a particular church is located. These boundaries have frequently crossed through cultural regions, dividing peoples and their churches, and creating continuing problems. We can see examples of such culturally insensitive political boundaries wherever Western colonization was active, but in Europe as well. The state church is a subtly powerful model that still shapes the ecumenical efforts of North American denominations. We struggle in some of our denominations with boundaries of judicatories that literally prevent meaningful mission within regions whose social structures have radically changed since those boundaries were drawn. National churches, state churches, people's churches *(Volkskirchen)*, and connectional churches in Western Christendom have frequently been insensitive to, if not repressive of, the cultural diversity within political boundaries.

Further, the issue of organizational unity in North America should be probed with a view to the specific character of North American culture, in which issues like efficiency, management, and power dominate. The influence of the corporate business ethos on North American denominations can be seen in present efforts to unite denominations, moving from top to bottom. Corporations may merge when their respective administrations or stockholders decide to do so. But denominational churches do not necessarily unite when their headquarters want to merge.

Next to these patterns of institutional unity we also contend with more sentimental concepts of unity that focus on feelings of oneness. Many conservative Christians like to stress that we are all one in Christ because we share similar emotional experiences and thus are all part of the invisible church. One independent missionary organization emphasizes in its statement of faith that "we believe in the spiritual unity of believers in our Lord Jesus Christ." This spiritual unity is not, however, a concrete, tangible reality. From the world's perspective, the witness remains divided and often competitive. A spiritual unity that is neither concrete nor institutional is, by definition, not incarnational. When the gospel becomes flesh, it takes on organizational forms that witness to the apostolicity, catholicity, and holiness of God's missionary people.

There is good reason to be skeptical about the assumptions that shape our understandings of unity in the Western tradition. But when we read the biblical record carefully, we discover that the biblical practice of unity focused on the church's faithful mission as it demonstrated the gospel of peace. Evangelical unity is a way of living out the gospel in community, a way of incarnating the love of God in Christ. It is not defined biblically in organizational terms at all, and certainly not as a centralized institution regulating all the New Testament communities under one central headquarters. It is also far more than a spiritual feeling or a pious idea. It functions concretely as communities practice accountability toward each other and submit to each other's guidance and admonition. Evangelical unity rejects the idea that any particular community is independent of all other communities. Dependence, connectedness, mutual love, shared responsibility, as well as submission to one another are the marks of the structures of connectedness that practice unity as apostolic witness. The biblical purpose of visible unity is to manifest the "unity of the Spirit in the bond of peace." This witness manifests to the world that there is "one body and one Spirit, just as you were called to the one hope of your calling, one Lord, one faith, one baptism, one God and Father of all, who is above all and through all and in all" (Eph. 4:4-6).

This call to unity must be effected in new and altered structures. We must ask whether our inherited assumptions about those structures are the only options in God's economy for the church. The church's oneness must carry out and demonstrate its mission. Unity is witness. To seek unity for the sake of faithful witness will reveal more options for the structures of the church than the organizational approaches that currently dominate our ecumenical efforts.

Toward Missional Structures of Connectedness

The task of transforming the connectional structures of the North American churches into missional structures is obviously daunting. But the task is unavoidable and necessary. Connectional structures are missiologically essential to the apostolicity, catholicity, holiness, and unity of the church. These marks of the church, as we have said, are not to be abstractions. We are to incarnate them both in the life and practice of the local congregation and in the connectional structures that relate the local and particular to the universal and catholic. The connectional structures of the church are needed to represent the missional unity that transcends all human boundaries and cultural distinctions. These structures will express the multicultural diversity that is part of God's good design for the church. That diversity is seen in different ways to organize the church, different approaches to public worship and liturgy, different systems of leadership and decision making, different patterns of theological reflection and doctrinal formulation. Yet in all those differences there is the necessary counterbalance provided by structures of connectedness that testify to one Lord, one gospel, and one mission.

What we propose as structures of connectedness will both authenticate and relativize the cultural diversity of the church. The legitimate variety of theological, liturgical, and organizational expressions of Christian faith and mission needs to be related to the common center of the gospel. This is how we demonstrate the infinite translatability of the good news.

The movement toward missional connectedness should be centrifugal, starting from particular communities and expanding to the global dimensions of the church, the community of communities. God's Spirit forms particular communities for mission in particular places and multiplies that mission by increasing the number of particular communities: the church moves from Jerusalem to Judea to Samaria and out to the ends of the earth. As this happens, the Spirit has shaped this church to become multicultural, multiethnic, geographically extensive, and organizationally diverse.

We see this movement in especially dramatic ways in the expansion of the Christian church throughout the twentieth century. Our history teaches us, however, that this process may degenerate as particular communities begin to see themselves as exclusive, as "the church the way it ought to be." Particularity can deteriorate into exclusivity: communities begin to assume that their version of the gospel is final and complete; communities develop practices that they see as the only true expression of Christian discipleship; communities begin to judge each other's authenticity, using themselves as their standard; communities translate the gospel into their cultures in such a way that they become captive to their context and serve other masters than their Lord. The result is the formation of communities cut off from the rest of the body, claiming to be the true church, or its true remnant. In their isolation, such communities rarely can see their own shortcomings, rarely repent, rarely experience the continuing conversion that is essential to Christian growth and faithfulness.

In like manner, structures of connectedness are susceptible to the misconception that they are themselves the reign of God. Rather, they are its servants. As they connect particular communities around the world, they share with those communities the task to be the sign, foretaste, and instrument of God's inbreaking kingdom. As human organizations, developed by human initiative seeking to be faithful to God's mission, they are just as sinful as every particular community and every individual Christian. The seductive impact of accumulated power often leads the connecting structures to betray the church's mission. They betray it when they develop corporate behaviors that are not "worthy of the calling to which they have been called." They do this when they bless wars, condone and even practice economic injustice, endorse slavery and racial discrimination, tolerate immorality among secular rulers and ecclesial leaders, and exploit their power to build their own wealth. In its structures of connectedness, the church lives out of repentance and forgiveness, but it is difficult, especially for larger and complex institutional structures, to practice such basic Christian disciplines. Their reform therefore almost always originates nearer the particular community and expands outward. A missional ecclesiology for North America will ask how our structures of connectedness engage in these essential ecclesial practices.

The missional ecclesiology for North America that we envision assumes that these structures of connectedness are theologically essential for mission. We cannot espouse a classic congregationalism that rejects connecting structures of accountability, cooperation, and decision making. The ecclesiology we propose, however, will insist that such structures be defined and evaluated by the church's mission. They are not divinely inspired institutions but functionally designed structures to support, complement, and enhance the mission of the church catholic, both particular and connected. They are not intended to replace organizational diversity with uniformity but to demonstrate oneness in Christ in all the ways that they witness to the one gospel. Unity is defined in terms of catholicity. Particular mission communities are helped to lead lives "worthy of the calling to which they have been called" when they are related to the church around the world so as to demonstrate the reconciling character of the gospel.

The Continual Conversion of the
Missional Structures of the Church

All structures change. Our concern is that this change in missional structures be intentional and evangelically shaped. The continuing organizational processes of the church, both particular and connected, need to interact with the gospel, the tradition, and the challenges of the particular cultural context. This should be a dynamic process in which the church responds to the challenges of social change and to the claims of the gospel as it is heard in new and transforming ways. These processes will have missional integrity when we incorporate into our structures, at every level, ways to examine ourselves and our institutions in the light of the gospel. It begins with our confession that we need the Holy Spirit's continual work to convert us, and it continues as we approach Scripture, the traditions, and the global experience of the church knowing that we always require forgiveness and renewal. For this reason, we constantly emphasize that the first mission of the church is always to itself. The church that itself is constantly being evangelized, that hears and responds to the invitation to receive and enter the divine reign of God, is the church that can be faithful in its witness to the world.

We know from an attentive reading of our history that we may expect the church to continue to reduce the gospel to a comfortable fit with its culture. Therefore we know that we need to repent of such reductionism. We know that the church will, again and again, fail to perceive opportunities for witness in its cultural context. We know that we need to repent of our lack of vision. We know that the church will allow itself to be seduced by power, fame, prestige, and wealth. We know thus that we need to seek God's cleansing and forgiving work to prepare us for our continuing mission. We know that we, as the church, will deny our Lord by allowing other masters to dominate and use us. We will have to break these idols and be restored to our proper place as Christ's disciples and apostles.

As our North American society continues to experience massive change, including a paradigm shift, we can claim and use unique resources to understand the processes that have produced and continue to shape us. Our work on a missional ecclesiology can supplement our biblical and doctrinal labors with insights gained from historical, anthropological, and sociological analyses. All of this helps us to see how we are conformed to this world. We may welcome the disestablishment of our traditional structures and the rapidly changing shape of our denominations as a God-given opportunity to shape ourselves for God's mission. We may not be able to foresee the outcome of this exile-like passage through which we are moving, but we can with all modesty mark out the trajectories of organizational reform that will move us toward greater missional faithfulness. We can start to set aside the institutional baggage that no longer serves the church, both particular and connected, in its mission. We can seek to run the race with clearer vision, based on what we have learned, attempted, and failed at in our history.

A missional ecclesiology must clearly identify and resist all attempts to equip the church merely for its maintenance and security. It must reject every proposal to restore the trappings and privileges of Christendom. It must boldly question every temptation to indulge in compromises with worldly power and jeopardize the institutional practice of servanthood after the model of Jesus. Wherever we see that we are structuring ourselves to serve national, ethnic, or cultural interests, we need to turn to Scripture and to the global church for guidance and correction. Wherever we or our sister communions see the resurgence of our old addictions to control, to management and planning God's future, to strategies to bring in the kingdom, we need humbly to seek God's strength to liberate us. The gospel of the inbreaking reign of God must be upheld as the sole criterion of the particular and connecting structures of the church. That gospel requires of the church that it be open to surprise, to testing, to suffering, as well as to the blessing of joy and peace.

In particular, a missional ecclesiology for North America will resist all attempts at uniformity of structure in favor of a missional unity in diversity. It will renounce the power games of democratic and representational polities in favor of creative new forms of collegiality and consensus formation. The "strong in faith" will be required in a missional ecclesiology to shape their desires and actions around the needs of the "weak in faith" (Rom. 14), as a testimony to the transformed understanding of power that we are learning from Jesus. In terms of the lessons of our long history, we will shape our structures of connectedness in the tradition of conciliarism, which we know to be more missiologically faithful than hierarchical structures. The connecting structures of the church will be designed as communities of communities, standing under and shaped by the same missional mandate that is normative for the church in all times and in all places: "You shall be my witnesses."

Bibliography for Research on a Missional Ecclesiology for North America

This bibliography draws together the literature that the members of the research team used and recommend as important for the formation of a missional church. The list includes most but not all of the titles cited in this book. The resources are grouped according to the following areas:

    A. Missional Theologies of the Church
    B. Signaling the Current Crisis
    C. Biblical and Theological Perspectives
    D. Historical and Sociological Perspectives
    E. Vision for Pastoral and Congregational Practice

A. Missional Theologies of the Church

Arias, Mortimer. *Announcing the Reign of God: Evangelization and the Subversive Memory of Jesus.* Philadelphia: Fortress, 1984.

Barth, Karl. *Church Dogmatics.* Vol. 4, *The Doctrine of Reconciliation.* Tr. G. W. Bromiley. Ed. Bromiley and T. F. Torrance. Edinburgh: T. & T. Clark, 1956-69.

Blauw, Johannes. *The Missionary Nature of the Church.* New York: McGraw-Hill, 1962.

Bosch, David J. *Transforming Mission: Paradigm Shifts in Theology of Mission.* Maryknoll, N.Y.: Orbis, 1991.

Braaten, Carl E. *The Flaming Center: A Theology of the Christian Mission.* Philadelphia: Fortress, 1977.

————. *The Apostolic Imperative: Nature and Aim of the Church's Mission and Ministry.* Minneapolis: Augsburg, 1985.

Christians, Clifford, Earl J. Schipper, and Wesley Smedes, eds. *Who in the World?* Grand Rapids: Eerdmans, 1972.

Clapp, Rodney. *A Peculiar People: The Church as Culture in a Post-Christian Society.* Downers Grove, Ill.: InterVarsity Press, 1995.

Guder, Darrell L. *Be My Witnesses: The Church's Mission, Message, and Messengers.* Grand Rapids: Eerdmans, 1985.

Hoekendijk, J. C. *The Church Inside Out.* Tr. Isaac C. Rottenberg. Philadelphia: Westminster, 1966.

Hunsberger, George R., and Craig Van Gelder, eds. *The Church Between Gospel and Culture: The Emerging Mission in North America.* Grand Rapids: Eerdmans, 1996.

Newbigin, Lesslie. *The Household of God.* New York: Friendship, 1953.

————. *The Open Secret: Introduction to a Theology of Mission.* Grand Rapids: Eerdmans, 1978. Rev. ed. 1995.

————. *Sign of the Kingdom.* Grand Rapids: Eerdmans, 1980.

————. *The Gospel in a Pluralist Society.* Grand Rapids: Eerdmans, 1989.

Scudieri, Robert J. *The Apostolic Church: One, Holy, Catholic and Missionary.* Fort Wayne: Lutheran Society for Missiology, 1995.

Shenk, Wilbert R. *Write the Vision: The Church Renewed.* Valley Forge, Penn.: Trinity Press International, 1995.

Snyder, Howard A. *The Community of the King.* Downers Grove, Ill.: InterVarsity Press, 1977.

Taylor, John V. *The Go-Between God: The Holy Spirit and the Christian Mission.* London: SCM, 1972.

Trueblood, Elton. *The Incendiary Fellowship.* New York: Harper & Row, 1967.

Van Engen, Charles. *God's Missionary People: Rethinking the Purpose of the Local Church.* Grand Rapids: Baker, 1991.

Van Ruler, Arnold A. "A Theology of Mission." In *Calvinist Trinitarianism and Theocentric Politics: Essays Toward a Public Theology.* Tr. John Bolt. Lewiston, N.Y.: Edwin Mellen, 1989.

Vicedom, George F. *The Mission of God: An Introduction to a Theology of Mission.* Tr. Gilbert A. Theile and Dennis Hilgendorf. St. Louis: Concordia, 1965.

Webber, Robert E., and Rodney Clapp. *People of the Truth: A Christian*

Challenge to Contemporary Culture. Rev. ed. Harrisburg: Morehouse, 1993.

World Council of Churches. *Mission and Evangelism: An Ecumenical Affirmation.* Geneva: WCC Publications, 1982.

B. Signaling the Current Crisis

Bosch, David J. *Believing in the Future: Toward a Missiology of Western Culture.* Valley Forge, Penn.: Trinity Press International, 1995.

Brueggemann, Walter. *Disciplines of Readiness.* Louisville: Theology and Ministry Worship Unit, PC(USA), 1989.

Callahan, Kennon L. *Effective Church Leadership: Building on the Twelve Keys.* San Francisco: Harper & Row, 1990.

Hall, Douglas John. *Has the Church a Future?* Philadelphia: Westminster, 1980.

————. *An Awkward Church.* Louisville: Theology and Worship Ministry Unit, PC(USA), 1993.

Hauerwas, Stanley, and William H. Willimon. *Resident Aliens: Life in the Christian Colony.* Nashville: Abingdon, 1989.

Hodgson, Peter C. *Revisioning the Church: Ecclesial Freedom in the New Paradigm.* Philadelphia: Fortress, 1988.

Hoge, Dean, R. Benton Johnson, and Donald Luidens. *Vanishing Boundaries: The Religion of Mainline Protestant Baby Boomers.* Louisville: Westminster/John Knox, 1994.

Keck, Leander E. *The Church Confident.* Nashville: Abingdon, 1993.

Lash, Nicholas. *The Beginning and the End of "Religion."* Cambridge: Cambridge University Press, 1996.

Lindbeck, George A. "The Sectarian Future of the Church," in Joseph P. Whelan, S.J., ed., *The God Experience.* New York: Newman, 1971. Pp. 226-43.

Mead, Loren B. *The Once and Future Church: Reinventing the Congregation for a New Mission Frontier.* Bethesda: Alban Institute, 1991.

Lesslie Newbigin. *The Other Side of 1984: Questions for the Churches.* Repr. Geneva: WCC Publications, 1984.

————. *Foolishness to the Greeks: The Gospel and Western Culture.* Grand Rapids: Eerdmans, 1986.

Placher, William. *The Domestication of Transcendence: How Modern Thinking about God Went Wrong.* Louisville: Westminster/John Knox, 1996.

Radner, Ephraim. "From 'Liberation' to 'Exile': A New Image for Church Mission," *Christian Century* 106, no. 30 (1989): 931-34.

Sanneh, Lamin. *Encountering the West: Christianity and the Global Cultural Process: The African Dimension.* Maryknoll, N.Y.: Orbis, 1993.

Thiselton, Anthony C. *Interpreting God and the Postmodern Self.* Grand Rapids: Eerdmans, 1996.

C. Biblical and Theological Perspectives

Abbott, Walter M., S.J., ed. *The Documents of Vatican II.* New York: Herder and Herder, Guild Press, American Press, and Association Press, 1966.

Banks, Robert. *Paul's Idea of Community: The Early House Churches in Their Historical Setting.* Grand Rapids: Eerdmans, 1980.

Barrett, Lois. *Doing What Is Right: What the Bible Says about Covenant and Justice.* Scottdale, Penn.: Herald Press, 1987.

Barth, Markus. *Ephesians.* Anchor Bible 34-34A. Garden City, N.Y.: Doubleday, 1974.

Berkhof, Hendrikus. *Christ and the Powers.* Tr. John Howard Yoder. Scottdale, Penn.: Herald, 1962.

Berkouwer, G. C. *The Church.* Tr. James E. Davison. Grand Rapids: Eerdmans, 1976.

Boff, Leonardo. *Trinity and Society.* Tr. Paul Burns. Maryknoll, N.Y.: Orbis, 1988.

Brownson, James V. "Speaking the Truth in Love: Elements of a Missional Hermeneutic." In George R. Hunsberger and Craig Van Gelder, eds. *The Church Between Gospel and Culture: The Emerging Mission in North America.* Grand Rapids: Eerdmans, 1996. Pp. 228-59.

Cobble, James F. *The Church and the Powers: A Theology of Church Structure.* Peabody, Mass.: Hendrickson, 1988.

Driver, John. *Understanding the Atonement for the Mission of the Church.* Scottdale, Penn.: Herald, 1986.

Dulles, Avery, S.J. *Models of the Church.* Expanded ed. Garden City, N.Y.: Image, 1987.

Fee, Gordon D. *Paul, the Spirit, and the People of God.* Peabody, Mass.: Hendrickson, 1996.

Ferguson, Everett. *The Church of Christ: A Biblical Ecclesiology for Today.* Grand Rapids: Eerdmans, 1996.

272

Gonzales, Justo L. *Out of Every Tribe and Nation: Christian Theology at the Ethnic Roundtable.* Nashville: Abingdon, 1992.

Gunton, Colin E. *The One, the Three and the Many: God, Creation and the Culture of Modernity.* Cambridge: Cambridge University Press, 1993.

Guroian, Vigen. *Ethics after Christendom: Toward an Ecclesial Christian Ethic.* Grand Rapids: Eerdmans, 1994.

Hall, Douglas John. *Thinking the Faith: Christian Theology in the North American Context.* Minneapolis: Augsburg, 1989.

———. *Professing the Faith: Christian Theology in a North American Context.* Minneapolis: Fortress Press, 1993.

———. *Confessing the Faith: Christian Theology in a North American Context.* Minneapolis: Fortress Press, 1996.

Hanson, Paul D. *The People Called: The Growth of Community in the Bible.* San Francisco: Harper & Row, 1986.

Hauerwas, Stanley. *Character and the Christian Life: A Study in Theological Ethics.* San Antonio: Trinity University Press, 1975.

———. *A Community of Character: Toward a Constructive Christian Social Ethic.* Notre Dame, Ind.: University of Notre Dame Press, 1981.

———. *In Good Company: The Church as Polis.* Notre Dame: University of Notre Dame Press, 1985.

Hays, Richard B. "Ecclesiology and Ethics in First Corinthians," *Ex Auditu* 10 (1994): 31-43.

Hunsberger, George R. "Is There Biblical Warrant for Evangelism?" *Interpretation* 48, no. 2 (1994): 131-44.

Johnson, Ben Campbell. *95 Theses for the Church: Finding Direction Today.* Decatur, Ga.: CTS Press, 1995.

Johnson, Luke Timothy. *Scripture and Discernment: Decision Making in the Church.* Rev. ed. Nashville: Abingdon, 1996.

Kraus, C. Norman. *The Authentic Witness: Credibility and Authority.* Grand Rapids: Eerdmans, 1978.

———. *The Community of the Spirit: How the Church is in the World.* Scottdale, Penn.: Herald, 1993.

Kraybill, Donald B. *Upside-Down Kingdom.* Scottdale, Penn.: Herald, 1978.

Küng, Hans. *The Church.* Garden City, N.Y.: Image, 1967.

LaCugna, Catherine Mowry. *God for Us: The Trinity and Christian Life.* San Francisco: Harper & Row, 1991.

Lohfink, Gerhard. *Jesus and Community: The Social Dimension of Christian Faith.* Tr. John P. Galvin. Philadelphia: Fortress, 1984.

MacIntyre, Alasdair. *After Virtue.* 2nd ed. Notre Dame: University of Notre Dame Press, 1984.

Minear, Paul S. *Images of the Church in the New Testament.* Philadelphia: Westminster, 1960.

Moltmann, Jürgen. *The Church in the Power of the Spirit: A Contribution to Messianic Eschatology.* Tr. Margaret Kohl. New York: Harper & Row, 1977.

Newbigin, Lesslie. *The Relevance of Trinitarian Doctrine for Today's Mission.* London: Edinburgh House Press, 1963. Republished as *Trinitarian Faith and Today's Mission,* Richmond: John Knox, 1964.

————. "The Form and Structure of the Visible Unity of the Church." In Otto Wack, et al., eds. *So Sende Ich Euch: Festschrift für D. Dr. Martin Pörksen zum 70. Geburtstag.* Korntal bei Stuttgart: Evang. Missionsverlag, 1973. Pp. 124-41.

Palmer, Parker. *The Company of Strangers: Christians and the Renewal of America's Public Life.* New York: Crossroad, 1986.

Paul, Robert S. *The Church in Search of Itself.* Grand Rapids: Eerdmans, 1972.

Rasmusson, Arne. *The Church as Polis: From Political Theology to Theological Politics as Exemplified by Jürgen Moltmann and Stanley Hauerwas.* Notre Dame, Ind.: University of Notre Dame Press, 1994.

Ridderbos, Herman. *The Coming of the Kingdom.* Tr. H. de Jongste. Philadelphia: Presbyterian & Reformed, 1962.

Russell, Keith. *In Search of the Church: New Testament Images for Tomorrow's Congregations.* Bethesda: Alban Institute, 1994.

Sanneh, Lamin. *Translating the Message: The Missionary Impact on Culture.* Maryknoll, N.Y.: Orbis, 1989.

Schweizer, Eduard. *Church Order in the New Testament.* Tr. Frank Clarke. Studies in Biblical Theology 1/32. Naperville: Allenson, 1962.

Snyder, Howard A. *Models of the Kingdom.* Nashville: Abingdon, 1991.

Volf, Miroslav. "Soft Difference: Theological Reflections on the Relation Between Church and Culture in 1 Peter," *Ex Auditu* 10 (1994): 15-30.

Wink, Walter. *Engaging the Powers: Discernment and Resistance in a World of Domination.* Minneapolis: Fortress, 1992.

Wolters, Albert M. *Creation Regained: Biblical Basics for a Reformational Worldview.* Grand Rapids: Eerdmans, 1985.

Yoder, John Howard. *The Royal Priesthood: Essays Ecclesiological and Ecumenical.* Grand Rapids: Eerdmans, 1994.

D. Historical and Sociological Perspectives

Ahlstrom, Sydney A. *A Religious History of the American People*. 2 vols. Garden City, N.Y.: Image, 1975.

Ammerman, Nancy. *Congregation and Community Life*. New Brunswick: Rutgers University Press, 1996.

Avis, Paul D. L. *The Church in the Theology of the Reformers*. Atlanta: John Knox, 1981.

Bellah, Robert, et al. *Habits of the Heart: Individualism and Commitment in American Life*. Berkeley: University of California Press, 1985.

Bibby, Reginald W. *Fragmented Gods: The Poverty and Potential of Religions in Canada*. Toronto: Irwin, 1987.

————. *Mosaic Madness*. Toronto: Stoddard, 1990.

————. *The Unknown Gods*. Toronto: Stoddard, 1993.

————. *There's Got to Be More! Connecting Churches and Canadians*. Winfield, B.C.: Wood Lake Books, 1995.

Carroll, Jackson W., and Wade Clark Roof, eds. *Beyond Establishment: Protestant Identity in a Post-Protestant Age*. Louisville: Westminster/John Knox, 1993.

Carroll, Jackson W., Carl S. Dudley, and William McKinney, eds. *Handbook for Congregational Studies*. Nashville: Abingdon, 1986.

Coalter, Milton J, John M. Mulder, and Louis B. Weeks. *Vital Signs: The Promise of Mainstream Protestantism*. Grand Rapids: Eerdmans, 1996.

Coalter, Milton J, and Virgil Cruz, eds. *How Shall We Witness?: Faithful Evangelism in a Reformed Tradition*. Louisville: Westminster/John Knox, 1995.

Crook, Stephen, Jan Palulski, and Malcolm Waters. *Postmodernization: Change in Advanced Society*. London: Sage, 1992.

Dudley, Carl S., Jackson W. Carroll, and James P. Wind, eds. *Carriers of Faith: Lessons from Congregational Studies*. Louisville: Westminster/John Knox, 1991.

Ellul, Jacques. *The Technological Society*. Tr. John Wilkinson. New York: Vintage, 1964.

Finke, Roger, and Rodney Stark. *The Churching of America, 1776-1990: Winners and Losers in our Religious Economy*. New Brunswick: Rutgers University Press, 1992.

Giddens, Anthony. *Modernity and Self-Identity*. Oxford: Oxford University Press, 1991.

275

Grant, John Webster. *The Churches in the Canadian Experience: A Faith and Order Study of the Christian Tradition.* Toronto: Ryerson, 1963.

————. *The Church in the Canadian Era: The First Century of Confederation.* Toronto: McGraw-Hill Ryerson, 1972.

Grenz, Stanley J. *A Primer on Postmodernism.* Grand Rapids: Eerdmans, 1996.

Hopewell, James F. *Congregation: Stories and Structures.* Ed. Barbara G. Wheeler. Philadelphia: Fortress, 1987.

Hough, Joseph C., Jr., and Barbara G. Wheeler, eds. *Beyond Clericalism: The Congregation as a Focus for Theological Education.* Decatur, Ga.: Scholars Press, 1988.

Hudson, Winthrop S. *Religion in America.* New York: Charles Scribner's Sons, 1965.

Hunter, James D. *Cultural Wars: The Struggle to Define America.* New York: Basic Books, 1991.

Luzbetak, Louis J. *The Church and Cultures: New Perspectives in Missiological Anthropology.* Maryknoll, N.Y.: Orbis, 1995.

Marty, Martin E. *The Modern Schism: Three Paths to the Secular.* New York and Evanston: Harper & Row, 1969.

————. *Righteous Empire: The Protestant Experience in America.* New York: Dial, 1970.

Milbank, John. *Theology and Social Theory: Beyond Secular Reason.* Cambridge, Mass.: Blackwell, 1991.

Niebuhr, H. Richard. *The Social Sources of Denominationalism.* Repr. Cleveland: World, 1957.

Richey, Russell E., ed. *Denominationalism.* Nashville: Parthenon, 1977.

Richey, Russell E., and Robert Bruce Mullin, eds. *Reimagining Denominationalism.* New York: Oxford University Press, 1994.

Roof, Wade Clark, and William McKinney. *American Mainline Religion: Its Changing Shape and Future.* New Brunswick: Rutgers University Press, 1987.

Roozen, David A., William McKinney, and Jackson W. Carroll. *Varieties of Religious Presence: Mission in Public Life.* New York: Pilgrim, 1984.

Tickle, Phyllis A. *Re-Discovering the Sacred: Spirituality in America.* New York: Crossroad, 1983.

Van Der Ven, Johannes. *Ecclesiology in Context.* Grand Rapids: Eerdmans, 1996.

Walls, Andrew F. *The Missionary Movement in Christian History: Studies in the Transmission of Faith.* Maryknoll, N.Y.: Orbis, 1996.

Walsh, H. H. *The Christian Church in Canada.* Toronto: Ryerson, 1956.

Williams, Raymond. *Keywords: A Vocabulary of Culture and Society.* New York: Oxford University Press, 1976.

Winter, Gibson. *The Suburban Captivity of the Churches: An Analysis of Protestant Responsibility in the Expanding Metropolis.* New York: Macmillan, 1962.

Winter, Ralph, and R. Pierce Beaver. *The Warp and the Woof: Organizing for Mission.* Pasadena: William Carey Library, 1970.

Wuthnow, Robert. *The Restructuring of American Religion: Society and Faith Since World War II.* Princeton: Princeton University Press, 1988.

E. Vision for Pastoral and Congregational Practice

Abraham, William J. *The Logic of Evangelism.* Grand Rapids: Eerdmans, 1989.

Ammerman, Nancy T. "SBC Moderates and the Making of a Postmodern Denomination," *Christian Century* 110, no. 26 (1993): 896-99.

Anderson, Ray. *Ministry on the Fireline.* Downers Grove, Ill.: InterVarsity Press, 1993.

Arbuckle, Gerald A. *Earthing the Gospel: An Inculturation Handbook for Pastoral Workers.* Maryknoll, N.Y.: Orbis, 1990.

————. *Refounding the Church: Dissent for Leadership.* Maryknoll, N.Y.: Orbis, 1993.

Arias, Mortimer, and Alan Johnson. *The Great Commission: Biblical Models for Evangelism.* Nashville: Abingdon, 1992.

Banks, Robert and Julia. *The Church Comes Home: Regrouping the People of God for Community and Mission.* Peabody, Mass.: Hendrickson, 1997.

Barrett, Lois. *Building the House Church.* Scottdale, Penn.: Herald, 1986.

Boff, Leonardo. *Ecclesiogenesis: The Basic Communities Reinvent the Church.* Tr. Robert R. Barr. Maryknoll, N.Y.: Orbis, 1986.

Brueggemann, Walter. *Biblical Perspectives on Evangelism: Living in a Three-Storied Universe.* Nashville: Abingdon, 1993.

Clark, Stephen B., ed. *Covenant Community and Church: A Statement on Catholic Covenant Community and a Selection of Documents.* Ann Arbor: Servant, 1992.

Cosby, Gordon. *Handbook for Mission Groups.* Waco: Word, 1975.

Dietterich, Inagrace. *Cultivating Purpose-Driven Churches.* Chicago: Center for Parish Development, 1996.

Dietterich, Paul. *The Transformation Zone.* Chicago: Center for Parish Development, 1996.

Farley, Edward. *Theologia: The Fragmentation and Unity of Theological Education.* Philadelphia: Fortress, 1983.

Foster, Charles R., and Theodore Brelsford. *We Are the Church Together: Cultural Diversity in Congregational Life.* Valley Forge, Penn.: Trinity Press International, 1996.

Fowl, Stephen E., and L. Gregory Jones. *Reading in Communion: Scripture and Ethics in Christian Life.* Grand Rapids: Eerdmans, 1991.

Fung, Raymond. *The Isaiah Vision: An Ecumenical Strategy for Congregational Evangelism.* Geneva: WCC Publications, 1992.

Gish, Arthur G. *Living in Christian Community.* Scottdale, Penn.: Herald, 1979.

Guder, Darrell L. "Evangelism and the Debate over Church Growth," *Interpretation* 48, no. 2 (1994): 145-55.

Hauerwas, Stanley. *Christian Existence Today: Essays on Church, World and Living in Between.* Durham: Labyrinth, 1988.

Hauerwas, Stanley, and William H. Willimon. *Where Resident Aliens Live: Exercises for Christian Practice.* Nashville: Abingdon, 1996.

Hinton, Jeanne. *Walking in the Same Direction: A New Way of Being Church.* Geneva: WCC Publications, 1995.

Hunsberger, George R. "The Changing Face of Ministry: Christian Leadership for the Twenty-First Century," *Reformed Review* 44, no. 3 (1991): 224-45.

―――. "Cutting the Christendom Knot." In Shin Chiba, George R. Hunsberger, and Lester Edwin J. Ruiz, eds., *Christian Ethics in Ecumenical Context: Theology, Culture, and Politics.* Grand Rapids: Eerdmans, 1995.

Hunter, George G., III. *Church for the Unchurched.* Nashville: Abingdon, 1996.

Hybels, Lynne, and Bill Hybels. *Rediscovering Church: The Story and Vision of Willow Creek Community Church.* Grand Rapids: Zondervan, 1995.

Johnson, Ben Campbell. *Rethinking Evangelism: A Theological Approach.* Philadelphia: Westminster, 1987.

―――. *New Day, New Church: Evangelism for Mainline Denominations.* Decatur, Ga.: CTS Press, 1995.

Jones, J. Gregory. *Embodying Forgiveness: A Theological Analysis.* Grand Rapids: Eerdmans, 1995.

Keifert, Patrick R. *Welcoming the Stranger: A Public Theology of Worship and Evangelism.* Minneapolis: Fortress, 1992.

Koenig, John. *New Testament Hospitality: Partnership with Strangers as Promise and Mission.* Philadelphia: Fortress, 1985.

Lee, Bernard J., and Michael A. Cowan. *Dangerous Memories: House Churches and Our American Story.* Kansas City: Sheed and Ward, 1986.

Lovell, Arnold, ed. *Evangelism in the Reformed Tradition.* Decatur, Ga.: CTS Press, 1990.

Mead, Loren B. *Transforming Congregations for the Future.* Bethesda: Alban Institute, 1994.

―――. *Five Challenges for the Once and Future Church.* Bethesda: Alban Institute, 1996.

Messer, Donald E. *A Conspiracy of Goodness: Contemporary Images of Christian Mission.* Nashville: Abingdon, 1992.

Mudge, Lewis S. *The Sense of a People: Toward a Church for the Human Future.* Philadelphia: Trinity Press International, 1992.

Nelson, C. Ellis. *Congregations: Their Power to Form and Transform.* Atlanta: John Knox, 1988.

O'Connor, Elizabeth. *Call to Commitment: The Story of the Church of the Saviour.* New York: Harper & Row, 1963.

―――. *Journey Inward, Journey Outward.* New York: Harper & Row, 1968.

―――. *The New Community.* New York: Harper & Row, 1976.

Ogden, Greg. *The New Reformation.* Grand Rapids: Zondervan, 1990.

Peterson, Eugene H. *The Contemplative Pastor: Returning to the Art of Spiritual Direction.* Grand Rapids: Eerdmans, 1989.

―――. *Five Smooth Stones for Pastoral Work.* Atlanta: John Knox, 1980.

―――. *Working the Angles: The Shape of Pastoral Integrity.* Grand Rapids: Eerdmans, 1987.

―――. *Under the Unpredictable Plant: An Exploration in Vocational Holiness.* Grand Rapids: Eerdmans, 1992.

Roxburgh, Alan J. *Reaching a New Generation: Strategies for Tomorrow's Church.* Downers Grove, Ill.: InterVarsity Press, 1993.

Russell, Letty. *Church in the Round: Feminist Interpretation of the Church.* Louisville: Westminster/John Knox, 1993.

Sample, Tex. *U.S. Lifestyles and Mainline Churches.* Louisville: Westminster/John Knox, 1990.

Schreiter, Robert J. *Constructing Local Theologies.* Maryknoll, N.Y.: Orbis, 1985.

Senge, Peter M. *The Fifth Discipline: The Art and Practice of the Learning Organization.* New York: Doubleday, 1990.

Senn, Frank C. *The Witness of the Worshiping Community: Liturgy and the Practice of Evangelism.* New York and Mahwah, N.J.: Paulist, 1993.

Shenk, David W., and Erwin R. Stutzman. *Creating Communities of the Kingdom: New Testament Models of Church Planting.* Scottdale, Penn.: Herald, 1988.

Snyder, Howard A. *Signs of the Spirit: How God Reshapes the Church.* Grand Rapids: Zondervan, 1989.

Stevens, Paul. *Liberating the Laity.* Downers Grove, Ill.: InterVarsity Press, 1985.

Trueblood, Elton. *The Company of the Committed.* New York: Harper & Brothers, 1961.

Wallis, Jim. *Agenda for Biblical People: A New Focus for Developing a Life-Style of Discipleship.* New York: Harper & Row, 1976.

Walton, Martin. *Marginal Communities: The Ethical Enterprise of the Followers of Jesus.* Kampen: Kok Pharos, 1994.

Warren, Michael. *Faith, Culture, and the Worshiping Community: Shaping the Practice of the Local Church.* Rev. ed. Washington, D.C.: Pastoral Press, 1993.

Watson, David Lowes. *Covenant Discipleship: Christian Formation Through Mutual Accountability.* Nashville: Discipleship Resources, 1991.

Westerhoff, John H. *Living the Faith Community: The Church that Makes a Difference.* San Francisco: Harper & Row, 1985.

Willimon, William H. *Shaped by the Bible.* Nashville: Abingdon, 1990.

Wright, N. T. *Following Jesus: Biblical Reflections on Discipleship.* Grand Rapids: Eerdmans, 1994.

Yoder, John Howard. *Body Politics: Five Practices of the Christian Community Before the Watching World.* Nashville: Discipleship Resources, 1992.